TEACHING
CREATIVE AND
CRITICAL THINKING
IN SCHOOLS

TEACHING
CREATIVE AND
CRITICAL THINKING
IN SCHOOLS

RUSSELL GRIGG
AND
HELEN LEWIS

Los Angeles I London I New Delhi
Singapore I Washington DC I Melbourne

Los Angeles | London | New Delhi
Singapore | Washington DC | Melbourne

SAGE Publications Ltd
1 Oliver's Yard
55 City Road
London EC1Y 1SP

SAGE Publications Inc.
2455 Teller Road
Thousand Oaks, California 91320

SAGE Publications India Pvt Ltd
B 1/I 1 Mohan Cooperative Industrial Area
Mathura Road
New Delhi 110 044

SAGE Publications Asia-Pacific Pte Ltd
3 Church Street
#10-04 Samsung Hub
Singapore 049483

Editor: James Clark
Editorial assistant: Diana Alves
Production editor: Nicola Carrier
Copyeditor: Gemma Marren
Proofreader: Emily Ayers
Indexer: Authors
Marketing manager: Dilhara Attygalle
Cover design: Naomi Robinson
Typeset by: C&M Digitals (P) Ltd, Chennai, India

Library of Congress Control Number: 2018943129

British Library Cataloguing in Publication data

A catalogue record for this book is available from the British Library

ISBN 978-1-5264-2119-7
ISBN 978-1-5264-2120-3 (pbk)

To Jack, Mildred and Dilys

CONTENTS

LIST OF FIGURES, PHOTOS AND TABLES

FIGURES

PHOTOGRAPHS

TABLES

ABOUT THE AUTHORS

Dr Russell Grigg is an Education Inspector for the Ministry of Education in the United Arab Emirates, based in Abu Dhabi. He was previously Associate Professor at the Wales Centre for Equity in Education and has worked for many years in teacher education. His interest in the teaching of thinking was triggered by reading the works of Edward De Bono as a student in the 1980s. He believes passionately in fostering creativity in teaching and learning, which is reflected in his writing. He is author of many books and articles on primary education including *Becoming an Outstanding Primary Teacher* (Routledge, 2014) and *Big Ideas in Education: What Every Teacher Should Know* (Crown House, 2016). He is co-editor of the *Wales Journal of Education* and has a particular research interest in the history of education in Wales. He is currently involved in research projects associated with the history of the inspectorate in Wales and the history of free school meals. Russell is a lifelong Swansea City supporter, through the highs and lows.

Dr Helen Lewis is a senior lecturer in Yr Athrofa: Institute of Education, at the University of Wales Trinity Saint David. She became interested in the teaching of thinking when working as a primary school teacher in inner London. Subsequently she learnt more about how teachers can make thinking visible in classrooms at Project Zero, Harvard University. Her PhD focused on the development and teaching of metacognition in early years' and primary classrooms and she has written widely in the field. Helen is qualified to train teachers in a number of thinking materials, sits on the committee of the 'Let's Think' Council Forum and is an Associate of Early Education. In her free time she enjoys walking her dogs, and is currently researching the impact of animal-assisted interventions in classrooms.

ACKNOWLEDGEMENTS

We are grateful to the many teachers and their pupils who provided fascinating real-life insights into how they promote thinking in their classrooms. These teachers made time in their very busy schedules to answer numerous calls, texts and emails, and made us very welcome when we visited. Pupils gave their time and their ideas freely and enthusiastically, and we enjoyed the time spent with them.

A special thanks go to:

Tania Morgan and the staff and pupils of Ysgol Y Bynea, Llanelli.

Russell Dwyer, Laura Luxton, and the staff and pupils of St Thomas Community Primary School, Swansea.

Sarah Di Tomaso and the staff and pupils of Oak Field Primary School, Barry.

Steve Lewis, and the staff and pupils at Tondu Primary School, Bridgend.

Yvonne Yorkshades, Primary PGCE graduate of the University of Wales Trinity Saint David.

Ian Longshaw, and the staff and pupils of Marown Primary School, Isle of Man.

Claire Lawton, and the staff and pupils of Danescourt Primary School, Cardiff.

Matthew Noyes, BA Education with QTS student, University of Wales Trinity Saint David.

Sharon Phillips, and the staff and pupils at Deri View Primary School, Abergavenny.

Ruth Harris, and the staff and pupils of Castle School, Narbeth.

Louise Muteham, and the staff and pupils of Whitchurch Primary School, Cardiff.

Rose Cope and the staff and pupils of Kingsdown and Ringwold CofE Primary School, Kent.

Barbara Murphy and the staff and pupils of St Robert's RC Primary School, Bridgend.

Sarah Cunningham, and the staff and pupils at Berrywood Primary School, Hampshire.

Martina Lecky, and the staff and pupils at Ruislip High School, Middlesex.

Judith Stephenson, and the staff and pupils at Barbara Priestman Academy, Sunderland.

Alona Yildirim, and the staff and pupils at the International IB school, Ankara, Turkcy.

We would also like to thank Richard Cummins and Clare Barden at Thinking Matters, and the Thinking School Hub for allowing us access to the materials on their website. We drew upon case studies from the following schools: Barton Court Grammar School, Kent; Rochester Grammar School, Kent; Portsmouth Academy for Girls, Portsmouth; Maidstone Grammar School, Kent; St Anne's CofE Primary School, Oldham; and Notting Hill Preparatory School, London and have included where possible examples of their good practice.

Finally, our thanks go to Diana Alves and her colleagues at SAGE, and Gemma Marren, for their support and patience through the editorial process.

INTRODUCTION

'

We don't need no education

We don't need no thought control

No dark sarcasm in the classroom

Teachers leave them kids alone.

'

Many readers will recognise the above lyrics, part of Pink Floyd's rock opera, *Another Brick in the Wall*, released in 1979. Some English teachers may flinch at the use of double negatives (don't … no), perhaps an ironic comment on the perceived failure of the educational system. Creatively, however, it sounds much better than a chorus of children singing 'We don't need any education.' The lyrics of the song and the circumstances when it was produced say a lot about the themes we discuss in this book: the value of education and the point of schooling, the balance between teacher direction and student independence and, most significantly, the role of schools in promoting children's thinking.

The song was composed by Pink Floyd's Roger Waters and reflects his own negative experience at school in the 1950s (Blake, 2008). Waters believed that schools suppressed rather than inspired children. But in 1979, when the group assembled in a north London studio to record the song, education was entering a period of considerable change. Just around the corner from the studio stood Islington Green, one of the city's largest comprehensive schools. When Pink Floyd's manager turned up at the school looking for children to sing on the record, he bypassed the headteacher's office and ended up in the music department. Alun Renshaw, the unconventional head of department, snapped up the opportunity to broaden his students' musical horizons. He immediately escorted a handful of excited youngsters to the studio where they were told to sing the words in the style of playground rant rather than a polished choir performance. Renshaw soon realised that the message might not present the school in a good light. Margaret Maden, the headteacher, expressed concern over the potential publicity, but it was too late. Pink Floyd went on to sell around 4 million copies of the song worldwide and it became an anthem for freedom of expression in countries such as Iran and South Africa. Maden became an education professor at Keele University, while a disillusioned Renshaw headed off to Australia because he could feel 'the clouds of conservatism heading towards the school system at the time' (Winterman, 2007).

Many years later, Maden reflected on the episode:

> I think schools, and I think children, need that kind of eccentric nutter, as long as they're producing the goods. A school couldn't have nothing but Aluns, it would collapse instantly, but just one like that is a very good idea. (Winterman, 2007)

Maden's comments illustrate the tensions between creative expression on the one hand, and the need for conformity and structure on the other. In education, this is often manifested in the enduring dichotomy of 'progressive' versus 'traditional' teaching characterised as follows:

- Traditionalists value the learning of facts, basic skills of literacy and numeracy, a subject-based curriculum, teacher-led instruction, the teacher's authority and test-driven assessment.
- Progressivists value the development of the whole child, pupil independence, cross-curricular teaching, discovery or inquiry-based learning, 'soft skills' such as problem-solving, creative thinking, teamwork and holistic assessment.

The caricature suggests that those who support the teaching of thinking skills, particularly creative thinking, tend to orientate themselves, or be associated with, the progressive camp.

This long running polarisation of views is both unhelpful and inaccurate. Even during the height of the debate over teaching styles and approaches, Wright (1977: 196) pointed out that the differences had been over-exaggerated and while there may have been some 'progressive' thinking confined to a few university departments of education, *thinking* was the operative word – what academics think, say and write is one thing, 'what teachers do in school is quite another'. In any event, classroom practitioners (unlike armchair pundits) are likely to settle for a mid-way position between these two extremes even if they may prefer to be ideologically closer to one end than the other. Many 'creative' disciplines such as dance or music build upon foundations of skills, knowledge and understanding that develop through drills and practice. Ballet students may practise for six to seven hours a day, six days a week, as well as doing daily Pilates and strength training sessions. Good teachers use a balance of approaches, including direct instruction and setting more inquiry-based tasks that demand collaboration, problem-solving and creative thinking.

One of the features of children's thinking as a subject is that it attracts interest from many groups. Neuroscientists, psychologists, sociologists, medical experts, religious ministers, social workers, journalists, parents and formal educators all have something to contribute. And, of course, children from a young age are aware of their thinking processes and can offer valuable opinions on the subject (Coltman et al., 2013). Given such broad interest, it is important to be clear about what we mean by thinking, which we discuss in Chapter 1.

Dictionary definitions of thinking, which see it as the act of using one's mind to produce thought or the process of reasoning, soon run into trouble among academics. Reasoning is only one element of thinking. Problem-solving, planning, decision-making, to name a few, are all equally valuable skills. The skills of thinking are defined as 'translatable mental processes which require learners to plan, describe and evaluate their thinking and learning' (Moseley et al., 2005: 24). At times, in this book, we use the term as a convenient shorthand although acknowledge that it is problematic. For one thing, it implies that the skills can be taught separately without being applied to specific contexts. Even then, there is a danger that general statements about thinking skills are included in lesson plans and schemes of work (e.g. as learning objectives), but without any clear indication of how these will be taught and developed over time.

Imagine setting a group of pupils the project to plan a family holiday abroad with a limited budget. The intended thinking skills might include: *planning* (e.g. dates, duration, family dietary and medical needs), *comparing* and *contrasting* (e.g. holiday destinations, prices, travel arrangements), and *evaluating* (e.g. how well the overall package meets the needs of the family). During the lesson, the teacher may be satisfied that the group is making good progress in demonstrating the thinking skills. They appear to be busy scanning holiday brochures and travel websites, developing useful literacy skills as a bonus. When the group reports back on the suggested holiday destination the teacher might conclude, via a tick-box, that they have demonstrated many useful skills. Unfortunately, this does not necessarily mean that they have become better all-round thinkers. Critics might suggest that such a lesson is at best introducing pupils to different types of thinking but is not helping them become more skilful thinkers. Tasks can be completed superficially and quickly, without much thought. On the other hand, if pupils are taught *how to* do things skilfully (e.g. how to gather relevant information), then through careful practice they should become capable and confident thinkers.

Anyhow, the skills of thinking alone are not enough. As Claxton (2008a) put it, we need to support pupils so that they are ready, willing and able to use them. Pupils must develop dispositions, social and emotional competencies and a knowledge base upon which to exercise their thinking. Many writers use terms other than thinking skills to indicate the broader competences that pupils need to develop. The phrase 'thinking-based learning' (Swartz et al., 2008) neatly encapsulates the skills, dispositions and values that pupils need to develop if they are make the most of their education. Thinking is very much a holistic business. Neuroscientists and cognitive psychologists are moving away from the notion that thinking is just the concern of the brain, recognising the influence of the body and emotions on how we think (Claxton, 2015). Often, good thinking takes place in a social context as ideas are shared and reflected upon.

No one knows for sure what someone else is thinking because it is a hidden process. In photo 1.1 we can only infer what the little girl is thinking. Of course, she can tell us and we can observe her at work, but whether she is thinking about the problem in hand, her lunch, going out with her friends or something that has upset her, only she knows. Even then, articulating critical thoughts (as opposed to general everyday thinking) can be challenging. In this example, the group was set the task of thinking how to improve a robot, which requires explanation and evaluation, skills that exercise a lot of mental energy and need practice.

Photo 1.1 Ultimately, thinking is a hidden process

Similarly, for teachers, making judgements on learning is not a straightforward matter. Learning involves the continuous long-term retention and application of knowledge and skills. Ideally, learning should lead to improved performance, which is often a measured output on a test or evaluation of some kind or another. Dweck (1989) distinguishes between those students who approach tasks from a *learning* or a *performance* perspective: the former students are more interested in developing their competence whereas the latter have a greater desire to do well and look good in front of others. The difference matters because students, who are mainly concerned with their performance, rather than their learning, tend to avoid challenging tasks due to fear of failure. This impacts on the goals that they set. As educators, there is a danger of being duped by performance over learning and thinking. Jo Boaler (1997), a leading expert in mathematics teaching, has shown that students can be learning the same content and gain similar examination results but due to the teaching approaches, leave their classes with different levels of understanding, confidence and capability in tackling mathematical problems in real-life.

In Chapter 3, we put forward arguments why *all* pupils should be taught how to improve their creative and critical thinking. They are entitled to be taught how to think better because this will help them with all aspects of their lives, whether following instructions, using technologies safely, composing music, finding space on the playing field or resolving personal difficulties. In short, becoming a good thinker makes children happier individuals and their overall wellbeing improves. Moreover, in the longer-term being able to think effectively will increase young people's employability prospects. The most successful educational systems in the world support the teaching of creative and critical thinking or aspire to do so.

Meta-analyses show that well-implemented thinking skills programmes and approaches are effective in improving pupils' performance as measured in standardised tests. Higgins et al. (2005) report that the overall effect size[1] is 0.74 (including cognitive, curricular and affective measures), based on a meta-analysis of twenty-nine studies which contained quantitative data on pupils' attainment and attitudes. This compares favourably with the average effect size of 0.4 in John Hattie's (2012) database. However, it is unclear whether the benefits are due to specific aspects of each programme's content or changes in the teaching and learning, which ensue. In the longitudinal Effective Provision of Pre-school Education (EPPE) project, evidence collected from 141 pre-school settings over a ten-year period was analysed (Siraj-Blatchford et al., 2006). The researchers identified effective settings (basing their definition of 'effective' on child outcomes) as offering children more opportunity to highlight and share their thinking with adults. High quality interaction is crucial, as is the teacher's role in supporting, promoting and provoking this.

---

[1]An effect size is a simple measure for quantifying the difference between two groups or the same group over time, using a common scale. In education, it is used to measure the effectiveness of a particular intervention.

Meta-analyses also show that interventions, which focus on developing metacognition, produce high effect sizes for very low costs, although it is important to look more deeply into why this might be the case. Many of the approaches reviewed in this book teach metacognitive strategies.

Chapters 4 to 10 provide the backbone of the book in setting out examples of approaches that are widely used to promote pupils' thinking. Chapter 4 reviews Visible Thinking Routines developed by researchers at Harvard University (Ritchhart et al., 2011). These are highly flexible and simple structures to develop thinking skills such as comparing and contrasting, reasoning and justifying. Chapter 5 focuses on Edward De Bono's (1985) Six Thinking Hats, which symbolise different types of thinking and attempts to move pupils beyond argumentative thinking. Chapter 6 discusses David Hyerle's Thinking Maps® (Hyerle and Alper, 2011), which combine the use of cognitive processes with the concept of a visual organiser. Tony Ryan's (2014) Thinkers Keys, comprising a set of twenty activities designed to unlock different cognitive processes, are introduced in Chapter 7. Philosophical approaches that give pupils space to think and enquire are outlined in Chapter 8. At their core is the notion that schooling does not simply serve economic purposes, as a preparation for work, but exists to broaden the mind by asking fundamental questions about life: what goodness, justice, truth and friendship mean. Cognitive Acceleration programmes (Shayer and Adey, 2002), which aim to accelerate pupils' thinking through challenge and dialogue, are discussed in Chapter 9. Finally, in Chapter 10 we turn to thinking dispositions or what Costa and Kallick (2000a; 2000b) call Habits of Mind. These are sixteen patterns of thinking that drive creativity and criticality.

These approaches are not presented as a definitive list but they illustrate the variety of practical ideas available to schools. We have selected these because of our experiences of seeing them in action – in a variety of school contexts, locally, nationally and internationally. Readers interested in finding out more about these approaches are directed to the Thinking Schools International website.[2] Although this is a commercial organisation, the website provides numerous free resources, which relate to some of the approaches we mention, and represents a good starting point for further research. It also includes case studies of schools using different approaches and these are a useful supplement to those discussed in Chapter 11. In our experience, many schools have developed the notion of a toolkit from which they select particular strategies and ideas. Hence although these chapters discuss approaches separately, inevitably there is overlap in the kinds of dispositions and skills they seek to promote.

In recent years, schools have been encouraged to reflect upon what works well in education (Marzano, 2003; Petty, 2006; Hattie, 2009; Higgins et al., 2014) and sometimes what doesn't work so well (Hattie, 2015). Schools are well supported by organisations

---

[2]www.thinkingschoolsinternational.com (accessed 20 June 2018).

such as the Education Endowment Foundation/Sutton Trust (EEF/ST). In America, the Best Evidence Encyclopedia,[3] run by Johns Hopkins University, provides objective evidence about the strength of evidence supporting a variety of programmes. One thing to bear in mind about guidance on 'what works' is that for any area of practice, including thinking skills interventions, the evidence points to what works *on average*. In most interventions, this conceals considerable variation in terms of efficacy. Questions need to be asked about who undertook the research, when and where it occurred, the size of the samples, the costs and the implications, if implemented. Even interventions that are widely held as having a significant impact on learners' progress need to be examined closely by school leaders before they are adopted or adapted for their specific context.

While we are confident that the approaches reviewed in Chapters 4 to 10 provide teachers with substance to work from, they should not be read as quick-fix solutions. Schools are examples of what sociologists call complex adaptive systems (Fidan and Balci, 2017). Put simply, there are many things going on in classrooms and each of these variables can affect each other and, most significantly, the quality of learning and teaching. Broadly speaking, these variables can be categorised as follows:

- physical (e.g. class layout, furniture, temperature)
- personal (e.g. pupils' and teachers' own personal circumstances)
- pedagogical (e.g. pupils' needs, ages, pupil–teacher relationships)
- institutional (e.g. policies, scheme of work, timetable).

Moreover, what happens in the classroom is nested within a broader ecological system including: school leadership styles, parental expectations, government policy, inspection requirements and societal values. Some of these factors are more temporary than others, but collectively they shape what happens in the classroom through constant interaction. And so, at any given time the quality of thinking, teaching and learning can ebb and flow.

In addition to the ideas mentioned in Chapters 4 to 10, there are other approaches to the teaching of thinking. These include the impactful Thinking Together Project based at the University of Cambridge, which has a strong focus on developing children's thinking through dialogue (Dawes and Warwick, 2012; Littleton and Mercer, 2013) and Bella Wallace's (2001; 2004; 2009) popular Thinking Actively in a Social Context (TASC), with its emphasis on children as 'equal partners' in thinking. There are also interventions that may not be explicitly badged as promoting pupils' thinking but clearly do so as part of a broader focus on their wellbeing. For example, Reading with Dogs is an intervention that aims primarily to engage reluctant readers and improve their literacy skills. In so doing, however, many pupils develop positive dispositions and attitudes towards learning. Early research findings are based on children's views of themselves as learners (measured

---

[3]www.bestevidence.org/ (accessed 20 June 2018).

on attitudinal scales), their reading scores on standardised tests and their engagement in lessons. Pupils and teachers report gains in dispositions such as enthusiasm, resilience and persistence, as well as fluency and enjoyment (Lewis, 2017a; 2017b; Lewis and Grigg, 2017).

Chapter 11 includes brief case studies of primary, secondary and special schools successfully promoting children's thinking in different contexts. Four general factors that contribute to their success are highlighted, namely effective planning, practices, professional learning and partnerships. We relate these to four Habits of Mind (asking questions and posing problems, thinking flexibly, remaining open to continuous learning and thinking interdependently) to reinforce the importance of leaders modelling thinking dispositions.

Every now and then the educational system is attacked for being little more than factories churning out fodder (Freestone, 2016). This was graphically depicted in the video that accompanied *Another Brick in the Wall*, as children marched through a meat grinder. One of us was leaving school at the time and doesn't recall anything quite as pessimistic as that. Nonetheless, there remain substantial concerns about many children's school experiences. The Children's Society's (2016) *Good Childhood Report* reveals that three in ten children and young people (aged 8–17) do not like school. This is based on surveys of more than 60,000 children conducted since 2008. Children's wellbeing at school is a complex subject and affected by many factors beyond the school gates. However, one leading teachers' union, the National Education Union (2015), acknowledges that children and young people too easily become 'commodities of the education system' as teachers are forced to focus on examination passes in a narrow range of academic subjects.

School leaders and teachers are understandably concerned about meeting external demands in a high-stakes system of accountability, where the prevailing discourse is dominated by test results and performance data. Naturally, school leaders, teachers, parents and children themselves want good examination results. But as Paul Collard, chief executive of Creativity, Culture and Education, points out: 'what we test is the acquisition of a narrow collection of facts, not whether we have the skills to succeed in employment, not whether we have the capacity to build and maintain, the ingredients of a fruitful adulthood' (Garner, 2014). And even Andreas Schleicher, education director at the Organisation for Economic Co-operation and Development (OECD), which administers the international Pisa tests, admits education needs to be much more about 'ways of thinking, which involve creative and critical approaches to problem-solving and decision-making' (Schleicher, no date).

But there is some good news. There are clear signs that the rigid system of schooling with its narrow focus is changing. For example, in Wales, the Donaldson Review of the curriculum highlights the case for change noting, for instance, that the high degree of prescription and accountability pressures has created a culture in which creativity has diminished and the professional contribution of teachers is underdeveloped (Donaldson, 2015). One of the four core purposes of the new curriculum in Wales is to develop 'enterprising, creative contributors' ready to play a full part in life and work. The expectation is that there is to be a strong emphasis on teaching pupils to think creatively to reframe and solve problems, take measured risks, express ideas and emotions through different media and identify and grasp opportunities. Further afield, as we note in Chapter 3, the changing role of schools is anticipated in countries that are regarded as having the world's leading educational systems, such as Finland, Singapore and Shanghai. The Chinese authorities recognise that it is one thing to have students who perform exceptionally well during examinations, but it is quite another to have a generation of creative and critical thinkers, which its society and economy needs. As one of their leading officials put it, schools need to move away from *tianyashi*, translated as force-feeding the duck (Crehan, 2016) – the cultural equivalent of Pink Floyd's meat grinder metaphor.

WHAT DO WE MEAN
BY THINKING?

INTRODUCTION

Imagine a school in which mathematics lessons were taught in the swimming pool or where children had voice-activated pencils. Or at a more mundane level, classrooms in which children did not scrape their knees on tables, had blinds to keep out the sun and enough space to move around, free from clutter. Imagine schools run on flexible timetables where children could spend more time studying their interests, or 'schools without walls' where children could learn outside with immediate access to animals and wild gardens. These were the responses of primary and secondary pupils to a competition in 1997 run by *The Guardian* called 'The School I'd Like'. It was re-run of a similar competition held thirty years earlier (Blishen, 1973). Both generations wanted more time to be creative, a theme that has continued in follow-up competitions and surveys. As one 6-year-old put it: 'Children sometimes have better ideas than adults. That is because the children's brains are new and not old' (Birkett, 2011).

There are schools around the UK that have taken up some of these ideas. For instance, quiet or sensory rooms are increasingly popular although they tend to be used for children with behavioural or learning difficulties. Even the more fanciful ideas have been supported by teachers and backed by academic research. Take the child who wanted to walk around the school on pink fluffy carpets in her socks. One study spanning twenty-five countries over ten years reports that children who learn in a 'shoeless' environment are more likely to behave better and obtain good grades than peers with footwear (Pells, 2016). The deputy head at one East Midlands primary school reports a calmer and more relaxed atmosphere after it was decided that children could wear slippers in class. The researchers claim that cleaning costs are lower, furniture lasts longer and children's reading improves – as they can read in more comfortable positions (Khomami, 2017). It is important then not to underestimate children's thinking capabilities.

Studies reveal that before children enter the world they are learning. Remarkably, their senses are so well developed that they can recognise sounds and face-like shapes before they are born (Knapton, 2017). The question of when babies first develop powers of conscious thinking is more debatable (Koch, 2009). We simply do not know whether this is in the womb, at birth or during early childhood. The field of baby research is a contentious one, but there are claims that six-month-old babies can reason and display far greater intelligence than was once thought (Saini, 2013). Scans suggest that their brains work incredibly hard just to look at a stranger's face and it takes about a thousand hours to commit this to memory (Livingstone, 2005). Around the age of one, children begin to point at things and effectively ask the question with their finger: 'What is this?' As young children explore their surroundings, they ask questions and make connections between new experiences and what they already know. By eighteen months, toddlers can make connections – if provided with a toy rake and an out-of-reach toy, they will realise that the rake can be used to retrieve the toy. Young children are keen to find things out. By the time they are four, one study suggests children ask their caregivers, on average, more than 100 questions every hour. Two-thirds of these questions are designed to elicit information such as the names and purpose of objects (Chouinard, 2007). By the age of seven, and with the right support, children can use 'thinking' language such as 'guess', 'know' and 'remember', reason logically, hypothesise, suggest alternative actions that could have been taken in the past and understand that the beliefs of others may be different from their own (Taggart et al., 2005).

In short, young children are natural thinkers – curious, imaginative and eager to learn. In this book, we explore how teachers can build on these traits and inclinations. We begin by considering the meaning, nature and scope of thinking.

WHAT IS THINKING?

Thinking can be defined in many ways. Edward de Bono (1976: 33) offered a concise definition that remains a useful starting point: 'Thinking is the deliberate exploration of experience for a purpose'. This is helpful because it highlights the deliberate and purposeful aspect of thinking which interests educators – the purpose may vary, from seeking to judge, plan, evaluate, create and so on. Smith (1992: 9) defined thinking as 'the business of the brain' although increasingly cognitive psychologists are recognising the influence of the whole body and feelings on how we think (Claxton, 2015). In physical terms, thinking is a biological process whereby brain cells (neurons) connect with each other through electrical impulses. Once neurons connect, they form a network of pathways. As these pathways are used repeatedly, the connections become permanent. These connections are strengthened through interactions with the environment and through natural maturity (Figure 1.1).

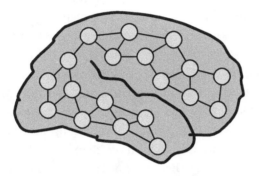

Figure 1.1 Neuron pathways

However, we remain very much in the dark about how these billions of neurons achieve thinking (Ramachandran, 2011; Solomon, 2015). Ignorance has led to speculation and misinformation. Hence neuroscientists have been busy correcting the myths that have emerged from the industry, such as we only use 10 per cent of our brain or that there are left- and right-brained people. Brain-based pedagogies such as brain gym and visual, auditory and kinaesthetic (VAK) learning styles have also been widely discredited (Coffield et al., 2004; Geake, 2009). Unfortunately, we are easily seduced into thinking that there is scientific credibility behind anything that features pictures of a brain. Measuring what goes on in the mind has remained one of the greatest challenges in the history of psychology (Wooldridge, 1994). And yet, despite the reservations associated with brain-based research in the next decade or so, it is forecast that neural implants could improve our powers of memory and reasoning by 30 per cent (Dodgson, 2017). Rather than struggle to learn a language, an implant might save the effort. The lines between artificial (computer) and human intelligence are becoming increasingly blurred.

On a more philosophical level, thinking can be defined as the ability to reason that sets humans apart from other animals (if not computers). This is expressed, for instance, in the application of logic to solve complex problems and the application of literacy skills. McLeish (1993: 1) estimated that in a lifetime (presumably spanning seventy or so years), each human learns, ponders and applies fifteen billion items of information. This is the process of thinking that we know so little about. As De Bono (1976: 8) put it, 'thinking is a most awkward subject to handle'. Even the notion of thinking as being a matter of reasoning is contentious. While we have the capacity to think rationally we often act very irrationally. Some people habitually leave things to the last minute, even though they know in plenty of time that they have a deadline to meet. From a rational perspective, many of us who are overweight know that it is in our best interests to reduce sugary foods, drink water rather than alcohol and walk several miles a day. The writer Dan Ariely (2010) points out that occasionally there are unexpected benefits from defying logical thinking. Trusting instinct can sometimes triumph over logic and considering every detail. Instinct draws upon in-built mental shortcuts (heuristics), which saves overly complicated analysis. Hence, we tune into our names if mentioned in a crowd and can filter out everything else we hear.

Historically speaking, the word 'think' has carried several meanings. It developed from Old English, first appearing in the supernatural poem Beowulf composed around 1,300 years ago (Barnhart, 1988: 1134). It originally meant to imagine something so strongly that it appeared real to oneself. It is now the seventy-ninth most widely used word in the English language, based on an analysis of more than two billion words by the Oxford English Corpus. Samuel Johnson's Dictionary of 1755 illustrated how, over the centuries, the word had evolved to have several meanings:

1. To have ideas; to compare terms or things; to reason; to cogitate; to perform any mental operation;
2. To judge; to conclude; to determine;
3. To intend;
4. To imagine; to fancy. (Lynch, 2004: 498–499).

These definitions demonstrate the critical, purposeful and creative aspects of thinking, although the imaginative element in the fourth definition has been relatively neglected.

Most modern dictionaries follow Johnson's first definition of thinking as the mental process of reasoning about something, usually an issue or problem. Adey (2002: 2) defines thinking simply as 'something we do when we try to solve problems'. But problem-solving is only one thinking skill. 'Thinking skills' is used as an umbrella term to cover a range of mental processes which require learners to 'plan, describe and evaluate their thinking and learning' (Higgins et al., 2005: 1). When they were first included in England's National Curriculum in 1999, five sets of skills were identified:

- Information-processing skills – to locate, collect and analyse information
- Reasoning skills – to give reasons, draw inferences and make deductions
- Enquiry skills – to ask relevant questions, pose and define problems, plan research, test conclusions and improve ideas

- Creative thinking skills – to generate and extend ideas, suggest hypotheses, apply imagination, and to look for alternative innovative outcomes
- Evaluation skills – to evaluate information, judge value and to have confidence in judgements (DfEE/QCA, 1999).

Since then, as we will discuss in Chapter 2, there have been significant revisions to the curriculum in England, which have seen thinking skills lose their explicit status although the phrase remains alive in other parts of the UK and further afield (e.g. Donaldson, 2015; OECD, 2016).

Winch (2010) offers a balanced and insightful discussion about the controversies associated with 'thinking skills' such as whether they can be genuinely regarded as skills, applied in a range of different contexts and taught independent of subject disciplines. He concludes that despite philosophical differences there is a consensus that no thinking skills intervention should be introduced without carefully weighing up its scope, limits and evidence of impact.

One of the limitations in using the term 'thinking skills' is the implication that teachers need only to focus on skills to develop thoughtful learners. Hence some writers prefer the broader term 'capacities' (Lucas and Spencer, 2017) or 'competences', which is a combination of knowledge, skills and attitudes. The importance of cultivating the right attitudes and dispositions towards learning and thinking is now widely recognised. A child may acquire higher-order thinking skills, such as the ability to read between the lines, but not be disposed to read regularly. Katz (1993: 16) describes dispositions as:

> A pattern of behavior exhibited frequently and in the absence of coercion and constituting a habit of mind under some conscious and voluntary control, and that is intentional and oriented to broad goals.

As discussed further in Chapter 10, by developing dispositions such as open-mindedness, curiosity and flexible thinking, children are more likely to become lifelong learners, effective problem-solvers and decision-makers.

In summary, several writers have confirmed that thinking and thinking skills may well be fluid concepts but argue that this should not put teachers off from promoting thinking in the classroom. For instance, Resnick (1987), suggests that thinking skills are hard to define, but possible to recognise, while McGuinness (1999) suggests that there are common processes and attributes that constitute thinking – these include collecting, sorting, analysing and reflecting. What is important to realise is that thinking can develop, change and improve with support, experience and direct teaching. Therefore, while defining and classifying thinking may be difficult, this should not put teachers off from pursuing thinking in the classroom.

TYPES AND QUALITY OF THINKING

In everyday life, we think in different ways. At times, this can be sequential as we process information in an orderly, linear manner. We make lists, follow directions, predict outcomes and recount events. On other occasions, we may think holistically to gain the bigger picture and see how different parts fit together. A good garage mechanic, doctor or computer technician will try to understand the whole 'system' and work through various scenarios before deciding upon the correct diagnosis and action. In academic disciplines, there is a need for both sequential and holistic thinking. For example, historians need to think about the chronology of events in determining when things happened in the past but they also need to study society as a whole: the relationships, values and beliefs, as they try to explain motives.

Designers use creative processes such as experimenting, creating prototype models and redesigning. 'Design thinking' places learners in the context of how designers operate. They need to solve technical problems but they also need to understand the product or service from the viewpoint of user and producer. Sharples et al. (2016) identify the teaching of design thinking as one of the innovative pedagogies that might transform education. Challenges can be set for pupils so that they begin to understand the design process. These challenges should include a setting (e.g. a local park), characters (e.g. parents, animals, children) and a potential problem (e.g. litter, vandalism, possible closure). The design process involves posing questions and considering alternatives (e.g. How might we keep the park clean? What if we redesign the pathways? Can we raise income by hosting an event?)

Much of our thinking can be very random and unplanned, such as when ideas come into our heads while out walking the dog or during a shower. We often carry out tasks such as driving and housekeeping without much conscious thought. However, we can easily slip into autopilot with potentially lethal consequences. Drivers who lose concentration, for example, cause nearly half of all car accidents; a poll of 27,000 drivers by the Automobile Association found that a quarter of 25–34-year-olds struggled to recall parts of their journey. In the classroom, we are more interested in the kind of conscious thinking, which we can influence. This thinking is deliberate and purposeful, whether helping children to recall historical facts, solve numerical problems or plan an outing. As De Bono (1991: 9) points out, we need to separate 'what goes on in our heads *all* the time from the more focused thinking that has a purpose' (our italics).

One particularly relevant concept here is 'metacognition' (Flavell, 1976), often simplistically described as 'thinking about thinking' (McGuinness, 1999; Hattie, 2009). It more accurately refers to the beliefs and knowledge individuals hold about their cognitive processes and their ability to manage these processes. As Figure 1.2 shows, metacognition involves processes beyond simply knowing (cognition). Metacognitive knowledge involves how we see ourselves as learners and thinkers. Metacognitive experience refers to how well we feel we are doing a task, i.e. the degree of confidence, satisfaction or puzzlement, while metacognitive tasks or goals describe what we intend to gain from a cognitive activity. Metacognitive strategies or skills refer to knowing which methods to use and when to use them, as well as monitoring and evaluating learning from the success (or failure) of the strategy used.

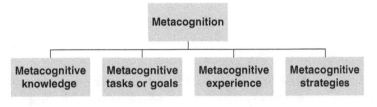

Figure 1.2 Overview of metacognition

Higgins et al. (2014) suggest that supporting metacognitive approaches to learning offers a high impact, low cost way to improve attainment. Examples include self-questioning (e.g. What else do I need?), providing regular time for personal reflection (e.g. Have I met my goal?), modelling think aloud strategies, and the use of checklists. Reflective, meta-cognitive learners will recognise flaws in their thinking and will review or amend their thinking strategies accordingly.

Several writers have highlighted the characteristics of good quality thinking. They describe this as purposeful, self-directed and active – as Halpern (2002: 1) points out, 'thinking is not a spectator sport'. It calls for active engagement. And yet there is often a mismatch between the kind of thinking expected in school and the demands beyond the school gates (Claxton, 2008b; Lucas and Spencer, 2017). Real-life learning usually happens when we are interested in getting something done – putting up a garden fence, passing a driving test, playing the piano, selling unwanted junk. Often there is a sense of urgency and the learning is 'just in time'. In school, on the other hand, learning is often presented in sixty-minute lessons and predetermined chunks, with little scope for pupils to decide on where, when, why and how they go about the tasks. One of the practical things teachers can do is provide a toolbox of thinking strategies from which learners can draw upon as and when needed to achieve the task in hand.

In this book, we focus on thinking critically and creatively. These are best regarded as related processes, covering a range of skills, dispositions and techniques. Beginning in the 1950s, the American psychologist J.P. Guilford (1897–1997) explored the relation-ship between critical and creative thinking in his general theory of intelligence. Guilford (1967) introduced the terms convergent and divergent 'production' (thinking). These were key mental operations, which were necessary to solve problems and generate ideas.

Guilford suggested that convergent thinking was the process of narrowing options to a single 'right' solution. The answer already exists 'out there' in the world but needs to be located, recalled or worked out systematically. In contrast, divergent thinking generates alternative answers and options without the limits of preconceived ideas. Creativity involves both imaginative (divergent) and disciplined (convergent) aspects of thinking (Lucas et al., 2012). Creative thinking involves making critical judgements, just as critical thinkers need to be curious and embrace divergent views.

THINKING CRITICALLY

Thinking critically is a process of questioning sources to make well-informed judgements. It is healthy scepticism and involves challenging assumptions. Unfortunately, it is rooted in negative connotations – the language of judgement, investigating, enquiries, criticism and critics do little to cheer the spirit. However, thinking critically does not mean simply finding fault or exposing weaknesses. Rather, it seeks a solid basis on which to judge something. And this should involve commenting on strengths, weaknesses and raising further questions, as is the case with a book or film review. These are the hard outcomes of thinking critically, produced by applying a range of skills. Many of these ancillary skills can be illustrated in the process of writing this book. We have synthesised relevant research, evaluated arguments, observed lessons, compared data in the case studies, explained key concepts, critiqued each other's writing, reflected on comments from reviewers and editors and made many revisions, hopefully to improve the published outcome. Analysis, synthesis and evaluation are among the higher-order thinking skills famously proposed by the American psychologist Benjamin Bloom (1913–1999) in his taxonomy of educational objectives.

Thinking critically also involves the ability to apply informal logic. Put simply, logic involves searching for what is true. The formal 'computer style' logic aims to produce a valid conclusion, i.e. it follows on from its premise. However, formal logic does not consider false premises or desirable results – the 'rubbish in, rubbish out' principle applies. Hence informal logic, which considers common sense and human values, should override reasoning. We have all misunderstood things and jumped to conclusions too readily based on inaccurate information.

Thinking critically involves inductive and deductive reasoning. While inductive reasoning begins with an observation and moves outwards to reach a generalisation, deductive reasoning works from a general premise, hunch or theory to find specific results. Typically, the reasoning follows the sequence: 'If a is greater than b and if b is greater than c, then a must be greater than c'. This deductive reasoning is well known in science and mathematics. In science, for example, it has led to the discovery of new planets in other solar systems, based on what was already known about the orbit of planets in our system.

In mathematics, children are set problems along the lines, 'If a football shirt costs £30, what will eleven cost?' Such cold reasoning is an antidote to imaginary thinking but it is not infallible. It is restricted by the capacity of one's working memory, which is typically limited to two or three premises at a time. When overloaded, people give in or guess. Cognitive Load Theory, developed in 1988 by psychologist John Sweller, suggests that processing new information results in a significant 'cognitive load' on working memory, and this can impact on learning. Therefore, teachers need to design learning experiences that reduce this 'load'.

Moreover, the human mind tends to go beyond the stated information and revert to real-world experience. For instance, we know that in buying a set of football shirts it may be possible to gain a discount and so eleven shirts may be less than £330.

There is evidence that very young children can use both inductive and deductive reasoning. They develop their reasoning skills from simply describing and explaining what they did to offering a convincing argument based on their observations and experimentation, using phrases such as 'I think that ... because'. When children justify their decisions, they begin to form a chain of reasoning. Making appropriate connections is central to logical reasoning. Consider the following example:

> Helen has no money, and she is unhappy.
>
> Helen has no money, therefore she is unhappy.

The first sentence includes two unrelated thoughts whereas in the second sentence the thoughts are connected, indicating a relationship. Words such as 'so', 'therefore' and 'because' are used to infer relationships. However, often we do not engage in conscious reasoning. We might simply listen to what someone says, take notes of what is happening around us, tell stories or watch television.

Critical thinkers often use analogies and metaphors in their reasoning to help the audience grasp the key messages. A similarity between two different things is highlighted to shed light on an issue. In *A Bee in a Cathedral: And 99 Other Scientific Analogies*, Levy (2011) provides analogies to illustrate how the world works. Examples include likening the Earth to a Scotch egg, how long it would take to drink the Pacific or get to the top of Mount Everest in an elevator and why an electron is like a bee in a cathedral. Children can play analogy games to help form connections. For instance, the names of objects, people and animals (e.g. table, egg, teacher, builder, map, cat) can be placed on slips of paper in a box and children are invited to pull out two and complete the sentence 'X is like Y because ...'. De Bono (1985) has used the well-known metaphor of hats, discussed in Chapter 5, to describe how we think. Less well known is his metaphor of action shoes to describe how we respond in certain situations (De Bono, 1991). Hence, when we think we need more information we should wear 'grey sneakers'; grey signifies the grey matter of the brain, the grey fog that needs to recede to make things clearer, while the sneaker represents a casual, quiet and unobtrusive approach.

The critical thinker is someone who evaluates and makes clear, rational judgements. This involves acquiring solid evidence to make informed decisions. It means developing the habit of spotting factual errors or inconsistencies in arguments and unsupported assumptions. Perhaps there is a lack of detail or poor referencing, which raises questions about the reliability of what is claimed. The language used may be overly emotive or stereotypes deployed. Pupils can use prompts and cues when evaluating their own and other people's work. De Bono (1993), for instance, offers the simple PMI technique where plus, minus and points of interest are noted. More complicated rubrics that identify criteria can be used as reference points to evaluate the extent to which learning outcomes are achieved. The American website RubiStar offers templates and allows users to generate their own criteria for evaluation.[1]

Critical judgements should be based on clear criteria. It is common practice for teachers and pupils themselves to judge the quality of their schoolwork by success criteria. When writing a report, pupils know that they need to give accurate information, answer questions, use captions and a title and include the author's name. In all walks of life, criteria are used to inform judgements. Architects judge the value of a building by its utility, safety and aesthetic appeal. Art critics consider features such as line, colour, space, light and shape. Interview panels refer to essential and desirable criteria when making judgements on the suitability of candidates. Thinking critically then involves the process of justifying and defending decisions. It is well illustrated in the fields of law and medicine. Judges and doctors need to make good, reliable judgements based on standards they follow, the evidence before them and the balance of probabilities.

Unfortunately, even the most serious of thinkers run into difficulties. One study (see Bryant, 2011) reveals how judges are more likely to grant prisoners parole early in the day or after lunch. This may be due to breaks improving the mood of judges by increasing glucose levels in the body. Thinking critically is constrained by our physiology. For cognitive psychologists, it involves creating mental models of a situation to manipulate it. Our thinking is subject to faulty reasoning because the mind is set up to make easier decisions rather than exert more effort by reasoning things through. Psychologists refer to a range of cognitive biases that affect how we think (Figure 1.3). These errors often occur because of holding preferences or beliefs that run contrary to the facts.

The existence of cognitive bias is one reason why schools should consider raising the profile of thinking skills in the curriculum. Another reason is the huge inflow of information available at our fingertips. Being able to think critically about the value of this information is of increasing importance, which is discussed further in Chapter 3.

---

[1] http://rubistar.4teachers.org/index.php (accessed 20 June 2018).

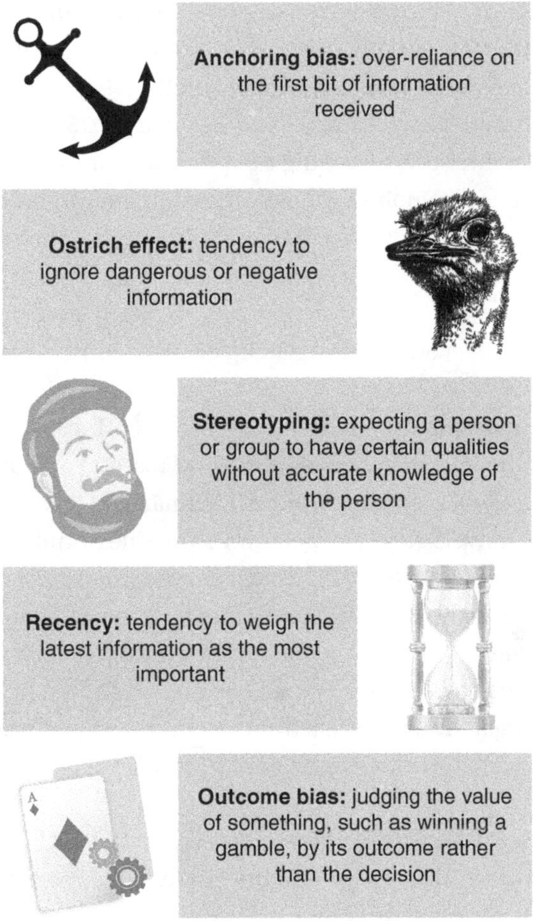

Figure 1.3 Five examples of cognitive bias

THINKING CREATIVELY

Academics have struggled to reach a shared view on what thinking creatively and creativity mean, reflecting their different starting points. As Pfenninger and Shubik (2001: xiii) put it, 'psychologists look inward and theologians upward'. Treffinger et al. (2002) identified over one hundred definitions! Most share two basic elements: novelty and value. At a simple level, being creative means making something that was not there before. De Bono (1992) pointed out that even 'creating a mess' is creative because the mess is new. However, simply doing something new is not necessarily original. In 1919, the French artist Marcel Duchamp made a parody of the *Mona Lisa* by adding a moustache and goatee. These additional brush strokes were unexpected but hardly original, given the painting already existed.

Philosophically, it could be questioned whether anything in the world is truly original. For example, authors essentially derive their work from rearranging existing letters of the alphabet, musicians select musical notes while artists produce art from nature, people and objects around them. Kounios and Beeman (2015) thus define creativity by suggesting that it is a matter of rearranging existing elements in a surprising way. Hence, a successful entrepreneur recombines well-known components, products or services that no one sells and everyone wants to buy. In copyright law, the threshold for originality is whether something comes from someone as the author or originator, rather than never having existed before. Tests of novelty or originality typically involve puzzles such as how many different uses can be made for a paper clip or brick, or how many items can fit into a matchbox.

In any event, originality is not enough. The nineteenth-century humourist Charles Lamb suggested that one way to roast a pig is to let it roam in a house and then set fire to the house. This is a novel but inappropriate idea. Kaufman and Sternberg (2010: xiii) suggest 'a creative response is novel, good and relevant'. Goodness implies a moral dimension to creativity. Simon Baron-Cohen (2011: 1) recalls when he was seven being told by his father that the Nazis turned Jews into lampshades and bars of soap. These were creative but heinous and morally repulsive acts. The Good Project at Harvard University, on the other hand, is concerned with exploring a set of principles about how to carry out 'good' work that is ethical, engaging and excellent. Its website includes resources for schools to involve children in discussions about excellence in a range of contexts across and beyond the curriculum.[2]

E.P. Torrance (1915–2003), who devised many creativity tests, used three definitions of creativity depending on his purpose and the context. For research, he focused on the creative process that he defined as:

> sensing difficulties, problems, gaps in information, missing elements, something askew; making guesses and formulating hypotheses about these deficiencies; evaluating and testing these guesses; possibly revising and retesting them; and finally communicating the results. (Torrance, 1988: 47)

This definition highlights the complexity of skills involved in creating something of value. Torrance also suggested an artistic definition of creativity, comprising amusing figure drawings and simple sentences along the lines, 'Creativity is ...'. For instance, 'Creativity is digging deeper', 'Creativity is looking twice', 'Creativity is cutting holes to see through' and 'Creativity is shaking hands with tomorrow'. Torrance's third definition is a 'survival' one, which he named after training US Air Force pilots in the 1950s

---

[2]http://thegoodproject.org (accessed 20 June 2018).

to survive emergencies and extreme conditions, e.g. lost at sea or in the jungle. In these circumstances, while the crew could be taught techniques from those who experienced similar situations in the past, they needed to use their imagination and so creativity was a matter of 'self-discovery and self-discipline' (Torrance, 1988: 58).

Studies of creativity focus mainly on the created outputs, the creator's personality, the thinking process or the environment in which creativity develops (Sternberg, 1988).

The created outputs

In modern society, there is a wide range of creative outputs, including objects, books, music, clothes, websites, behaviours, ideas and organisations. It is customary for people knowledgeable in the respective field to judge as 'gatekeepers' the creativity of an output, based on established norms, standards or criteria. For instance, in the Creativity International Graphic Design Awards, a panel of design professionals judge entries on a scale of 1 to 10 based on the following criteria: design, usability, theme/idea, execution and follow-through. Outputs are usually judged as creative if they meet a high standard, show originality and value, all of which are subjective and open to interpretation. Technically speaking, anything that has been created which has not been made before counts as an invention, whereas creativity involves the capability or act of conceiving something original or unusual (Sloane, 2007).

Personality traits or dispositions

Several writers (Torrance, 1962; Shallcross, 1981; Feist, 1999) have also focused on identifying the essential characteristics of the creative mind. These include: open-mindedness, persistence, curiosity, self-confidence, independence and intrinsic motivation. Merely possessing these characteristics is no guarantee that creative outputs will follow, particularly if the environment is not conducive to creative expression. Moreover, there are also negative personality traits associated with creative people, such as hyperactivity, rebelliousness, sarcasm, disobedience and egocentricity (Runco and Pagnani, 2011). However, an over-emphasis on traits is unhelpful because it implies that creativity is a matter of genetics, fixed at birth, rather than something that can be nurtured in everyone.

Studies of the most creative minds reveal patterns essential to our understanding of creativity. Gardner (2011) reports that the most significant breakthroughs in the lives of geniuses such as Sigmund Freud, Albert Einstein and Pablo Picasso were not 'Eureka' moments but took at least ten years for the initial idea to be conceived and another ten years for the idea to be accepted. He also found that they experienced greater emotional turmoil than most of us but had support from someone reassuring them that they were not crazy. In a more recent study of 160 of the greatest philosophers, writers, composers and artists ever to have lived, Currey (2014) draws several key lessons. The majority were early risers, frequent walkers and kept to a tight schedule. Legend suggests that the neighbours of the German philosopher Immanuel Kant (1724–1804) could set their clocks by his 3.30 pm walk.

The most creative people are usually very motivated individuals. They love what they do and are intrinsically driven by the subject rather than any promised rewards or external goals. Their passion means that they follow their interests, which calls for resourcefulness, single-mindedness and perseverance. The film director Henry Jaglom likened the joy of creating to 'being on a bicycle going downhill' (cited by Hennessey and Amabile, 1988: 11). This exhilarating experience relates to Csikszentmihalyi's (1996) concept of 'flow' that describes the highly focused, intense state of consciousness when someone is fully engrossed in what they are thinking and doing. More recent studies of motivation by Pink (2011) highlight a move from a Motivation 2.0 world (based on rewards and punishments) to a Motivation 3.0 world (based on inherent satisfaction in the work itself). However, it is worth noting a recent shift in our understanding of creativity, from individual creativity to 'participatory creativity'. This acknowledges that those associated with creative works have not existed in isolation, rather their ideas draw on the historical, cultural and political context in which they live (Clapp, 2017).

The creative thinking process

John Cleese (1991), the English actor and comedian, once said that 'creativity is not a talent; it is a way of operating'. One of the earliest theories put forward to explain this process was based on observations and a study of famous inventors (Figure 1.4). The English psychologist Graham Wallas (1926) suggested in *The Art of Thought* that the process begins with understanding the task in hand (inception or preparation), which involves identifying and exploring the problem from different directions and collecting background information. During the incubation stage, the problem is put aside without much deliberate thought. The brain begins to make connections with previous experiences necessary to formulate ideas. The idea emerges (the 'Aha' moment) during the illumination stage and may follow a gut feeling. Finally, the idea is then implemented and tested (realisation), first personally and then with others (verification).

Wallas provided practical suggestions on how to improve productivity, which modern psychologists would endorse (Sternberg, 2003; Gardner, 2007). For instance, he advised during the incubation stage that people should take frequent breaks and return to problems rather than trying to solve them in one sitting. He strongly advocated 'uninterrupted day-dreaming' and walking to relax the mind (Wallas, 1926: 59).

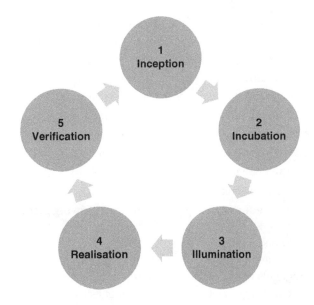

Figure 1.4 The Wallas stage model of creativity

There are other factors at work in the creative process, including luck (favourable chance). The Russian author Leo Tolstoy (1904: 42) once said, 'a work that pleases a certain circle of people is accepted as art, then a definition of art is devised to cover these productions'. Simply being in the right place with the right people can make a difference to whether an idea moves forward. The developments behind many technologies, including the airplane, air conditioning, radio, photography, microwave and the Apple iPhone, had significant slices of luck. However, the likelihood of benefiting from a break is very much in the hands of individuals who are proactive and persistent in their approach. They are resilient enough to handle setbacks, what the business community considers 'brilliant failures' (Schoemaker, 2011). There are important implications here for educators in cultivating dispositions, which we discuss in Chapter 10.

The concept of innovation is sometimes used interchangeably with creativity. However, technically creativity is the generation of a new idea whereas innovation describes its application or implementation. A staff meeting may generate lots of ideas but unless something gets implemented then there is no innovation. Risk is needed for something to become an innovation. But the risk can be small, for instance, extending or shortening the lesson to allow more flexibility for teachers (Hampson et al., 2010).

The creative learning environment

What is deemed to be creative is shaped by the socio-cultural context within which it is produced. Something may be valued at one time, but not another. The work of Vincent van Gogh and Franz Schubert were either ignored or deplored as worthless for most of their lifetimes. Changes in fashion, style or social conventions can elevate something as creative even though the artist or product has not changed.

Where you think sometimes matters as much as what you think. One study reports that the school environment can affect a learner's progress by as much as 25 per cent over a year (Barrett et al., 2013). Creativity follows the interplay between the individual's own personality, the environment and the creative process itself. In the school context, the creative learning environment means more than the physical layout of the buildings and furniture. It includes the pedagogical approaches and the psychological climate in which children are encouraged to be creative. One systematic review of the literature on creative learning environments in education suggests that the following factors stand out:

- flexible use of space and time
- availability of appropriate materials
- opportunities to regularly work outside the classroom/school
- 'playful' or 'games-bases' approaches with a degree of learner autonomy
- respectful relationships between teachers and learners
- opportunities for peer collaboration
- partnerships with outside agencies
- awareness of learners' needs
- non-prescriptive planning (Davies et al., 2013).

Another interaction highlighted as effective in early years' settings is 'sustained shared thinking' (SST) where meaning is jointly constructed through dialogue (Siraj-Blatchford et al., 2002). This term refers to the sharing of thinking and to the importance of the sustained nature of such an interaction. This emerged as an analytical node within the 2004 Effective Provision of Pre-school Education report (EPPE; Sylva et al., 2004), which was a longitudinal study of practice in early years' settings. SST occurred most commonly in effective settings, where researchers observed higher cognitive outcomes (Siraj-Blatchford, 2009). As such SST has been described as 'effective pedagogic interaction' (Sylva et al., 2010: 257) and it most commonly occurs in 1:1 interactions between adult and child (Siraj and Asani, 2015). There is a clear link to principles such as co-construction and participation advocated by theorists such as Vygotsky (1962). For example, during SST interactions, effective teachers use a variety of techniques such as scaffolding, challenge, discussion and modelling to promote learning (Sylva et al., 2010). A key component of the learning and thinking environment is the provision for dialogue.

LANGUAGE, COMMUNICATION AND THINKING

Socio-cultural and socio-constructivist theories of cognitive development propose the importance of cultural materials, tools and signs (e.g. words) and social interaction in mediating learning (Siegler and Alibali, 2005). These conceptions are generally traced to Vygotsky (1962), Leontiev (1978) and other theorists who see cognition as a complex social phenomenon rather than a mental process separate from the world. Learning involves a process of 'enculturation', acquiring the jargon, behaviour, beliefs and norms of a new social group (Brown et al., 1989). Language is central to this immersion in culture.

Thoughts have been described as 'sentences in the head' (Ohreen, 2004: 34), illustrating the close relationship between language, communication and thinking. The case for promoting spoken dialogue as a means of supporting children's intellectual development has been made forcefully elsewhere (Mercer and Littleton 2007; Alexander, 2008). It is underpinned by rigorous theory drawing upon the fields of psychology, philosophy and linguistics (Vygotsky, 1962; Bruner, 1983; Wells, 1999). And yet in practice, classroom talk and its importance for critical and creative thinking is perhaps the most neglected element of pedagogy. Alexander's (2010) dialogic model sets out principles for teachers to work from. Teaching becomes dialogic when it is:

- collective (teachers and children addressing learning tasks together)
- reciprocal (teachers and children listening to each other, sharing ideas and considering alternative viewpoints)
- supportive (children articulating their ideas freely, without fear of embarrassment over 'wrong' answers)
- cumulative (teachers and children building on their own and each other's ideas in a coherent, logical manner)
- purposeful (teachers planning classroom talk with clear goals in mind).

This model is built upon a social constructivist view of learning, i.e. it is assumed that through interaction the learner builds an understanding of the world as mental structures or patterns. The theory runs that children sharpen their thinking as they interact with those around them, especially adults (Pritchard and Woollard, 2010).

The initial stimulus for an idea often comes from working with others. The power of others in shaping how people think and behave is well known and can be a positive force (e.g. voluntary work, keep fit groups) or a negative force (e.g. football hooligans, jihadist cells). What psychologists call 'groupthink' (Janis, 1972) can result in the distortion of reasoning and common sense as individuals unquestionably follow the word of leaders (Bond, 2015). By providing regular opportunities for debate and argumentation, teachers can reduce the likelihood of groupthink. The approaches we have selected (Chapters 4–10) all value dialogue and discussion. The use of role play, modelling and problem-based learning in which real-life scenarios are examined from different perspectives, can also build up children's capacity to think independently while well-planned and organised collaborative projects (especially those that involve members of the wider community) develop communication and problem-solving skills. Fostering a strong, supportive classroom spirit and school identity can go a long way in creating a climate conducive to thinking creatively and critically. Children need the confidence and opportunity to talk regularly in different contexts and with different people about their ideas. Johnson (2011) highlights that many good ideas come from conversations with people from different disciplines and backgrounds who combine their hunches in what he calls 'liquid networks', named after the eighteenth-century coffee houses where writers would meet, argue and develop ideas. When social interaction involves pupils in describing, explaining and justifying their views, it becomes a powerful means of developing metacognition (Kuhn and Dean, 2004; Siraj-Blatchford, 2009).

THINKING AND EMOTIONS

Our ability to think well is affected by how we feel and our inclinations. To state the obvious, at any given task children can respond in different ways depending upon how they feel. Research indicates that there is a tendency to notice information that reflects or is congruent with our prevailing mood (Newton, 2014). So, for example, if we are sad then we tend to focus on the more depressing features of a text, film or conversation. Someone who is anxious tends to interpret ambiguous scenarios as a threat to themselves. A simple statement such as 'There was a fire in the room' can be interpreted in lots of ways. A person might think about a family huddled around a nineteenth-century cottage with a kettle on the hob and bread toasting over the fire. Or this could be viewed as a raging inferno about to engulf the whole house. Students feeling happy are more likely to think about the former whereas sad and anxious students are more likely to interpret the fire as a major risk (Newton, 2014: 31). It is also the case that students in a positive mood tend to reason in a more superficial manner, failing to see the detail of an argument.

Research also shows that the brains of adults who have suffered emotional trauma, for example as victims of child abuse, change for the worse (Baron-Cohen, 2011). The empathy circuit within the brain is damaged. Baron-Cohen examines why people behave with zero degrees of empathy, committing horrendous crimes. He concludes that they think only of themselves (single-minded attention) rather than someone else's mind at the same time as their own (double-minded attention). For Baron-Cohen and others, empathy needs to have a greater place in education and society at large. Without this and other regulatory feelings, our thinking can be highly logical but profoundly wrong. Hence emotions have been described as providing 'the rudder to guide judgement and action' (Immordino-Yang and Damasio, 2007: 3).

Increasingly, educational psychologists acknowledge the significance of emotion in understanding how children think and behave (Phelps, 2006). The psychologist Tali Sharot (2017) illustrates the power of emotion over reason with a story of how Donald Trump won a televised debate over the causes of autism. Ben Carson, an expert pediatric neurosurgeon, provided many facts to show that there was no direct link between child-hood vaccines and autism. However, the audience was swayed not by research reports but by Trump's anecdote of a nurse inserting a horse-sized syringe into a 'beautiful child', who a week later caught a tremendous fever, 'got very, very sick and is now autistic'. Parental anxiety overtook reasoning and Carson's argument was dead in the water.

Current psychological models support dual processing theories. Daniel Kahneman (2012), Nobel Laureate in Economics, helps explain what this means in his book *Thinking, Fast and Slow*. System 1 is fast, intuitive and emotional, whereas System 2 is slower and more logical. Both are equally important and have their strengths and limitations. To illustrate, Kahneman (2012: 7) gives this scenario:

> An individual has been described by a neighbor as follows: 'Steve is very shy and with-drawn, invariably helpful but with little interest in people or in the world of reality. A meek and tidy soul, he has a need for order and structure, and a passion for detail.' Is Steve more likely to be a librarian or a farmer?

In this illustration, many of us would conclude that Steve is more likely to be a librarian than a farmer. This is based on preconceived, stereotypical ideas of what librarians are like. We may not be aware of, or decide to ignore, statistical factors such as there are many more farmers than librarians in the country. And, logically, the likelihood is that more farmers will be 'meek and tidy' than those who care for books. Kahneman points out that we often rely on resemblance as default thinking: the resemblances of one thing, in this case someone's personality, to another we hold in our memory.

Kahneman concludes that to improve judgement and decision-making requires con-siderable effort in developing System 2 thinking. But he acknowledges that questioning one's intuition is uncomfortable even though relying on System 1 thinking leads to over-confidence, extreme predictions and inaccuracies. In Chapters 4–10, we outline some of the approaches teachers can adopt in slowing down children's thinking so that they are less impulsive and prone to error. However, there is a salutary warning. Despite extensive research spanning more than forty years, Kahneman acknowledges that in his own think-ing he has only improved in his ability to recognise situations in which errors are likely. He has also made much more progress in identifying the errors in the thinking of others than his own.

Among the implications for educators is to encourage students to be open about how they feel, to promote self-regulatory strategies and emotional competencies. Expert teach-ers tend to be skilled at responding appropriately to their students' emotions, even from observing their facial expressions and vocal tone. In any event, emotional intelligence can be learned through practice and training (Goleman, 1995). Moreover, there is growing evidence that students benefit considerably from teachers who model a positive outlook (e.g. 'I can do this with a bit more effort') and provide explicit instruction on how to overcome barriers (Seligman, 2002; Dweck, 2006; Hattie, 2009). It is important for learners to recognise that learning is often hard work and that stress is not inherently bad; it can be harnessed in a positive way to increase alertness and responsiveness to challenges, such as finishing a project on time. The responsibility of teachers is not to eliminate classroom stress but to create an environment in which intellectual risks are encouraged and all learners feel valued, safe and secure.

SUMMARY

Thinking is a vast subject. Inevitably then, there are many different views on what thinking means. At a basic level, it involves exercising the mind. However, our thinking is affected by many factors, including previous experiences, the language we use, the company we keep and how we feel.

- Thinking critically involves a range of skills including reasoning, evaluation and analysis. Critical thinking is not straightforward and is prone to cognitive bias.
- Thinking creatively means generating ideas that are novel and useful.
- Studies of creativity focus largely on the created outputs, the creator's personality, the thinking process or the environment in which creativity develops.
- Children and young people have the capacity to think well. Teachers have a responsibility to develop children's thinking skills.

2

WHAT CAN WE LEARN FROM THE HISTORY OF THINKING, CHILDHOOD AND SCHOOLING?

INTRODUCTION

In 2016, Paul Dix asked teachers to nominate the greatest educational fads or gimmicks over the last twenty years.[1] The responses included learning styles, Brain Gym and Personal Learning Thinking Skills. The latter was originally introduced in 2005 as part of government reforms of education for 14–19-year-olds (DfES, 2005). The framework set out skills that young people would need to enter the workplace and adult life as confident and capable individuals. These skills included creative thinking (e.g. generating ideas and questioning assumptions) and independent enquiry (e.g. evaluating information, judging its relevance and value). On 15 February 2011, the framework was consigned to the National Archives. It seems appropriate then to take stock and reflect on what we can learn from past efforts to teach thinking. Where did this 'nice [but impossible] idea', as the blogger put it, originate?

---

[1] www.teachertoolkit.co.uk/2016/07/10/education-fads/ (accessed 3 November 2017).

In this chapter, we trace the origins and development of thinking in the broader context of ideas about childhood and schooling. This should prove instructive in understanding where the teaching of thinking fitted into the priorities of past educational systems, how these have changed and why, metaphorically speaking, 'thinking skills' deserve to be brought out of the National Archives. This chapter also serves another purpose. It illustrates how much of the discourse in education, which forms the backdrop to the teaching of thinking, and ideas around curriculum reform, effective pedagogy and the respective roles of teacher and learner are recurring themes in history. The overview offers an anchor point at a time when those entering the teaching profession have so little input on the history of education in their initial teacher training. The chapter focuses on developments as seen through a Western lens. However, interest in Eastern thinking has increased in recent years following the leading performance of educational systems in countries such as Singapore, Hong Kong and South Korea (see Chapter 3).

THE ANCIENT MIND

A new field of enquiry called cognitive archaeology skilfully pieces together the material remains from the distant past to try and figure out what people thought long ago. Archaeologists (Renfrew, 2007; Coolidge and Wynn, 2009) reckon that the making of the first stone tools required considerable planning (e.g. to collect raw materials some distance away) and imagination, as no one would have known what the finished tools would look like. The stone workers (knappers) had to visually rotate in their minds, images of what would happen to a stone if it were struck in a certain way and then imagine how it would then look from the other side. And this was the kind of intellectual effort needed to make everyday objects. Consider the thinking involved in the building of major cromlechs such as Stonehenge. One study suggests that the Stone Age architects had the geometrical skills to rival Pythagoras – but they lived 2,000 years before the Greek 'father of numbers' was born (Keys, 2008). Our prehistoric ancestors were nothing like the cartoon figure, Fred Flintstone.

We also find the origins of creativity in prehistoric times. We can only speculate about what was going on in our ancestors' minds tens of thousands of years ago when they first picked up natural crayons and began painting their bodies and environment. When cave art in Spain and France was rediscovered in the nineteenth century it was assumed that the art was made for its own sake as prehistoric people were thought too primitive for the higher kinds of reason (Bruno, 2017). More recent interpretations see these earliest creative expressions as records of the histories of tribes, their rituals and beliefs before writing served that purpose. Victor Shamas (2018), an American psychologist, has spent more than thirty years studying what it *feels* like to create something. He believes that since prehistoric times people have always shared the same dual motivation: to produce something fresh, unlike anything that has gone before; and a spiritual transcendence to connect with something greater, an ideal or hidden truth. Imagine then the determination of prehistoric artists who spent months with little light or oxygen in the dark recesses of caves. They certainly were not motivated by commercial gain. They understood the intrinsic value of being creative, to express feelings, inspire others and connect with the supernatural. The production of stone tools and cave art are only two examples of our longstanding abilities to think creatively and critically. At least in terms of thinking capacity, archaeologists conclude that there is little difference between modern and ancient minds. The creative explosion of prehistoric art has been described as 'when the final major re-design of the mind took place' (Mithen, 1996: 174).

THINKING IN THE FIRST SCHOOLS

Our earliest glimpses of the teaching of thinking in formal education can be traced to the ancient Greeks, who created the first educational system more than 2,500 years ago. The unqualified elementary schoolteacher was only responsible for teaching children basic skills. Young children's moral education was entrusted to a pedagogue or family servant, who escorted the children (boys only) to and from school. Literally and metaphorically, the pedagogue held a lantern to light their path. While the primary teaching focused on reading, writing and counting, largely through recitation and drill, the secondary schools introduced textual criticism, grammar and the natural sciences of mathematics, music and astronomy. There were also gymnasiums for training in sport. Although we can trace here the beginnings of critical thinking being taught, this did not extend to creative thinking. Marrou (1956: 175) pointed out:

> The schoolboy of antiquity was not obliged to be original: all that was required of him was that he should learn to write and criticize according to certain rules.

In higher education, there was an emphasis on the teaching of philosophy, logical thinking and rhetoric or effective speaking, all highly regarded in society. The itinerant teacher Protagoras (486–411 BC), for instance, once charged 10,000 drachmas for a course on rhetoric at a time when one drachma was a skilled worker's daily wage (Worthington, 2007). For ambitious young Athenians who wanted a career in politics, learning how to win an argument then was an appealing proposition. The most successful rhetoric contained:

- Logos (Greek for 'word') – logical facts and figures, to appear knowledgeable
- Pathos (Greek for 'suffering' or 'experience') – imagination and feelings, the emotional impact

- Ethos (Greek for 'character') – personal anecdotes, to convince the audience of the speaker's trustworthy character and credibility
- Kairos (Greek for 'right time' or 'opportunity') – maintaining the appropriate tone, structure and timing.

Today, the most acclaimed public speeches are built on similar principles. In a review of the best Technology Entertainment and Design (TED) talks, some of which have attracted millions of viewers, Anderson (2018: 10) identifies the importance of connecting to audiences with personal stories, focusing on one big idea and asking the question: 'Who does this benefit?' As he acknowledges, public speaking is 'an ancient art, wired deeply into our minds'.

The philosopher Plato (427 BC–347 BC) established the first institution of higher education in Western history, known as the Academy. It was originally a garden where intellectuals gathered. In a sense this was the birthplace of thinking 'as a very special kind of psychic activity, very uncomfortable, but also very exciting' (Havelock, 1963, quoted by Gleck, 2012: 37). Fundamental questions were raised about humanity, the ideal society and the purpose of education therein. Plato believed that we come into the world equipped with hard-wired innate ideas (e.g. about love, morality and mathematics), which could be stirred through reflection. Aristotle (384 BC–322 BC), Plato's star pupil, challenged this and argued that the source of learning is experience. As Gaarder (1995: 89) explains in the wonderfully erudite *Sophie's World*, Aristotle 'got down on all fours and studied frogs and fish' whereas Plato was more interested in the eternal world of ideas. Prinz (2012) points out that the entire history of Western philosophy is a set of footnotes on this seminal debate: whether knowledge is acquired through perception (the senses) or thinking (reason). Aristotle maintained that the distinguishing feature of what makes us human is the ability to make rational decisions and his system of logic provided the blueprint for Western education.

Although the ancient Greek world was very different from our own, it remains the key anchor for modern debates over how children should learn. For example, Plato suggested that the education of young children should be play-based because 'nothing that is learned under compulsion stays with the mind' (quoted by Thomas, 2013: 4). And yet, Greek schools were characterised by a didactic, heavy-handed style of teaching and corporal punishment designed to instil memory recall, discipline and obedience. Put crudely, the Greek philosophers put a marker down as to whether schools should instruct children and transmit knowledge or cultivate independent thinking and discovery. The suicide of Socrates in 399 BC raised further questions about the extent to which free speech and thinking should be tolerated. Socrates was accused of corrupting young minds through his continual questioning and probing. He maintained that his philosophical enquiry was a means of answering the big question, 'How should we live?' The scholar Gregory Vlastos (1991), who spent his academic life studying the Greek philosophers, concluded that the Socratic method was 'among the greatest achievements of humanity' because this opened up philosophy to the 'common man'. The legacy can be found not just in movements such as Philosophers in Pubs[2] and Philosophy for Children (Chapter 8) but social networking services such as meetup.com, which bring people together to discuss their passions.

However, several modern writers (De Bono, 1994; Finn, 2015) blame the ancient Greeks for undervaluing creative thinking that did not feature strongly in their formal schooling. It is noteworthy that the Greeks had a rich vocabulary for critical thinking – 'critic', 'critical', 'criterion' and 'criticism' all stem from their literary judges (*krites*) – but not an equivalent stock of words for creativity.[3] Critical thinking certainly offered structure and logic so necessary when processing information in the Greek quest to 'know thyself'. And yet this has also meant that Western schooling, built on the Classical model, has largely ignored the more expressive, emotional and creative aspects of education. This is despite the pleas of individuals such as the Roman writer Cicero (106 BC–43 BC) for a broad-based education in the liberal arts (*artes liberals*), which at the time was effectively training in how to be a good citizen. Philosopher Martin Nussbaum (2010) believes that this remains essential for democratic societies because it involves fostering critical thinking, problem-solving and an understanding of others.

MEDIEVAL SCHOLASTIC THINKING

Throughout the medieval period and beyond, the grammar school curriculum was modelled on 'the seven liberal arts': grammar, rhetoric and dialect (*trivium*) and arithmetic, geometry, music and astronomy (*quadrivium*). The Trivium provided grounding in the rules of language necessary to study any subject. John of Salisbury (*c.* 1120–1180) argued it was the basis of independent learning because once these were grasped, students did not need the help of a teacher to understand the meaning of books or to find solutions to problems. Robinson (2013) suggests that the Trivium was a *way* of knowing rather than just what was learned: grammar (knowing), rhetoric (communicating) and dialect (questioning). Far from being a medieval relic, Robinson argues that a contemporary trivium would offer much to modern-day students.

Historians have traditionally dismissed education in the Middle Ages as a period of stagnation where 'practically nothing' was added in terms of ideas (Curtis and Boultwood, 1965: 93). This is not true. The words 'scholar' and 'scholarship', for instance, come from

---

[2]http://philosophyinpubs.co.uk/ (accessed 20 June 2018).

[3]However, the Greek root (*krainein*) for the Latin verb *creare* meant to 'fulfil' and by this definition, anyone who fulfils his or her potential can be described as creative (Pope, 2005: 60).

the medieval practice of writing critical remarks (*scholia*) in the margins of texts. Scribes also introduced word separation in Classical texts, which had previously been single blocks with very little or no punctuation. While this kind of scholarship was limited to the major libraries and monasteries of the medieval world, there is a little bit of evidence to suggest that a few teachers offered their students momentary respite from the tedious exercises in rote learning and translation that characterised medieval schoolrooms. For example, an eighth-century teacher called Aldhelm enjoyed writing his own riddle books designed to test how 'quick-witted' children were, as well as providing a source of pleasure. He also wrote dialogues in which, unusually, children asked the questions rather than the teacher (Godfrey, 1907: 35–36). At the higher levels of study, in the top fee-paying schools, scholars engaged in disputations that undoubtedly involved applying skills in logical thinking (Orme, 2006).

In the twelfth century, leading schoolmen ('scholastics') combined mainly Greek pagan thinking with Christian teaching to produce 'scholasticism'. This was an approach to critical thinking that featured the forerunners of the lecture (*lectio*) and debate (*disputatio*). The medieval Church, which was inseparable from society, harnessed critical thinking for its own purpose in identifying and refuting (or burning) heretics. Students engaged in theological arguments, led by the likes of Thomas Aquinas (1225–1274) and William of Ockham (*c.* 1288–*c.* 1348). Aquinas developed natural theology, in which he used reason and the experience of nature to provide arguments for the existence of God. Ockham introduced the principle that among competing hypotheses, the one with the fewest assumptions should be chosen. 'Ockam's Razor', as it is called, is still referred to in rational thinking as a means of shaving away any material that is superfluous and opting for the simplest explanation.

The aims of schooling the poor in the Middle Ages were to inculcate industrious habits and to remind them of their station in life in a very hierarchical society. This was not the time or audience for teaching critical or creative thinking. But as one expert points out, for the clear majority, 'It was not an unrealistic upbringing for their situation at that time' (Jewell, 1998: 91).

THINKING IN THE RENAISSANCE AND THE ENLIGHTENMENT

In the fifteenth century, a group of intellectuals known as humanists started to question the scholastic, medieval approaches to learning. John Colet (1467–1515), for example, regarded the manner of disputations that aimed simply to win arguments as valueless. He told the Dutch scholar Erasmus (1466–1536): 'We seek not for victory in argument but for truth' (quoted by Curtis and Boultwood, 1965: 117). Erasmus criticised slavish rote learning, arguing that the gaining of knowledge could only be achieved through purposeful, intelligent thinking. He would undoubtedly be satisfied with the strapline of the modern-day European Commission Erasmus+ projects: 'Enriching lives, opening minds'.

Renaissance scholars worked on the premise that religion, art, human nature, law and other aspects of life were open to criticism. The natural philosopher Sir Francis Bacon's (1561–1626) *The Advancement of Learning* (1605) has been held up as one of the first texts in critical thinking. He believed that truth could be established not by rational argument, as Aristotle maintained, but through real-world investigation (empiricism). Thus, Bacon is credited as being the creator of modern science. He was responsible for moving the study of nature from 'armchair speculation' and abstract reasoning, to experimentation and first-hand observation through the scientific method (Henry, 2017).

The invention of the printing press in the fifteenth century was undoubtedly one of the most significant milestones in the history of literacy, thought and education. It was the engine of creative thinking in art, science and literature. The actual invention and operation of the printing press was a highly creative process by itself. Images originally designed to be placed on walls or parchments now appeared in woodblocks and engravings, reworked by potters, cabinet-makers, glaziers and tapestry weavers. A new generation of artists emerged. Their ideas were circulated and preserved in print, thus elevating them to 'immortal' status. Incidentally, the word 'stereotype' is derived from the printing press, when plates (called stereotypes) were used to produce identical copies of one page. Today, one of the functions of critical thinking is to challenge stereotypes such as people from the same country or race are alike, as if they have all been stamped from one plate.

The story of the printing press is also instructive in highlighting the dangers of creativity, which most people assume is a good thing. If someone is called 'creative' then this is naturally taken as a compliment. In describing the impact of the printing press, Eisenstein (1982: 254) points out that the 'creativity of one generation proved more burdensome to the next'. Playwrights, poets, composers and writers were caught up in an increasingly frantic pursuit of novelty. Critics were quick to judge the quality of printed work and so artists were expected to spend more time researching their subjects, i.e. more time in the library than the workshop to ensure accuracy of fine details, such as whether Saint Jerome wore a red hat as was the fashion among contemporary cardinals. The 'correct' presentation of historical subjects assumed greater importance than imaginative thinking.

The collection of ideas, values and beliefs known as the Enlightenment (*c.* 1650–1800) placed an emphasis on human rational capacity to advance knowledge and improve social conditions. Before the Enlightenment, Christian intellectuals saw education in terms of transmitting truths necessary for salvation. The essence of the Enlightenment was to suggest that reason, experience and exploration, rather than superstition and belief in received wisdom, were the key to the good life. The author Steven Pinker (2018), in *Enlightenment Now*, points out that the uplifting Enlightenment principles of applying reason, science and humanism remain highly relevant in an age of cynicism, doubt and fear. The implied purpose of education was to liberate rather than constrain. But, as Phillips (1996) points out, some of the leading figures of the Enlightenment recoiled at the implications of their philosophy because they had no intention of over-throwing the established order. Rather, they wanted to redefine it.

René Descartes (1596–1650), the most famous rationalist, was a very restless spirit, moving house at least eighteen times in twenty-two years. Due to childhood illness, he often slept until noon and valued his bed as 'the best place to think' (Zeldin, 1994: 192). Descartes cast doubt on the reliability of learning through the senses because they can deceive. He was right. Consider how optical illusions distort appearances and we know that amputees experience sensations such as itching and pain from missing limbs. Instead, Descartes looked inwards and developed a systematic approach to doubting something until it could be proved. His famous dictum, 'I think, therefore I am', was his conclusion that the very act of doubting was a form of thinking and therefore assurance that he was alive. As Zeldin (1994: 192) put it, Descartes made 'the historic and heretical pronounce-ment that curiosity was something all people had, that nothing could prevent it, and that it increases inevitably with knowledge'.

The Enlightenment is particularly relevant to our overview because it signalled new thinking over how our mind works, the way childhood was understood and the purpose of education. Richard Mulcaster (1531–1611), a sixteenth-century schoolmaster, believed that educators should seek to enhance children's natural capacities: 'whereto nature makes him toward, but that nurture sets him forward' (quoted by Prinz, 2012: 8). He was the first to use the terms 'nature' and 'nurture', which became central to the enduring debate about whether intelligent behaviour is determined by biology or the environment, and which has only recently been resolved as a kind of score draw (Ridley, 2003; Dowling, 2007; Kovas et al., 2013; Polderman et al., 2015).

This was a period when elaborate theories of consciousness first developed, which rec-ognised that the mind was not a passive receptor but an active processor of information (Bullard, 2016). The philosopher John Locke (1632–1704) put forward the theory of men-tal association where an idea is triggered by association with another idea. For example, he suggested children's fear of the dark was associated with the stories about goblins and spirits they were told at night by 'foolish maids' (Locke, 1690: 8). Locke is often associ-ated with the 'blank slate' view of the mind, a phrase first coined by Thomas Aquinas. Locke actually said that children were like 'white Paper, or Wax, to be moulded and fash-ioned as one pleases' and that 'nine parts of ten are formed by upbringing or education' (Locke, 1690: 217), but he added that 'due weight should be given to the tenth part'. In other words, learning was largely a matter of nurture but not exclusively so. Locke's most famous work, *Some Thoughts Concerning Education* (1693), became the most influential book about thinking in Western history for the next 200 years. Locke gave all kinds of weird and wonderful child-rearing guidance, for example on sleeping, diet and footwear, but the key point was that he recognised the need to strengthen children's powers of reasoning through experience. He likened children to newly arrived travellers to a strange country who had to learn the customs and ways of life. Locke hinted at the plasticity of children's thinking: 'I imagine the minds of children as easily turned this or that way as water itself' (quoted by Thomas, 2013: 20). Locke did not, however, say much about the importance of feelings and he regarded imaginative thinking as 'a source of mischief' (Quick, 1907: 222). His focus was on the education of the young gentleman fit for seventeenth-century society.

A more romantic notion of childhood can be traced to the Swiss philosopher Jean-Jacques Rousseau (1712–1778). He believed that children were not born in sin, as the Church taught, but innocent and naturally good. It was the corrupting influence of adults that children needed to be protected against. His most famous work, *Emile* (1762), based on the development of a fictitious pupil in the care of his tutor, sets out how children should be educated and its purpose, namely to achieve happiness. Children should learn through trial-and-error, observation, play and exploration. They should enjoy the 'Age of Nature' (0–12 years) to run around free from constraints, including reading books,[4] and acquire knowledge through first-hand experience.

Rousseau's enlightened view of childhood didn't prevent him from allowing his own illegitimate children to be sent to an orphanage. However, his writings influenced succeeding generations of progressive thinkers, including Johann Pestalozzi, Robert Owen, Friedrich Fröebel, Rudolf Steiner and Loris Malaguzzi. Over time, the respective state policies towards education, particularly in the early years, have been shaped by their child-centred views. However, the short-term impact of a handful of European thinkers on mainstream education should not be overstated. Before the nineteenth century, most children were not even attending school. Those who were in classrooms received little encouragement to express their views, think independently or follow their interests. Things continued very much as they had always done, characterised by rote learning, the teaching of Scripture and basic skills in reading, writing and arithmetic.

CHALLENGING THE INDUSTRIAL MODEL OF EDUCATION

The industrial revolution heightened political interest in providing mass education to ensure that Britain had the necessary basic skills to remain economically advanced. From

---

[4]The exception was *Robinson Crusoe*. Ironically, children's books were invented during the Enlightenment.

the 1830s, gradually a dual system of Church and state-funded elementary schools operated very much on a factory model of 'producing' an obedient, literate and God-fearing workforce. A few voices, such as the Scottish philosopher Thomas Carlyle (1795–1881), saw the potential of education 'to impart the gift of thinking to those who cannot think' (quoted by Williams, 1958: 82). Radical reformers such as the Chartist William Lovett (1800–1877) envisaged 'Schools for the People' in which children and adults had access to 'useful works on politics, morals, the sciences, history and such instructing and entertaining works as may be generally approved of' (Kelly, 1970: 141). For most in authority, however, this was not the time to expand minds – as one school inspector lamented, he had never heard a child 'ask a question of its teacher on the subject of the lesson' (Martin, 1979: 51).

There were exceptions. Richard Dawes (1793–1867) opened an excellent school at King's Somborne, Dorset in 1842. He was the local rector, a keen scientist and eager to train children in how to observe and think logically. Hence his pupils calculated wind speeds from cloud shadows, worked out water pressure on fish in streams and compared animals' teeth. He set up a library so children could take books home to read to their parents. The children formed clubs to carry out their investigations. No doubt they were engaged in much reasoning, inferring and other higher-order thinking skills. Dawes regarded the conventional schools as 'a deception, retarding the cause of education rather than advancing it' (quoted in Stewart and McCann, 1967: 133). And yet the Victorian education policy-makers and teachers largely achieved their objectives. Basic literacy levels increased from approximately 73 per cent (female) and 80 per cent (male) to 97 per cent for both men and women (Lawson and Silver, 1973). The system of schooling contributed to preserving the social order and most young people had respect for their elders.

Historians trace more 'progressive' tendencies in the curriculum and pedagogy to a series of official publications, the *Handbook of Suggestions for the Consideration of Teachers* (1905–1957). The remarkable Robert Morant, Permanent Secretary to the Board of Education, introduced these handbooks. He has been described as 'an educational buccaneer, a desk-bound Francis Drake' (Eaglesham, 1967: 39). Primary teachers responded to suggestions from both the Board of Education and Her Majesty's Inspectors of School that children should be taught in creative ways and learn through first-hand experiences such as visits to local parks and museums. For the first time in their lives, such visits allowed thousands of London children to see the River Thames while others were amazed at the sight of a cow in the flesh. Teachers had scope to provide 'realistic studies' by making lessons relevant. For instance, rather than write an imaginary letter to a child in France, children corresponded with French pen pals. Technologies were also embraced by a growing number of schools. By the 1930s, around 800 schools were reported to be using projectors to show films and about 5,000 made some use of the wireless (Lowndes, 1937: 172). In practical subjects, such as woodwork and metalwork, the emphasis was placed on giving children simple tools and materials to work independently as soon as possible. In drama, children were taught creative skills such as puppetry.

Official encouragement for schools to provide a richer curriculum and to develop children's thinking capabilities was further endorsed in the Hadow Report of 1931: 'the development of [children's] critical powers should be encouraged, so that, as time goes on, the child should be taught to rely more upon his independent initiative and enterprise' (Board of Education, 1931: 43). The Hadow Committee discussed how primary schools could promote children's 'higher mental capacities' in real-life contexts. It was scornful of teachers who concentrated merely on instruction in reading, writing and arithmetic without giving 'meaning' to these skills by relating them to children's 'living interests'. The Hadow Report signalled a progressive turn in the very notion of what schools were for: 'a good school is ... not a place of compulsory instruction, but a community of old and young, engaged in learning by cooperative experiment' (1931: Introduction), while 'the curriculum is to be thought of in terms of activity and experience rather than of knowledge to be acquired and facts to be stored' (1931: section 75).

Members of the Hadow Committee drew upon the sentiments of John Dewey (1859–1952) and Maria Montessori (1870–1952). Dewey argued that schools were more interested in meeting curriculum demands ('covering the ground' as he put it) and transmitting knowledge rather than nurturing the mind. In *How We Think* (Dewey, 1910), Dewey explained that education was not about learning facts but developing criticality and reflective thinking. This was best achieved through practical problem-solving, an approach generally termed instrumentalism, which remains hugely influential in primary education today. Montessori looked upon the infant school as an idealised home with exemplary family role models. These views stood in contrast to the traditional factory model of education with its emphasis on efficiency, repetitious teaching methods and little scope for children's creative thinking.

The spirit of educational reform and reconstruction that followed the Second World War, embodied in the 1944 Education Act, offered new freedom and opportunity for all. A primary sector from 5 to 11 years was established with progression to secondary education. The 'elementary' tradition, which saw schools concentrate on teaching 'the basics' within a strong religious framework, now competed with a 'developmental' (child-centred) view of education and the arrival in middle schools of a secondary (subject-centred) view (Blyth, 1965). The rise of developmental psychology over the next twenty or so years pointed in a new direction where primary schools were not just seen as places of instruction but centres of child life in general.

These sentiments gathered pace during the largely optimistic and confident spirit of the 1960s. The landmark Plowden Report made it clear that 'at the heart of the educational process lies the child' (DES, 1967: 7). Based on visits to schools, members of the Plowden Committee concluded that formal lessons tended to replace more creative approaches in the junior years. They were critical of problem-solving tasks that were 'simply mechanical sums in disguise' – for example, 'calculating how many men would take how many hours to dig so many yards of ditch if it took another lot of men a different number of hours to dig a different length of ditch' (DES, 1967: 237). These did little to develop constructive thinking. Instead, the Plowden Report recommended authentic problem-solving using the school and local environment, such as how much water is being wasted in 24 hours, a week or a year, when a tap is left dripping in a cloakroom. It was critical of the teaching of punctuation and grammar because they hindered creativity. There are commentators who identify the problems of modern-day education to such thinking (Phillips, 1996; Peal, 2014).

Despite an immediate backlash to Plowden's child-centred philosophy (Bantock, 1969), the government endorsed the importance of teaching children to think critically and creatively, stating that the primary school should 'help children develop lively, enquiring minds; giving them the ability to question and to argue rationally, and to apply themselves to tasks' (DES, 1977: 6). However, it was also acknowledged that some less able and experienced teachers had fallen into a 'trap' by applying freer methods uncritically and at the neglect of teaching basic skills. Ironically then, teachers' own critical thinking skills were called into question. Too many did not monitor pupils' development of skills in English and mathematics closely enough. While most children acquired these reasonably well, those who did not floundered (Bassey, 2012). By the 1980s, only 10 per cent of schools were doing 'learning by discovery' as advocated by Plowden, the same as in 1967 (Galton, 1995). Ricard Mayer (2004), an American cognitive psychologist, suggests that in each decade since the mid-1950s, despite solid evidence questioning the effectiveness of discovery learning, a similar approach pops up under a different name (problem-based learning, inquiry learning, experiential learning, constructivist learning) and the cycle repeats itself.

The Plowden Report was influenced heavily by the work of the Swiss psychologist Jean Piaget (1896–1980). His cognitive theory suggested that the child actively interprets the world and constructs knowledge (as opposed to receiving it). Using his own children as subjects, he observed that children think differently from adults. They consistently gave wrong answers to certain types of problems. For instance, if the water from a tall jar was poured into a shorter, fatter one, young children would say that the taller jar contained more water. Plowden took on board Piaget's theory uncritically and agreed that children should learn at their own pace through distinct stages of learning. It is not necessary to rehearse these here, nor the criticisms that have been capably covered elsewhere (Mooney, 2013; Gray and MacBlain, 2015). However, it is worth noting that Piaget's central idea about children constructing their own mental worlds dominated teacher training over the second half of the twentieth century.

Lev Vygotsky (1896–1934) and Jerome Bruner (1915–2016), most closely associated with social constructivist theories of learning, addressed several shortcomings in Piaget's work. They highlighted, for example, a more prominent role for language and the skilful contribution of more knowledgeable others (e.g. adults or older peers) to the development of children's learning and thinking. They did not accept the concept of 'readiness', arguing for a less rigid view of children's intellectual development. In short, they paved the way for current views on the fluid, multiple nature of intelligence (Gardner, 2000) and the importance of high-quality talk in the classroom (Alexander, 2008).

The importance of culture and the environment in shaping how children think was illustrated by the pioneering work of Reuven Feuerstein (1921–2014). He fled Romania for Palestine during the Nazi persecution and taught child survivors of the Holocaust, which spurred his interest in meeting the needs of refugee children. The improvements in learning they made following interventions led Feuerstein to conclude that intelligence was not fixed or limited by genetic inheritance. Some culturally deprived children regarded as unteachable made good progress, illustrating the potential for growth. Feuerstein's ideas were expressed decades before neuroscientists' groundbreaking findings on brain plasticity. He developed mediated learning programmes that supported *all* children's higher-order thinking, including those with learning disabilities. Feuerstein believed that children's intelligence could be modified and should not be predefined by stages. Here he differed from Piaget, one of his teachers at the University of Geneva. For instance, Piaget claimed that young children could not solve analogy problems before the stage of formal operations. However, Feuerstein showed through his experiments that this was not so, provided they were presented with stimuli in a systematic way and were helped to organise information (Feuerstein et al., 2015).

MODERN TIMES

The last quarter of the twentieth century was a time when education was increasingly subjected to centralisation, privatisation, parental choice, greater teacher accountability and a focus on performativity (forces collectively described as 'neoliberalism'). A subject-based National Curriculum was introduced and, although later slimmed down, left teachers increasingly in the role of curriculum deliverers rather than innovators. Despite the political rhetoric of modernisation and 'a third way' (between the old left and the Conservative right), New Labour elected in 1997 continued many of the policies developed by the previous Conservative government. Although non-statutory, the introduction of national literacy and numeracy strategies in 1998 and 1999, along with literacy and later numeracy hours, effectively meant that teachers were increasingly being told not only what to teach but *how* and *when*.

Interest in thinking skills developed in the late 1980s and 1990s as part of broader discussions around improving standards. Philip Adey and Michael Shayer led a research team from King's College, London. They developed classroom materials for the teaching of science called *Cognitive Acceleration Through Science Education* (Shayer, 1988), discussed further in Chapter 8. The authors shared Feuerstein's premise that any pupil could make good progress if taught in the right way. They developed a similar approach in mathematics and English through *Let's Think* materials (Chapter 6), with statistically significant learning gains reported (Adey and Shayer, 1994; Shayer and Adhami, 2007). Elsewhere, a Thinking Skills Research Centre was established at Newcastle University with academics sponsored by various bodies to investigate the impact of thinking skills lessons (Hall et al., 2005). In 1998 Professor Carol McGuinness was commissioned by the Department for Education and Employment to undertake a literature review and evaluation of the most successful approaches (McGuinness, 1999). Consequently, thinking skills became one of six key skills to be embedded across the national curriculum in England. They were badged as universal skills helping pupils to focus on 'knowing how' as well as 'knowing what' – learning how to learn.

The role of schools in promoting creativity also attracted growing interest. A report on the arts in school (National Advisory Committee on Creative and Cultural Education, 1999) attempted to reinvigorate the arts curriculum, while the Creative Partnerships initiative (2002–2011) linked schools to artists, architects, scientists and other creative thinkers, albeit with mixed results (Ofsted, 2006; Bragg and Manchester, 2011). The introduction of the government strategy *Excellence and Enjoyment* (DfES, 2004) encouraged teachers to take a creative approach to the curriculum and provided a bank of professional development resources to this end. However, critics claimed that New Labour's policies on personalised learning indicated a return to child-centred ideology – 'Plowden with tests'.

It proved difficult to retain a focus on creativity and enjoyment within what was effectively a two-tiered curriculum, along with league tables, testing and a competitive market. Even within the core subjects of English, mathematics and science, concerns were raised over narrow, teaching-to-the-tests pedagogy. Paul Andrews (2004), chair of the Association of Teachers of Mathematics Council, pointed out (largely in vain) that 'children must be helped to see maths as a creative, imaginative and problem-solving set of challenges'.

The election of the Coalition and then Conservative governments in 2010 and 2015, signalled a decline in official support for thinking skills in England. When the revised curriculum was introduced the stance taken by Michael Gove, then education minister, was that knowledge precedes thinking and what matters most is ensuring that children develop a solid base of core knowledge to build upon (Gove, 2013). A hundred leading university academics published an open letter in the media complaining about a return to rote learning and 'an endless list of spelling, facts and rules' (*The Independent*, 19 March 2013). These academics wanted the government to give teachers greater professional autonomy in making decisions about the curriculum. Their support for the central value of creativity in the curriculum echoed the views of teachers and others in the Cambridge Primary Review (2006–2009), the largest review of primary education since Plowden. Witnesses were united in complaining about the loss of 'creative' teaching and opportunities for children to be creative, over the past twenty years. They expressed concern over the dominant conception of childhood as a time of preparation for adulthood, which had stifled creativity, enjoyment and imagination (Alexander, 2010). Unfortunately, the comparatively high level of curriculum prescription in England and a narrow focus on attainment in a few subjects has had a negative impact on creativity in primary and secondary schools (Warwick Commission, 2015). One primary head goes so far as to suggest that 'We now create clones, not individual children with unique ideas and the ability to think outside the box' (Harris, 2016).

This is not the case, however, in the policy rhetoric surrounding the education of young children (0–5 years in England). The Tickell Review (2011) highlighted playing and exploring, active learning, and *creating and thinking critically*, as the three characteristics of effective learning. Despite fears that government plans for more formal learning and assessment reforms (the 'nappy' curriculum) would undermine the role of play in the early years (Paton, 2012), the principles outlined by Tickell remain in place in the latest statutory framework for the education of young children (DfE, 2017) in England, while there are similar endorsements for play-based learning in Wales, Scotland and Northern Ireland.

Nonetheless for older primary and secondary school children, the official policy steer in England shaped by testing regimes and the sanctity of data has veered away from the rest of the UK. In Wales, the new curriculum is designed, among other purposes, to develop learners who are enterprising and creative contributors to society. In Northern Ireland, one of the principles underpinning the curriculum is encouraging creativity and providing opportunities for children to engage in exploration, problem-solving and decision-making. In Scotland's Curriculum for Excellence, creativity has a high profile with an emphasis on providing young people with the skills to manage life's uncertainties and rapid changes. In contrast, the national curriculum in England is couched in knowledge-centred terms with references to the teaching of creativity and critical thinking buried deep within specific subjects, reflecting the view that thinking skills can only be taught within a subject context. Hence teachers are expected to demonstrate the skills and processes essential to writing, such as thinking aloud, in the collection and redrafting of ideas.

The thinking skills adopted throughout the UK are broadly similar although there were a few anomalies illustrating the difficulties in defining their nature and scope. Take problem-solving skills as an example. In England, problem-solving features as a separate key skill *outside* thinking skills whereas in Wales it is linked to critical thinking, in Northern Ireland it is associated with decision-making, while in Scotland it is not listed. In Wales, thinking skills were originally introduced as part of a non-statutory *Skills Framework for 3–19 Year Olds* and tied closely to an Assessment for Learning agenda (Stewart, 2014). The most recent curriculum review (Donaldson, 2015) suggests thinking skills form part of a statutory set of wider skills across the curriculum.

Table 2.1 Thinking skills across UK curricula, 1999–2015

Country	Framework	Thinking Skills
England	Among the Key Skills in the National Curriculum	Before 2013 • Information-processing • Reasoning • Enquiry • Creative thinking • Evaluation After 2013 No explicit reference but thinking skills integrated In subjects
Northern Ireland	Part of the Thinking Skills and Personal Capabilities Framework	• Managing information • Problem-solving and decision-making • Being creative • Working with others • Self-management
Wales	Wider skills within Donaldson Review	• Critical thinking and problem-solving • Planning and organising • Creativity and innovation • Personal effectiveness
Scotland	Skills for Learning, Life and Work within the Curriculum for Excellence	• Remembering • Understanding • Applying • Analysing • Evaluating • Creating

This chapter has put into historical context the development of the teaching of thinking in schools and society. The overriding question – what is the purpose of education? – has been batted around from one generation to the next. It seems like every twenty-five to thirty or so years there is a crisis of confidence in what education is for. Thomas (2013) suggests it all comes down to two basic positions: either schools exist to transmit facts and established ideas, the best of our cultural heritage, or they aim to foster independent thinking, questioning, discovery and self-awareness. While common sense suggests that they should do both, this is much more difficult to do in practice when schools are subjected to high-stakes external accountability and political pressures where only what is measurable seems to be valued. Some sociologists (e.g. Hargreaves, 1994) have argued that schools have not changed much (or enough) in their history when compared to other institutions, such as hospitals. Schools retain outmoded practices (e.g. holidays built around the farming year) and, to put it bluntly, resemble little more than examination factories. This begs the question: is it more important for primary schools to teach easily assessable basic knowledge and skills and prepare children for secondary schooling, or should education be less instrumental and focus on nurturing the potential of each child? More broadly, is education about meeting the needs of society and the economy, or about developing wider creative and intellectual capacities? These questions are considered in the next chapter where we discuss why the teaching of thinking skills is so important.

SUMMARY

- The Greek legacy of critical thinking has shaped much of our educational system, although some writers suggest that this has been at the expense of creativity.
- The Enlightenment signalled new thinking on childhood with its emphasis on children's freedom to discover and create for themselves. The implied purpose of education was to liberate rather than constrain young minds.
- The priorities of mass education, which followed industrialisation, were to meet the needs of the economy by producing literate, numerate and socially adept citizens. Generally, there was little desire or scope for the teaching of critical or creative thinking to the working classes.
- The influence of developmental psychology and progressive thinkers meant that periodically in the twentieth century (e.g. 1930s and 1960s) play, imagination and creative thinking had a strong presence in primary schools.
- Particularly in recent years, in England a premium has been placed on a knowledge-rich curriculum. This contrasts with more explicit support for thinking skills elsewhere in the UK.

3

WHY TEACH THINKING SKILLS?

INTRODUCTION

In 1946, the 'Wild Man from Sugar Creek' died. This was the name given to Eugene Talmadge, a highly educated, trained lawyer who became governor and chief executive of Georgia, in America. Talmadge earned the name because of his lively personality and the support he received from white farmers for his political views. As an indicator of his intellectual status, Talmadge wore the Phi Beta Kappa badge. This is one of the nation's most distinctive symbols of wisdom dating back to the American Revolution. No one doubted Talmadge's intelligence. An 18-year-old college student acknowledged Talmadge as 'one of the better minds' in Georgia, someone who could 'think critically and intensively'. But he was also a highly divisive figure. Upon Talmadge's death, his son said that a third of the people would follow his father to hell and a third of them wanted him in hell. He was against racial integration and viewed black people as inferior, including the college student, who was called Martin Luther King. After Talmadge's death, King (1947: 10) wrote:

> The function of education is to teach one to think intensively and to think critically. But education which stops with efficiency may prove the greatest menace to society. The most dangerous criminal may be the man gifted with reason, but with no morals ... We must remember that intelligence is not enough. Intelligence plus character – that is the goal of true education.

There are many people who are sharp, critical thinkers. But without moral purpose their thinking should not matter a jot. The same is true for creative thinking. It is remarkable how some of the world's cleverest scientists and architects could design and create the apparatus of concentration camps and conduct experimental 'research', before returning home to family meals, laughter and classical music. In this chapter, while we set out the case for promoting critical and creative thinking in school, this sits within a large caveat. Teaching children to be smart thinkers is not enough. As King said, there has to be a focus on moral development, character building as they say in the United States.

We put forward five central arguments for the teaching of thinking in school. First, if education is taken seriously, we maintain that one of children's basic human rights is to be taught how to think well. Second, if schools are successful at doing this, then pupils' love of learning will be enhanced across the curriculum and beyond school life. Third, when people are good at applying their thinking the evidence clearly shows that their overall wellbeing improves. Fourth, developing critical and creative thinking within schools improves young people's prospects for getting decent employment that benefits themselves, their families and society at large. Finally, if we consider what underpins the most successful educational systems in the world (at least judged by standardised test scores), it transpires that they make time for the teaching of creative and critical thinking or aspire to do so.

CHILDREN AND YOUNG PEOPLE HAVE A RIGHT TO DEVELOP SKILLS IN CREATIVE AND CRITICAL THINKING

Children's rights have occupied policy-makers and reformers for at least a century, while the notion of protecting vulnerable children dates back to ancient times. Since the 1960s there has been a concerted effort not only to protect children and young people but to empower them. The 1989 Children's Act gave children the right to express themselves in thought and action, recognised in the United Nations Convention Rights of the Child (Article 13: Freedom of expression and Article 14: Freedom of thought, belief and religion). Participation rights should allow children to be part of the decision-making processes in school and to learn how to express opinions responsibly, key aspects of becoming a good citizen. Many children benefit from attending 'Rights Respecting (RR) Schools', a UNICEF supported whole-school approach to embedding the UN Convention on the Rights of the Child (UNICEF, 2017). UNICEF recognises the efforts of these schools in taking children's voices seriously.

However, we know relatively little about how children enact their rights in the classroom and the challenges practitioners face to support these rights (Bae, 2009). There are suggestions that there is a gap between the very positive rhetoric and classroom realities in which children's views are effectively disregarded and where they remain passive in their thinking (Venninen et al., 2014). This may be because there is insufficient critical reflection in schools on the concepts underpinning legislation and guidance. Or it may denote a more fundamental scepticism over the capabilities of children. School councils, which should be an ideal democratic forum (Apple and Beane, 1995) for the generation of critical and creative ideas, are often tokenistic affairs. Rarely do children and young people engage in discussions over substantial matters, such as improving the quality of learning or curriculum content. To get the most from school councils and other forums, school leaders need to be more proactive in engaging pupils in significant decision-making (Whitty and Wisby, 2011; Bennett, 2012).

Unfortunately, the Children's Commissioners in the UK point to inconsistencies in the quality and provision for children to participate in school life (UK Children's Commissioners, 2015). Even in Wales, where children's rights have been held up as 'emblematic' of successful devolution, the picture is variable (Lewis et al., 2017). The Foundation Phase curriculum (3–7 years) is based on a play-based pedagogy, experiential learning, social interaction and creative expression. However, despite considerable Welsh government investment, evaluations of the learning experiences of young children present a mixed picture. While their enthusiasm for learning, behaviour and wellbeing are generally reported to be positive, more than four in ten practitioners observed in an evaluation study made little or no effort to involve children in their planning (Taylor et al., 2015).

That said, the question of children's rights to think and learn independently is not a straightforward topic. As Robinson (2014: 20) points out, many pupils themselves feel:

> conflict in their thinking between wanting to lead aspects of their own learning, while simultaneously wanting teachers to take charge of their learning as teachers are perceived as more knowledgeable and able to provide the information pupils need to help them achieve well in national tests and examinations.

Teachers also struggle with the dilemma of supporting autonomous thinkers while responding to pressures to achieve good examination results by taking control of pupils' learning. However, there are case studies of schools (see Chapter 11) that have successfully steered a path through these challenges.

The need for children to engage in creative learning is particularly pressing for those from low-income families. Around one in four (27 per cent) children in the UK live in poverty (McGuinness, 2016: 10). This statement takes on added significance when considering what this means for children in a typical week. These families often cannot afford to pay for their children to benefit from extracurricular clubs or school visits and have more limited opportunities to take their children to museums, galleries, heritage sites or holidays abroad. Higher social groups account for 87 per cent of all museum visits in the UK (Warwick Commission, 2015: 34). Parents fear the psychological impact on children seen to be missing out on these experiences or appearing 'the odd one out' (Hill et al., 2016: 3).

Hence there is a powerful social justice argument for promoting creativity in school. Based on substantial research evidence, the Cultural Learning Alliance (CLA, 2017) presents a strong case to justify more curriculum time for the arts. These include improvements in cognitive skills, higher attainment in core subjects and, in the longer term, better employment prospects, less chance of criminal behaviour, and substantial improvements in health. Students from low-income families who take part in arts activities at school are three times more likely to get a degree (CLA, 2017: 1).

Despite the overwhelming evidence that well-conceived creative learning opportunities benefit *all* children, particularly those from low-income families, there have been significant cuts to the arts in England over recent years. This has resulted in fewer teachers and less curriculum time in the creative arts. In primary schools, for example, the Warwick Commission (2015: 34) reports that the proportion of children engaged in dance activities has fallen from 43 per cent (2008/9) to 30 per cent (2013/14). Outside school, working-class communities have lost many of their traditional haunts (working men's institutes, local libraries, town halls, community centres) that provided cultural experiences for young people. Given this loss of 'cultural capital' (the knowledge, skills and experiences gained through exposure to the arts), schools have an even more important role in providing opportunities for all children to gain equal access to our rich cultural heritage. It is the birth right of the fifteen million children in the UK.

LEARNING HOW TO THINK CRITICALLY AND CREATIVELY SUPPORTS LEARNING IN ALL OTHER AREAS OF THE CURRICULUM

The inspectorate bodies endorse the importance of thinking skills in supporting pupils' all-round learning. The Ofsted handbook for schools makes it clear that inspectors will consider 'the extent to which children are active and inquisitive learners who are creative and think critically' (Ofsted, 2017: 63). Estyn, the Welsh inspectorate, evaluates the extent to which pupils 'develop their thinking skills ... and apply these to new situations' (Estyn, 2017: 15). In Education Scotland's self-evaluation guidance to schools, there is an expectation that 'staff, learners and partners engage regularly in critical and creative thinking' and where these opportunities are embedded, practice is said to be 'highly effective' (Education Scotland, 2015: 24). Finally, the Education and Training Inspectorate (ETI) in Northern Ireland examines the extent to which 'children work independently and with others, demonstrating and developing skills such as problem solving, decision making, managing information and thinking critically and creatively' with effective practice in this area based around how well teachers 'focus on explicit thinking' (ETI, 2017: 4, 7).

Every discipline has its specific skills and techniques that are not transferable to other subject contexts, e.g. playing a musical instrument, working through a mathematical formula, forming a scientific hypothesis or choreographing a dance. Indeed, the notion of transferability has attracted considerable criticism, with some academics (e.g. Johnson, 2010) contending that the skills of thinking critically or creatively in one subject field are not necessarily the same in another. The more specialised the field, the less likely the possibility of transfer. Consider the skills of professional footballers. Fullbacks rarely make good strikers. Even within the midfield, there are attacking and 'holding' players who are selected to play in different games because of their well-honed skill set and depending on particular contextual factors, e.g. the opposition's strengths. The key point is that critical thinking depends upon contextual knowledge. As Willingham (2008: 21) puts it:

> If you remind a student to 'look at an issue from multiple perspectives' often enough, he will learn that he ought to do so, but if he doesn't know much about an issue, he can't think about it from multiple perspectives.

Willingham is an oft-quoted critic of the idea that schools can teach a set of generic thinking skills devoid of subject context. Pupils cannot think well and apply their thinking to real-life without something of substance to think about. Otherwise, lessons will be relegated to a pooling of ignorance. Our argument is not to teach thinking skills in isolation, as a set of exercises. Rather, it is to firstly acknowledge the value of creative and critical thinking in and between different subjects and then to use appropriate contexts (subject-specific or cross-curricular) to develop these skills. And, as Siegel (2010) reminds us, there is no contradiction in holding both subject-specific knowledge and mastery of thinking skills as important. What matters is not how the curriculum is organised, but the quality of teaching and learning. The following section overview shows the importance of critical and creative thinking in all areas of the curriculum. The respective professional associations are a good starting point for readers keen to know more about how these skills can be developed in subject contexts.

English language and literature

English is a rich, continually evolving language. The *Oxford English Dictionary* typically adds 4,000 or so words, senses and subentries each year. In 2017, these included 'YOLO' (an abbreviation for 'you only live once') and 'clicktivism' (someone who supports a political or social cause by means of the Internet). Each generation makes its mark on the language. Shakespeare left us words such as 'bedazzled', 'cold-blooded' and 'fashionable'. Modern technology has produced its own lexicon. The term 'wearables', once an eighteenth-century description of things worn, now describes smart watches, fitness trackers and smart glasses. Exploring new words, their etymologies and meanings, reminds children of the inventive nature of language.

The imagination is continually at work when reading and listening to stories. Inviting pupils to respond to what they have read or heard through discussion, drawing, painting, modelling, composing a piece of music, dance, mini play or a PowerPoint presentation, often provides deeper insight into their thinking. The creative thinking involved in the process of writing needs to be demonstrated to pupils, as much as the outcomes themselves. This inevitably means generating and rejecting ideas, cutting chunks of text, replacing words, drafting, redrafting, working to time constraints, checking information, coping with roadblocks and distractions, communicating ideas and juggling the tension between the creative and critical elements. This is rarely a linear process, but a constant toing and froing.

Inviting authors and poets into class is often the best way to demonstrate this. One of the concerns authors have is that teachers are inadvertently damaging children's creative writing through their interpretation of the National Curriculum. Well-intentioned teachers encourage pupils to move away from using simple words such as 'big', 'bad', 'good', and 'said' and replace them with the likes of 'enormous', 'terrible', 'wonderful' and 'exclaimed'. The message to pupils is that more complicated, longer words are better alternatives. Cecilia Busby, the children's author, recalls visiting a classroom and reading a description of her character Sir Bertram Pendragon in the novel *Frogspell*: 'He is a gruff, burly knight with a deep voice and a large moustache who also happens to enjoy whacking his enemies with his big sword'. The teacher interrupted and told Busby "the word 'big' is one of the banned words in our classroom" (Flood, 2015). One of the enduring myths about creative writing is that it is about using flowery words. Students at Masters-level courses in Creative Writing are often taught the opposite – to write in a direct and simple way.

Pupils can experience the satisfaction of linguistic creativity by being exposed to a wide range of genres and contexts, including the use of:

- puns, e.g. insect puns bug me; whiteboards are remarkable
- jokes, e.g. What do you call an alligator in a vest? An investigator
- riddles, e.g. You answer me, but I never ask you a question. What am I? (a telephone)
- magazine articles, e.g. *First News, Minecraft World, Okido*
- newspaper headlines, e.g. 'Puddle splash victim vows revenge' (*Western & Somerset Mercury*, 31 January–6 February 2013)
- notices and shop signs, e.g. Grate Expectations (fireplace specialists), Surelock Holmes (locksmiths), A Fish Called Rhondda (Fish and Chip Shop, Pentre, Wales)
- place names, e.g. Lost (Aberdeenshire), Nasty (Hertfordshre), Great Snoring (Norfolk), Pity Me (Durham), Barton in the Beans (Warwickshire)
- poems, acrostics, ballads, limericks, sonnets, epigrams
- classics, e.g. techniques used by famous authors to engage readers such as making villains ugly and heroes beautiful (see Tolkien's *Lord of the Rings*), use of names to conjure up images (for instance, Dickens's Uriah Heap)
- stories from different cultures, places and times, e.g. see http://worldstories.org.uk/

- texting, e.g. creative 'translations' of famous films and books such as ChRLE & t chocl8 factrE and Alice in 1derl& (Crystal, 2010: 193)
- song lyrics with an imaginative mood, e.g. 'Imagine' by John Lennon, 'Over the Rainbow' by Judy Garland
- nursery rhymes and their modern-day revisions, e.g. *Three Little Pigs, True Story of the Three Little Pigs* (Scieszka, 1989), *The Three Little Wolves and the Big Bad Pig* (Trivizas, 1993)
- short stories, e.g. Ernest Hemmingway's six-word story, 'For sale: baby shoes, never worn'
- recitations and performances, e.g. three-minute talks, Mastermind quizzes
- advertising slogans, e.g. 'Think Different' (Apple), 'Play On' (Lego), 'Grace, Space, Pace' (Jaguar), 'Think Small' (Volkswagen) and 'Impossible is Nothing' (Adidas).

The examples can be used to stimulate pupils to create their own ideas. For instance, they might create a new name for a road, building or housing estate. They might suggest an appropriate town for twinning purposes. In 2012, councillors at Dull (Perthshire) twinned with Boring (Oregon) and, more recently, there has been talk of extending the link to the Australian region of Bland.

The important point is that teachers should take opportunities to highlight creative thinking in a wide range of literary contexts. *The Sun* newspaper, the most popular in the UK, has established a reputation for creative headlines, among other things. Even Celtic football supporters may have offered a reluctant smile at the headline when they lost 3–1 to Inverness Caledonian Thistle in the Scottish cup in 2000: 'Super Caley Go Ballistic Celtic Are Atrocious' (*The Sun*, 9 February 2000). When one of us was teaching Year 6 pupils many years ago, in order to illustrate the use of puns, headlines were taken from a book called *Hold Ye Front Page! 2000 Years of History on the Front Page of The Sun* (Roberts and Perry, 1999). Pupils were inspired to write their headlines following these examples:

- The birth of Christ (A Star is Born)
- The Roman Invasion (Send 'Em Rome)
- The Norman Invasion (Stormin' Normans)
- The American Revolution (Yanked Apart)
- The first airplane (All Wright on the Night)
- The rise of Hitler (Nazi Piece of Work).

Compared to the rest of the UK, teachers in England have less professional autonomy in deciding upon the 'what' and 'how' of teaching English, with the curriculum mapping the core knowledge about language and the use of systematic synthetic phonics (Cremin, 2015). In Scotland, for instance, one of the intended outcomes for pupils in literacy and English is for them to 'reflect on and explain [their] thinking skills' while they also explore the wide range of ways in which they can be creative in language (Education Scotland, 2012). However, the national curriculum programme of study for English does stipulate that teachers should discuss 'a wide range of stories, poems, plays and information books', while there are expectations that pupils at Key Stage 2 will be taught to read critically and make critical comparisons across texts (DfE, 2014). Certainly, there are opportunities for teachers to develop critical reading and writing skills by referring to conflicting newspaper reports of the same event, and getting pupils to evaluate books, films, websites and commercial products. To think critically and creatively about texts, pupils need to develop their questioning skills so that they regularly challenge what is written and reflect upon unusual features (e.g. pictures, captions, table of contents) as well as the content itself.

Mathematics

The history and very nature of mathematics is bound up with critical thinking. When pupils think critically in mathematics, they make logical decisions or sound judgements about what to do and think. Teachers can support pupils in developing criteria to decide on the most appropriate strategy to solve problems. For instance, in deciding whether to make a model, draw a diagram, compile a list or create a table or graph, pupils might consider how long this is likely to take (time), the material needed (resources), whether the strategy helps them understand the problem (appropriateness) and their feelings about the strategy (confidence). By promoting critical thinking in mathematics, teachers encourage independence and self-regulation, deep engagement with the subject, confidence and competence with mathematical processes such as reasoning, representing and communicating. This can be achieved by:

- offering regular mathematics challenges
- asking a range of questions and prompts to scaffold the thinking process, e.g. What do we need to carry out this investigation? (before); Is there a different or better way to carry out this task? (during); What difficulties did we face and how did we resolve them? (after)
- design and create mathematical board games
- telling stories that feature mathematical puzzles to resolve for the stories to progress, e.g. the Indian myth, Sissa's Reward[1]
- presenting open-ended problems with no predetermined solution strategies
- teaching flexible thinking strategies (e.g. analysing a word problem with 'what I know' and 'what I need to find out')
- inviting pupils to present evidence of thinking in different ways (e.g. pictures, numbers, words, poems, blogs, models).

Mathematical educators have worked hard to highlight the creative side of the discipline. Organisations such as NRICH[2] provide resources and ideas to support teachers.

---

[1]See https://nrich.maths.org/1163/index (accessed 20 June 2018).
[2]https://nrich.maths.org (accessed 20 June 2018).

Creativity in the field involves generating new and useful solutions to real-life or simulated problems using mathematical models, as well as posing and solving mathematical questions (Striraman and Lee, 2010). The most creative professional mathematicians are highly motivated and reflective individuals who enjoy tackling complex, time-intensive, non-routine problems (Striraman, 2004). In schools, the challenge is to provide extended periods for problem-solving and mathematical investigations. The creative side of mathematics, however, offers an important opportunity to motivate and engage all pupils, particularly those who have negative attitudes towards the subject. Take the fundamental mathematical concept of patterns, which has obvious links to art. The famous Dutch artist M.C. Escher (1898–1972) used art to explore a range of mathematical ideas. Despite not doing well at mathematics in school, he studied architecture and used geometry to create drawings and prints. His work inspired further mathematical investigations in tiling. Chapter 9 explores how Cognitive Acceleration approaches support creative and critical thinking in mathematics.

Science

In the early years, young children can develop their thinking in science by exploring their environment (both in and out of school), observing phenomena, asking questions, discussing ideas and solving problems. Establishing inviting play areas, such as a bakery, building site or garden centre, opens up lots of possible departures into creative science. Montessori considered all children were like 'young explorers' (Standing, 1998: 104) eager to investigate their worlds and make 'what if' discoveries (Photo 3.1).

To undertake the process of scientific enquiry effectively inevitably means using a range of critical thinking skills (e.g. classifying materials, comparing findings, evaluating the reliability of claims). One of the key challenges for teachers is ensuring that pupils genuinely undertake scientific enquiry themselves, rather than follow through prescribed teacher-led experiments. However, there is considerable support for teachers seeking to enthuse pupils and develop their scientific thinking. STEM Learning,[3] for example, offers many starting points on imaginative themes such as 'Accidental Discoveries', 'Save our Bees' and 'Einstein's Birthday Party'. The British Science Association runs an annual British Science Week, a ten-day celebration of science, technology, engineering and mathematics for all ages. Its website includes activity packs, guidance and small grant funding opportunities.[4]

In recent years, there has been an increasing focus on highlighting the creative possibilities within science education (DeHaan, 2009; Cutting and Kelly, 2015). The use of

---

[3]www.stem.org.uk (accessed 20 June 2018).

[4]www.britishscienceweek.org (accessed 20 June 2018).

Photo 3.1 Young children exploring outdoors

Source: Danescourt Primary School

concept cartoons, for example, encourages pupils to imagine other viewpoints and possibilities. Analogous thinking helps to understand scientific phenomena and ideas. The pumping capacity of the human heart, for instance, is better understood knowing that it would take a human heart less than eighteen days to fill an Olympic-sized swimming pool (Levy, 2011). As a goal, scientific creativity is about seeking to foster the ability to see things in novel and unusual ways. The stimulus may come from telling stories of famous scientists (e.g. Archimedes, Leonardo da Vinci, Marie Curie) and their discoveries or exploring scientific principles in everyday lives and posing 'What if ...?' questions. Teachers need to ensure that pupils are introduced to the appropriate content knowledge, which is a prerequisite for creative thinking in the subject.

Information and communication technologies

Technological change is one of the most powerful global trends of recent times and this presents significant opportunities and challenges for educators. Technologies demonstrate that creativity is a democratic process, rather than confined to a handful of great inventors and painters. The Westminster government has raised the bar in terms of what is expected of schools, replacing ICT with computer science in 2014 so that the needs of business and industry could be met more appropriately. While this is recognised as potentially 'game-changing', the impact is not likely to be for a generation. The House of Commons (2016) acknowledges the challenges in addressing the 'digital skills crisis', citing infrastructural issues (e.g. one in five pieces of IT equipment in schools is ineffective, while only 35 per cent of ICT teachers hold a relevant qualification).

In the realm of digital literacy skills, there have been many calls for schools to spend more time equipping children and young people with the critical thinking necessary to make sense of the information deluge they experience. It is estimated that we are bombarded with the equivalent of 174 newspapers of data each day (Alleyne, 2011). A survey of 2,000 UK consumers by the software company Adobe found that one in two people are distracted by the volume of daily information, typically spread over five screens, and eight out of ten complained of information overload (*Daily Express*, 14 December 2015). Learning to find the right information online and determine its truthfulness has become increasingly important in a post-truth era of 'fake news', i.e. websites that deliberately spread propaganda, hoaxes and disinformation. A 2017 survey found that only 4 per cent of adults could identify all three true stories presented within a selection of six, and 49 per cent said that at least one of the three fake stories was true (Channel4.com, 2017). 'Fake News 2' is around the corner, with predictions that computers will soon be able to fake the human voice (Welser, 2018). Although misinformation is not a new phenomenon, the rise in digital media has escalated the issue to the extent that governments and other bodies around the world are providing guidance on spotting fake news. In 2017 the parliamentary Digital, Culture, Media and Sports Committee concluded that one solution was to spend more time on teaching critical thinking (Thorrington, 2017). Although there are ethical questions over who decides what is truth and how this should be regulated (Picton and Teravainen, 2017), Professor Michael Peters (2017: 565) has put forward a strong case for teaching critical thinking:

> Criticality has been avoided or limited within education and substituted by narrow conceptions of standards, and state-mandated instrumental and utilitarian pedagogies ... If education is equated almost solely with job training rather than a broader critical citizenship agenda for participatory democracy, we can expect the further decline of social democracy and the rise of populist demagogue politicians and alt-right racist parties.

The communication aspect of technologies has enormous critical and creative potential. For example, pupils develop a range of creative writing skills by using the widely acclaimed Night Zookeeper online materials inspired by a love of animals.[5] While there are concerns over the time children and young people spend on video games, studies suggest that gaming can 'do serious good' by improving perception, resilience and problem-solving (Eichenbaum et al., 2014). There are similar debates over the role of social media, while an estimated three-quarters of 10–12-year-olds have social media accounts (Doward, 2017). What is agreed is the need for children to be taught how to use such technology appropriately. The nature of how most children use social media creates an 'echo-chamber' (Kershaw, 2017) in which they only hear from viewpoints like their own. Therefore, schools need to ensure that children are introduced to broader opinions in our diverse society and can stand back and evaluate the truthfulness of claims made.

Undoubtedly, technologies offer huge scope for thinking creatively in computer graphics, animation and multimedia presentations. Consider the creative energies behind developments over the last few decades: Bluetooth (2000); iPod (2001); Skype (2003); Facebook (2004); YouTube (2005); Twitter (2006); Apple iPhone (2007); BBC iPlayer (2007); Spotify (2008); 4G (2008); Apple iPad (2010); Instagram (2010); Google driverless car (2012). Then there are technologies that have been around for a while, but are only beginning to have an impact on our lives. The 'internet of things' (IoT), for example, was a term coined in the 1980s but it is only in recent times with the development of products such as smartwatches and smart speakers, such as Amazon Echo (available in the UK in 2016), that the technology is changing lives. The key point then is that generating ideas takes time.

In a fascinating book *Now You See It*, the digital innovator Professor Cathy Davidson (2011) reveals how for many years she has been using technologies to change the way American students learn. Davidson tells the story of 'Project Classroom Makeover' when in 2003 she was given a set of iPods to develop educational apps. In those days, there weren't any. When she asked her university students to play around with the technologies *during* lecture time, Davidson took a brave decision in reversing the roles of teacher and learner. This was a learning experiment a few years before Jeff Howe introduced the concept of crowdsourcing. Davidson (2011: 65) explains:

> Crowdsourcing thinking is very different from relying on top-down expertise. If anything, crowdsourcing is suspicious of expertise, because the more expert we are, the more likely we are to be limited to what we even conceive to be a problem, let alone the answer.

The student responses were overwhelming and included: downloadable audio files of lectures and course support materials which they could listen to anytime and anywhere;

---

[5]http://nightzookeeper.com (accessed 20 June 2018).

classes in languages, music and other subjects; podcasts; social networking to share and critique ideas; diagnostic uses for medical students stretching to those training in remote areas; and engineering students who took apart the iPods to figure out how new features could be added. This was a significant conceptual breakthrough: a commercial product being taken by the customer and adapted for their use. It illustrates powerfully what has now become something of a cliché in discussions about how we move learners from being consumers to producers of knowledge.

Even before pupils start working on computers they should be taught to engage in computational thinking. This describes looking at problems in a way that technologies can help to solve them. A calculator can help solve a word problem in mathematics but the nature of the problem needs to be understood first. Similarly, if making a computer animation, pupils should first learn to plan the sequence, perhaps using a storyboard. They can then use the appropriate hardware and software. Computational thinking involves concepts and skills such as understanding algorithms (sequence of instructions), applying logic (e.g. predicting and analysing), abstracting (i.e. removing unnecessary detail) and evaluating (making judgements). It also calls for approaches such as tinkering (experimenting), creating, debugging (finding and fixing errors) and collaborating. Key Stage 1 pupils might predict the movement of floor robots, explain their reasoning and write their own commands using programs such as Scratch or Kudu. Key Stage 2 pupils are expected to design programs with specific goals in mind, reflecting their logical reasoning and ability to detect and correct errors. Platforms such as Touch Develop encourage users to create their own programs by looking at the work of others.[6]

Humanities

The essence of the humanities is exploring what makes us human. It involves asking questions about fundamental aspects of our lives: who we are, what we value and believe, where we have come from, where we are heading, how we relate to others, where we belong. In Religious Education, for example, these big questions include:

- Can religion help people find peace?
- Is happiness the purpose of life?
- If God made the world, why isn't it perfect?
- How do we know what is true?

Source: www.reonline.org.uk/

---

[6]www.touchdevelop.com (accessed 20 June 2018).

Thinking critically and creatively is integral to the humanities. Historians, archaeologists and museum curators need to be critical of their source material and creative in how they reconstruct and represent the past. Geographers ask questions about relationships between different peoples, nations and cultures. They need analytical skills to make sense of patterns, for example trends in migration, trade and climate change. They need both critical acumen and creative thinking in exploring what might happen in the future if current trends continue. Any serious study of religion, at any level, requires an enquiring mind. It calls for critical judgements in exploring preconceptions, challenging bias and reflecting on human experience. Religious Education should also include opportunities for pupils to experience exciting, inspirational and creative times. They should express meaning in creative ways, for instance through art, dance, artefacts and rituals.

The enquiry approach is central to history, geography and Religious Education (Grigg and Hughes, 2018). Through planning, finding, selecting and using information, pupils can develop important thinking skills. They can learn to classify and interpret evidence, conduct fieldwork, make predictions, use maps, explore possible solutions to local issues and examine opinions from a range of sources. Creativity and initiative can be demonstrated when pupils:

- explore their natural environment (e.g. through sensory trails)
- use improvisations, role play and story-telling
- experiment with different ideas (e.g. design a house for a hot or cold country)
- develop a sense of place through play (e.g. using puzzles, picture maps, jigsaws)
- engage in collaborative projects (e.g. creating an eco-garden)

Davidson, mentioned earlier in the context of students thinking creatively in the use of technologies, tells the story of her mother-in-law, who was a teacher in remote Canada. The village was called Mountain View in the foothills of the Rockies. Inez Davidson's classes comprised a mix of native peoples and Mormons. The total population was 200 people in 200 square miles. In the 1970s the electricity supply was intermittent and temperatures dropped to between 20 and 40 degrees below zero in the winter. And yet despite the challenges, the school attracted considerable interest because of its success in sending students to higher education. One of the secrets was Davidson's enquiry-based approach to the curriculum. One project involved asking students to find another place in the world called Mountain View and to link up with a pen pal. This was a time before the internet and mobile phones. The challenge called for remarkable ingenuity and creative thinking among the students. Since this was a Mormon area, some of the children made contacts with those who had been missionaries all over the world. One child spoke to an elderly Chinese man who ran the local general store and who had come over to Canada to work on the railroad, along with many Chinese immigrants. He wrote a letter to someone in a town called Mountain View in China. Through the project, the children learned about places, cultures, languages, customs, history, beliefs and the world became a smaller, interconnected place. The project lasted beyond the year because children made lifelong friends, visiting other Mountain Views all over the world. It is a powerful illustration of the impact teachers can have on children's lives and the value of creative thinking, which is central to the humanities.

The arts

By their nature, the arts (music, dance, visual arts and drama) offer opportunities for children to think creatively – hence the term 'the creative arts'. There is substantial international evidence that when 'well taught, the arts provide young people with authentic experiences that engage their minds, hearts and bodies' (Arts Education Partnership, 1999: ix). Take music as an example. Through music, pupils can create sound effects to accompany stories or films, combine elements to create musical ideas, create a recording of their own music, and compose raps or chants relating to a particular theme, e.g. fireworks, the weather or the Victorians. In groups, pupils can combine a range of instruments to create contrasting moods and atmospheres, for instance during a storm or Roman invasion. They can also create musical 'conversations' for everyday life, e.g. a café scene. There is compelling evidence that a musical education strongly supports pupils' academic development and cognitive skills (Hallam, 2010).

The visual arts such as drawing, painting, ceramics, sculpture, filmmaking and photography provide further opportunities for pupils to develop a range of creative skills and dispositions. Design and technology provides an ideal subject to explore the creative thinking behind buildings, everyday products and processes. By learning to use various materials, instruments, tools and techniques, children can develop problem-solving skills (e.g. 'How do I use this material to make a model?'), observation skills (e.g. to notice fine details), perseverance (e.g. to keep going to complete a project) and accountability (e.g. understanding that actions such as not arriving on time for a film rehearsal affect others). Imaginative play, improvisation and drama enable children to make and explore new worlds. They learn to communicate through verbal and non-verbal means, reading facial expressions, intonation, gesture, mime and movement. They generate possible responses in role, cooperate with each other and learn to adapt their speech for different audiences and purposes.

The arts provide enormous potential for satisfaction as children learn to express and come to terms with a full range of emotions and thoughts. This can be illustrated simply by choosing a piece of art (painting, sculpture, weaving, artefact, musical extract) for children to explore as 'art detectives'. This could be a masterpiece, something produced by a local artist or from within the school. The following generic questions can encourage children to think critically about the work:

- What can you see?
- What might be happening?
- What materials do you think the artist used?
- If you could 'step inside' the picture what might you hear/see/smell?
- What might be happening outside the picture?
- What title would you give this picture if you were to hang it in a gallery?
- How might we find out more about this art?

Physical education

Physical education (PE) enables pupils to think critically and creatively in all areas: through movement, athletics, dance, games, gymnastics, swimming, outdoor and adventurous activities. High-quality PE is evident when pupils show balance, poise, control, develop stamina, work well in teams and apply a wide range of skills and techniques in different contexts. These cognitive skills and dispositions include decision-making (e.g. when to pass or move into space), planning (e.g. which resources to use), risk-taking (e.g. new dances), analysis (e.g. whether strategy and tactics were effective) and evaluation (e.g. how performance could improve next time). By their very nature, outdoor and adventurous activities are problem-solving experiences. Invariably these call for teamwork and imagination. Pupils can demonstrate their critical skills in many ways, from undertaking health and safety checks of the school grounds to reviewing the performances of themselves and their peers. Combining ideas and areas of experience, for instance music and swimming, or dance and history, can encourage creative thinking.

Dance has increased in popularity in recent years, through television shows such as *Strictly Come Dancing* (since 2004) and *Britain's Got Talent* (since 2007), becoming the second most popular physical activity after football. Consider the audience's emotional response to the performance of Attraction (Shadow Theatre Group), to win *Britain's Got Talent* in 2013.[7] Dance moves the heart, head and body. It offers not only the opportunity for pupils to develop artistic skills, but also team-working, problem-solving, observing, evaluating, verbal and non-verbal communication. Dance promotes creative and critical thinking at all ages. One research study shows that older people's thinking improves when they participate regularly in social dances because they learn new movements and socialise with others, which perks up ageing brains (Reynolds, 2017).

---

[7]www.youtube.com/watch?v=CvQBUccxBr4 (accessed 20 June 2018).

LEARNING TO THINK CREATIVELY AND CRITICALLY SUPPORTS CHILDREN'S OVERALL WELLBEING

Although there are different definitions and views of wellbeing, a general starting point is that the concept simply describes the quality of someone's life experiences. Leading experts in positive psychology identify creativity as one of twenty-four character strengths (Peterson and Seligman, 2004). Organisations which have more positive energy find that they generate more ideas and productive ways of doing things. In short, creativity is directly correlated to happiness. School leaders who promote creative teaching and learning are likely to see happier staff and pupils.

Wellbeing can be measured using external social indicators. This is the approach taken by organisations such as UNICEF, although in more recent times subjective measures have also been included. Bodies such as the Children's Society favour self-reported assessments because, regardless of how things appear to others, only the individuals experiencing life know how this makes them feel. These are personal judgements and it is now recognised in the research and educational communities that young children are capable of expressing views that provide valid and reliable evidence for their wellbeing.

The concept of wellbeing in education recognises the importance of the affective dimension of learning. Children's capacity to learn is influenced by a wide range of factors beyond their intellectual abilities, including relationships, family support and their attitudes to school. A.S. Neill, headteacher at Summerhill, famous for its emphasis on pupils' freedom, was highly critical of schools and universities because he thought they 'develop the intellect to the neglect of the emotions' (Neill, 1972: 231) whereas his school attempted to do the opposite. He asked:

> Is education to mean better scientists, engineers, doctors, instead of more balanced, happier, more tolerant human beings? A good education would mean both. (Neill, 1972: 484)

Schools have come a long way since then with many successful programmes designed to provide emotional support for learners. Neill's question, however, remains relevant at a time when concerns over children's wellbeing are frequently in the news. The Children's Society claims that children and young people's happiness is in decline based on their surveys of more than 60,000 children over a decade (The Children's Society, 2018). It reports that more than half of the children surveyed revealed that they faced three or more serious problems in their lives, such as bullying.

And yet it does not have to be this way. Although there are no simple answers to complex problems involving health, education and poverty, we know that creativity and the arts can make a significant contribution to people's health and wellbeing. This is illustrated in the *Be Creative Be Well* community project based in the most disadvantaged areas of London. Of 3,862 participants, 76 per cent reported increased physical activity and 85 per cent more positive feelings (Ings et al., 2012: 16). The researchers report: 'Artists model creativity as play and by involving people in play help to create a sense of wellbeing' (Ings et al., 2012: 18). The likes of dance, storytelling, music and craft enabled individuals to express their identity and build confidence. As one volunteer at an after-school club put it: 'The arts activities – dancing, drawing, modelling, drumming – have made a huge difference. It's not just through maths and English that people communicate who they are' (Ings et al., 2012: 58).

HAVING GOOD CRITICAL AND CREATIVE THINKING SKILLS INCREASES YOUNG PEOPLE'S PROSPECTS FOR EMPLOYABILITY

Around one in eight UK firms work within what are called the creative industries such as advertising, music, computer services, the media, architecture and performing arts (NASUWT, 2017: 5). This is a fast-growing and expanding sector of the economy employing around 2.9 million people. The Cultural Learning Alliance makes it clear that the educational system needs to prepare young people for the kinds of skills demanded by this sector:

> In a world where the generation of signs and symbols is as important as the manufacture of nuts and bolts, we need to invest more, not less, in the creative and imaginative skills of young people. Our economy will be strengthened by them. (CLA, 2017: 17)

A recent report by the innovation foundation Nesta and Pearson (Bakhshi et al., 2017) identified three sets of skills that will be needed by 2030, when children entering formal education will be making decisions about their careers:

- interpersonal skills, e.g. relating to others
- higher-order cognitive skills, e.g. originality, fluency of ideas
- systems skills, e.g. the ability to identify, understand and act upon connections.

Winthrop and McGivney (2016) scanned the educational policies of 102 countries and found that communication, creativity, critical thinking and problem-solving were the twenty-first-century skills most frequently identified. In the UK, the top ten skills and abilities associated with the rising occupations, such as hospitality, sports and leisure services, are set out in Table 3.1.

Table 3.1 Top ten skills, abilities and knowledge predicted for 2030 in rising occupations

Skills (S) and Abilities (A)	Meaning
1. Judgment and Decision-Making (S)	Considering the relative costs and benefits of potential actions to choose the most appropriate one.
2. Fluency of Ideas (A)	The ability to come up with a number of ideas about a topic.
3. Active Learning (S)	Understanding the implications of new information for both current and future problem-solving and decision-making.
4. Learning Strategies (S)	Selecting and using training/instructional methods and procedures appropriate for the situation when learning or teaching new things.
5. Originality (A)	The ability to come up with unusual or clever ideas about a given topic or situation, or to develop creative ways to solve a problem.
6. Systems Evaluation (S)	Determining how a system should work and how changes in conditions, operations and the environment will affect outcomes.
7. Deductive Reasoning (A)	The ability to apply general rules to specific problems to produce answers that make sense.
8. Complex Problem-Solving (S)	Identifying complex problems and reviewing related information to develop and evaluate options and implement solutions.
9. Systems Analysis (S)	Determining how a system should work and how changes in conditions, operations and the environment will affect outcomes.
10. Monitoring (S)	Monitoring/assessing performance of yourself, other individuals or organisations to make improvements or take corrective action.

Source: adapted from Bakhshi et al. (2017)

One of the key implications for educators is that they will need to focus on developing the skills and abilities associated with critical and creative thinking, such as problem-solving and fluency of ideas, if young people are to stand a good chance of employment in the future. This research goes beyond the generic 'twenty-first-century skills', sometimes criticised for being too fuzzy, by providing a more nuanced understanding of what needs to be taught to prepare children for future employment. The researchers strike an optimistic and reassuring note: 'we can all stop agonizing about machines taking over our jobs' (Bakhshi et al., 2017: 2). It is widely agreed that children will need to learn things that technologies cannot do – personal and emotional competences such as getting on with others and handling setbacks appropriately. But they will also need to think critically and creatively. Surveys regularly report that employers rank these as among the most sought-after skills (CBI/Pearson, 2016).

Creative and critical thinking are central to successful business. The European Commission's *EntreComp Framework* identifies fifteen competences that make up entrepreneurship and a staggering 442 learning outcomes (European Commission, 2016). Despite its unwieldy nature, EntreComp is a useful reference point for schools seeking confirmation of why creative and critical thinking matters in the modern business world. An entrepreneurial mindset includes demonstrating competences such as: spotting opportunities, taking the initiative, working with others, coping with ambiguity, uncertainty and risk, and creativity. These can be developed from an early age through charities such as Young Enterprise, which uses a network of local experienced business advisers to work with schools. Since 2014, its 'Fiver Challenge' gives primary pupils a month to set up a mini business and create a product or service that they can then sell or deliver at a profit and engage with their local community.[8] Previous winners have created products such as pom poms, greeting cards and sweets. Teachers report that the project develops a raft of skills and dispositions, including creativity, teamwork, communication, resilience and financial literacy (Young Enterprise, 2016). The process of transforming ideas into value for others, whether social, financial or cultural, is at the heart of what it means to be entrepreneurial.

The World Economic Forum (2015) identified sixteen 'crucial proficiencies' for education in the twenty-first century (Figure 3.1). These comprise 'foundation literacies', which

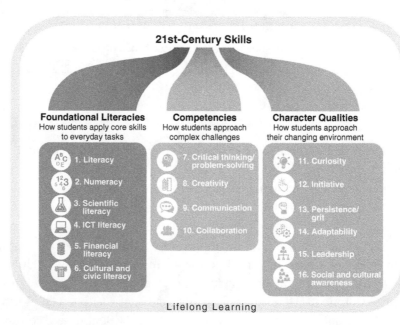

Figure 3.1   Twenty-first-century skills

Source: World Economic Forum (2015)

---

[8]www.fiverchallenge.org.uk (accessed 20 June 2018).

represent how students apply core skills in everyday life. But these are not enough for students to thrive. They also need competencies to critically evaluate knowledge, imagine and devise new ideas, and work well as a team to convey information. The 4 Cs of critical thinking, creativity, communication and collaboration are finally supplemented by a set of 'character qualities' that describe how students approach their environment. These are also known elsewhere as Habits of Mind and include persistence, curiosity and initiative. One of the World Economic Forum's recommendations is for governments to devote more resources, including technologies, to develop competencies and character qualities. What is clear from the World Economic Forum is that skilled jobs are increasingly demanding the ability to solve complex problems and effectively analyse information. This calls for qualities such as persistence, curiosity and initiative.

Unfortunately, there is evidence that too many children are leaving formal education without these competencies. In 2010, a rigorous American study of more than 2,300 undergraduates at 24 institutions, found that 45 per cent of these students demonstrated no significant improvement in skills such as critical thinking during their first two years of college (Arum and Roksa, 2010). An international survey of a thousand teachers in 2014 found that more than half acknowledged that critical thinking was missing from students leaving school (Stewart, 2014). In another study of Chinese students at a university in England, one Chinese student told her lecturer: 'We have no idea of how to be critical and critical of what' (Matthews, 2016). An independent review (Hutchings, 2015) of the impact of accountability measures on children and young people suggests that the success of schools should be judged by how pupils are engaged in creative learning, enjoy schooling, are suitably prepared for the next stage of their education or work (if it is available) and contribute effectively as members of society.

MANY LEADING EDUCATIONAL SYSTEMS IN THE WORLD HAVE CRITICAL AND CREATIVE THINKING AT THE CENTRE OF THEIR CURRICULA

Based on results from the Programme for International Student Assessment (PISA) and the Trends in International Mathematics and Science Study (TIMSS), many of the top-performing educational systems value thinking skills explicitly. Table 3.2 is based on five countries, which have performed consistently well over recent years. The Finnish National Board of Education introduced a revised National Core Curriculum in 2016. One of its reasons was to rethink the concept of what learning should be about. It wants a greater emphasis on the importance of students' own experiences, feelings and joy, as well as a focus on learning to learn in dialogue with others. Seven transversal competences, including thinking and learning to learn, have been developed to support a shift from what to how to learn. What is remarkable about the recent reforms in Finland is that these have been implemented not at a time of crisis but when the educational system has won plaudits from all over the world.

Table 3.2 Key competencies among five of the world's leading educational systems

Country	Competencies and skills
Singapore	Social and emotional competencies: • Self-awareness • Self-management • Social awareness • Responsible decision-making • Relationship management Twenty-first-century competencies: • Civic literacy, global awareness and cross-cultural skills • Communication, collaboration and information skills • Critical and inventive thinking
Finland	Seven transversal competences: • Thinking and learning-to-learn • Looking after oneself • Cultural competence, interaction and expression • Multiliteracy • ICT competence • Competence for the world of work, entrepreneurship • Participation and influence, building the sustainable future
Canada (Ontario)	Three essential skills: • Literacy • Numeracy • Thinking skills
New Zealand	Five key competencies: • Thinking • Relating to others • Using language, symbols and texts • Managing self • Participating and contributing
Australia	Seven general capabilities: • Literacy • Numeracy • ICT capability • Critical and creative thinking • Personal and social capability • Ethical understanding • Intercultural understanding

The Australian government and businesses recognise the importance of fostering creativity and critical thinking in school. A report by the Foundation for Young Australians (Canny, 2016) analysed more than four million job advertisements over a three-year period to identify the skills most wanted by employers. Following digital literacy, the greatest demands were for critical thinking (increased by 158 per cent) and creativity (up by 65 per cent). Jobs that demanded these skills also paid more. Acquiring decent problem-solving skills could earn an additional $7,745 a year. This premium pay reflects the value employers place on these skills. In the Australian future, jobs are forecast to demand enterprise skills (such as creativity and critical thinking) 70 per cent more than jobs of the past (Canny, 2016: 13).

In Ontario, students acquire essential skills as part of their Ontario Skills Passport. The five thinking skills are broken down as follows:

- Job Task Planning and Organizing – The planning and organization of one's own work.
- Decision Making – The making of any type of decision, using appropriate information.
- Problem Solving – The identification and solving of problems.
- Finding Information – The use of a variety of sources, including written text, people, computerized databases, and information systems.
- Critical Thinking – Making judgments by using criteria to evaluate ideas and information and the related consequences. (Ontario Ministry of Education, 2018)

Teachers are provided with descriptors for levels 1–4 for each essential skill to support consistency in assessment, tracking and planning over time.

In Singapore, the 21st Century Competencies (21CC) Framework is represented as a circle with an inner ring of core values; a middle ring of social and emotional competencies such as responsible decision-making, self-awareness and self-management; and an outer ring of three emerging twenty-first-century competencies, which include critical and inventive thinking (CIT) taught within subject contexts. An infusion approach is adopted and there is a strong emphasis on real-life investigations.

Of course, there are dangers in policy borrowing given the significant cultural differences between countries. The Global Education Reform Movement (GERM) is based on a business model that values competition, privatisation, performance-related rewards and accountability through tests. Pasi Sahlberg points out that none of the GERM elements are present in Finland, which has consistently performed well in educational comparisons. As he says, 'Lessons from Finland help you to kill 99.9 per cent of GERMs' (Sahlberg, 2012). Nonetheless, it is hard to escape the conclusion that critical and creative thinking are held in high regard among policy-makers and practitioners in the leading educational systems in the world.

The arguments for creativity and critical thinking do not rest only on how these skills benefit individual learners. Families, communities and society at large also gain when children are developing these skills.

SUMMARY

◯ All children have the right to learn to think creatively and critically.
◯ If schools teach these skills well, then pupils should develop confidence and capability across the curriculum.
◯ Creative learning leads to wide-ranging benefits including improved wellbeing and better employability prospects.
◯ The most successful educational systems in the world support the teaching of creative and critical thinking or aspire to do so.

VISIBLE THINKING ROUTINES

INTRODUCTION

There is something about the word 'routine' that suggests little more than a boring, repetitive habit. In the film *Groundhog Day*, the main character Phil is stuck in a time warp (2 February, which is Groundhog Day) and nothing that he does to try to get out of this makes any difference – the daily routines never change. For most of the film he seems doomed to repeat this day forever, and this is not perceived to be good thing! However, teachers often value routines in daily classroom practices. They use many routines, for example, to line up quietly, to tidy up and bring the schoolday to a close. These are designed to support children to become part of an accepted classroom culture. In terms of developing thinking, routines can also be very valuable, 'freeing up brain space to dream, to create fresh ideas, to solve problems' (Hevrdejs, 2012: 2). This chapter explores Visible Thinking Routines (VTRs), resources designed to help make thinking visible and accessible to children (Ritchhart et al., 2011).

BACKGROUND

VTRs offer simple, structured strategies for teachers to develop thinking skills, such as comparing and contrasting, reasoning and justifying. VTRs originated through the work of researchers at Harvard's Project Zero (PZ). Founded by philosopher Nelson Goodman at the Harvard Graduate School of Education in 1967, PZ is based on multi-disciplinary research. The underlying philosophy of PZ is that good thinking is as much a matter of disposition as it is of skill. Motivations, attitudes, values and Habits of Mind, all play key roles in good thinking. To a large degree, these elements determine whether people use their thinking skills when it counts. Learning is a consequence of thinking, and developing a culture of thinking is critical if we want to produce the feelings, energy, and even joy that can propel learning forward and motivate learners to do what at times can be hard and challenging mental work. As such, research at PZ includes enquiry into questions such as: 'What are the ingredients of good thinking?' 'Can good thinking be taught? How?' and 'What does good thinking have to do with good learning?'

VTRs are one of Project Zero's four themes within the Thinking Dispositions strand of enquiry. There are six principles underpinning VTRs, which relate to what is known about the development of effective thinking and learning. The first principle is that learning happens because of thinking carefully about something. Learners develop an understanding of a concept when they think about it and explore it in depth. Therefore, good thinking is needed as a prerequisite for good learning. This means that teachers need to provide stimuli that provoke opportunity for careful, deep thinking.

The second underlying principle of VTRs is the belief that good thinking comprises skills, but pupils also need to have the dispositions to use these skills. Dispositions such as curiosity, resilience, scepticism and imaginativeness all make for good thinking (Perkins et al., 2000). Pupils need to be willing as well as able to think.

The third principle is that the development of thinking often best occurs as a social endeavour. While we can sharpen our thinking through meditation and solitary musing, we often learn from interacting with those around us and build understanding together. Sometimes we learn 'untruths' as well as 'truths' from our peers! Hence, the environment in a classroom should be one that fosters and ensures thoughtful, social learning, which is embedded and pervasive, rather than sporadic or 'bolted-on'. However, we must also realise that good thinking requires the individual to make sense of the learning themselves, to internalise it, and so time to reflect as an individual is also crucial.

Fourthly, making good thinking visible is very important. Teachers need to think of ways of making things explicit, to support both the social and individual nature of learning. Thinking happens in our heads, invisible to others and often invisible to us. Effective thinkers make their thinking visible and they externalise their thoughts through speaking, writing, drawing, or some other method. They document thoughts to reflect on them later. Because thinking is an invisible process, young children need to learn the words associated with thinking, use props to help them work through each stage of thinking and see models of good thinking in practice (McGuinness, 1999). In other words, if we can help make the thinking process visible, children will be supported in gaining an understanding of how to think more effectively.

The fifth underlying principle of VTRs is that good thinkers operate in a supportive learning environment, which allows them to 'feel the force' of effective classroom cultures. Researchers suggest that there are eight 'forces' that shape all classrooms (see Table 4.1)

Table 4.1 Cultural forces within thinking classrooms

Cultural Force	Description
Time	Allocating time for thinking by providing time for exploring topics in more depth as well as time to formulate thoughtful responses.
Opportunities	Providing purposeful activities that require students to engage in thinking and the development of understanding as part of their ongoing experience of the classroom.
Routines and structures	Scaffolding students' thinking in the moment as well as providing tools and patterns of thinking that can be used independently.
Modelling	Modelling of who we are as thinkers and learners so that the process of our thinking is discussed
Language	Using a language of thinking that provides students with the vocabulary for describing and reflecting on thinking.
Interactions and relationships	Showing a respect for and valuing of one another's contributions of ideas and thinking in a spirit of ongoing collaborative inquiry.
Physical environment	Making thinking visible by displaying the process of thinking and development of ideas. Arranging the space to facilitate thoughtful interactions.
Expectations	Setting an agenda of understanding and conveying clear expectations. Focusing on the value for thinking and learning as outcomes as opposed to mere completion of 'work'.

Source: Ritchhart (2002)

Depending on the classroom culture, these forces can support or undermine thoughtful learning (Ritchhart, 2002).

Finally, the sixth principle is that schools must develop cultures of thinking for teachers as well as for pupils – developing one's thinking is a lifelong endeavour. Professional learning communities, which foster rich discussions of teaching, learning and thinking, should be a fundamental part of teachers' experiences. Such opportunities provide the foundation for nurturing thinking and learning in the classroom. Regular opportunities for teachers to discuss teaching, thinking and learning are therefore essential.

VTRs can support teachers to create a classroom culture of thinking which addresses these principles, making thinking visible, and immersing children into a rich environment of thinking. Ritchhart (2002) points out that effective teachers establish cultures of thinking from the very first moment pupils enter the room. For instance, they may discuss with students directly the value of dispositions such as curiosity and enquiry. They may devise open-ended problems to solve or may support dialogues around a topical issue. In such a culture, thinking is valued and given time, rich opportunities for thinking exist in the day-to-day classroom experience and models of thinking are present in the form of seeing teachers and peers as fellow thinkers. The development of understanding is the basis of VTRs. To teach for understanding, 'key thinking moves' are recommended (Figure 4.1).

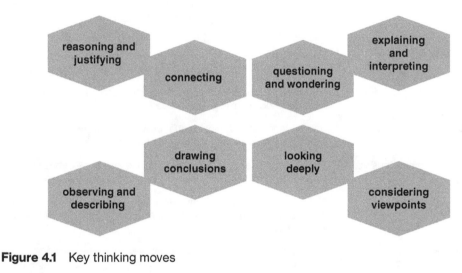

Figure 4.1 Key thinking moves

Source: after Ritchhart et al. (2011)

The routines act as scaffolds for children, and typically consist of a series of questions and prompts. VTRs have a few, clear steps (often three) so that they are simple to embed into practice. To become 'routine' they need to be used frequently, and the intention is that children will become familiar enough with the routines to use them quickly, increasingly independently and almost automatically. Once embedded, these routines can be transferred to situations beyond the classroom, and applied to many aspects of daily life.

INTRODUCING THE RESOURCES

There are over thirty VTRs, based on four key thinking ideals, Understanding, Fairness, Truth and Creativity. Some of the most popular VTRs are summarised in Table 4.2.

Table 4.2 Overview of selected Visible Thinking Routines

Visible Thinking Routine	Key thinking	What part of the lesson?	How to organise?
Think–Pair–Share	Promotes understanding through active reasoning and explanation, and encourages students to understand multiple perspectives.	At any point during the session. Pairs of children.	1. Pose a question. 2. Have students consider the question on their own (1–2 mins). 3. Students discuss the question with their partner and share their ideas and/or contrasting opinions (3 mins). 4. Re-group as a whole class and solicit responses from some or all of the pairs (3 mins).
Connect–Extend–Challenge	Make connections between new ideas and prior knowledge and take stock of ongoing questions, puzzles and difficulties.	During the plenary or mini-plenary of a session. Individuals, pairs, groups or the class.	Present the stimuli and activity. 1. How does this connect to your current understanding of the topic? 2. What new ideas did this task provide, which have extended your thinking? 3. Are there still challenges in your thinking – gaps and further questions to ask?
I used to think … Now I think	Reflect on their thinking about a topic or issue and explore how and why that thinking has changed.	Plenary or mini-plenary	At the end of a task, activity or topic allow the children time to reflect on how their thinking has changed. 1. What did they know at the start of the topic? (perhaps revisit early work here). 2. How has their thinking changed? 3. What helped them to think differently – was it a resource, an activity, a friend or something different? 4. What would they like to find out next?

(Continued)

Table 4.2 (Continued)

Visible Thinking Routine	Key thinking	What part of the lesson?	How to organise?
See–Think–Wonder	Make careful observations and thoughtful interpretations – careful selection of stimuli helps stimulate curiosity and sets the stage for inquiry.	At the start of an activity, or as the main activity itself.	1. What do you see? 2. What do you think? 3. What do you wonder?
3–2–1 Bridge	This routine encourages pupils to identify initial thoughts, ideas and questions about a topic and then connect these to new thoughts, ideas and questions after they have undertaken some learning.	Before an activity or topic and after.	Write down 3 ideas, 2 questions and 1 analogy about a topic. After learning, complete another 3, 2, 1. Make the bridge by sharing initial thoughts and how these may have changed with others, considering how initial ideas provide a starting point.
Circle of Viewpoints	Consider different and diverse perspectives involved in and around a topic, and understand that people may think and feel differently about things.	As an activity or as a precursor to some persuasive or creative writing.	Take the perspective – e.g. of a character in a story or in a historical event. Research this person and their perspective on the situation. Justify, explain and elaborate on your perspective to others.

Effective and appropriate use of VTRs helps to create patterns of learning and thinking that become part of the intellectual character of a child (Perkins, 2003). Each VTR is therefore aimed at developing specific thinking processes, such as making connections or comparisons, providing explanation, considering different perspectives or justifying an opinion. VTRs emphasise thinking being developed through talk and discussion, and have been used in early years' settings, primary and secondary schools and into university and wider educational venues (e.g. galleries and museums) in the United States, the Netherlands, Sweden, Belgium, Australia and increasingly in the UK (Ritchhart and Perkins, 2008).

THE VTRs IN PRACTICE

For classroom practitioners, the appeal of VTRs is as follows:

- they are easy to teach
- they relate to particular types of thinking

- they are easy to learn so that children can use them with increasing independence within day-to-day activities
- they are flexible enough to be used across many themes, subjects or areas of learning
- they are adaptable, to meet the needs of children of all ages and stages of development
- they act to help establish a structure to classroom dialogue – guiding (but not forcing, leading or dictating) the discussion
- they enhance children's cognitive development
- they raise children's and teachers' awareness of the thinking processes that happen during learning. This helps focus discussion and reflection.

The following examples show how different VTRs can be used in different ways, across the curriculum and across age groups.

See–Think–Wonder

Year 1 and Year 4 pupils from Bynea Primary School in Carmarthenshire could use the routine See–Think–Wonder when they looked at paintings of children at Christmas time in a local stately home. Following a successful inspection, the school had a focus on developing thinking and oracy in their school development plan, and wanted to promote opportunities for this beyond the classroom. VTRs were ideal activities to undertake while 'out and about' on a school trip. Year 1 pupils were studying the local area, while the Year 4 pupils were learning about the Victorians. The VTRs suited both age groups and topics. On the visit, the children worked in groups of three and had magnifying glasses to look very closely at the paintings. The teachers supported them to use appropriate vocabulary when describing what they saw and what they thought. The Year 1 pupils concentrated on objects and colours and saw 'a boy with curly yellow hair' and 'a big teddy bear', while the Year 4 pupils extended their descriptions to use more elaborate vocabulary: 'I saw a young child wearing a silken shirt', 'I can see a child who is wearing old-fashioned clothes and who has golden, shiny, curly hair'. The children were encouraged to make at least ten observations, which were then shared with the rest of the class.

After this, the children talked to one another about what they thought about the picture. The pupils were encouraged to use their observations to justify their thinking. For example, responses included:

> I think the painting is from a long time ago because the clothes are funny (Year 1).
>
> I think that this is a painting of a rich child because he looks clean and has fancy clothes and presents, and hasn't been cleaning the chimneys or working hard (Year 4).

Once the children's thoughts had been gathered, the teachers asked them what they wondered about the painting – and what questions they would ask the painter or the child if they could speak to them. This generated rich and interesting questions, which the teachers felt would not have emerged without the 'see and think' part of the routine. Questions included:

> I would ask the painter who the boy was and why he was painting him.
>
> I wonder why the boy doesn't look very happy – perhaps he is lonely 'cos he hasn't got family with him in the picture.
>
> I wonder whether he is like a celebrity and that's why he is in a painting – I'd want to know more about him and whether he lived in this house.

The teachers felt that the use of the VTR was helpful in focusing the children's attention on the painting, and in supporting them to think more deeply about it. As one teacher noted: 'normally we would have rushed past this painting, glancing at it quickly, with them probably more focused on what time packed lunch was. Instead they spent time looking and thinking about the painting, and connecting it to what they have already learnt about their topic. It captured their attention in a way that a simple worksheet couldn't have done'. Spending more time examining the resource is a way of 'slow looking', which Tishman (2018) suggests helps us gain a deeper knowledge of the world and uncovers complexities that we sometimes miss at first glance.

After pupils became familiar with the routine, encouraging them to use the three elements of See–Think–Wonder spontaneously, and not necessarily separately, can lead to some powerful opportunities for deeper thinking (Cale, 2011). For example, Laura Luxton, a Reception class teacher at St Thomas Community Primary school in Swansea, introduced her pupils to See–Think–Wonder during a term's residency at a local museum. In this innovative project the Reception class was based in the museum, and learnt through their practical explorations of the museum's collection (King's College London, 2017). They used the routine with some of the museum exhibits several times during the term. During a walk around the local area, the children spotted an interesting statue. They started to use the elements of See–Think–Wonder independently and spontaneously. This led to some thoughtful comments, as illustrated below.

> **I see ...** A man. A statue. An old man. A sleeping man.
>
> **I think ...** He's a sailor. He's tired from watching the sea. He is worried about something. He's happy because he's smiling. He is being blown around because he is tipping forward. He has lost his boat.

I wonder... What the bell is for? Why are his eyes closed? Is he scared? If he was on his own? Why he can't stand up straight? Did he ring the bell and who came to help him?

Laura consequently used this routine with several different starting stimuli. She found that the use of the routine provided a useful insight into pupils' prior knowledge and understanding, and provided an opportunity to make learning relevant and personal to pupils. For example, she used the image of a girl with a red balloon created by the mysterious graffiti artist Banksy in 2002 with her class of 4–5-year-olds. Arguably Banksy's most iconic piece, the words 'There Is Always Hope' are written just behind a young girl, who can be seen reaching for a balloon in the shape of a heart. There has been much debate within the art community about the true meaning of this piece of art, with a variety of ideas involving love, innocence and – obviously – hope. The pupils in Laura's class were not aware of the image, or its title, but it was chosen as a stimulus for discussion on the Welsh Valentine's Day (*Santes Dwynwen*), which falls on 25 January each year. Laura projected the image on the interactive whiteboard for discussion using the See–Think–Wonder routine. The responses are included in Table 4.3.

Table 4.3 Responses of 5-year-olds using the See–Think–Wonder routine to 'Girl Floating with Red Balloons' (Banksy)

SEE Heart, heart balloon, balloon flying, person, trying to get balloon, heart, balloon is red, floating away, something on the wall, writing, stairs, wall, girl with a dress on, a pipe, string, little box, ribbon, lamppost, plant.

THINK The box is an electric box, looks pretty, she's on a street, on the road, think she's alone, trying to catch it, let balloon go as an accident, think she's 6 years old [this was followed by other guesses of age 3–16], walls are dirty, she's in town, there's a shop next to her selling balloons, think it was in the war time – my Bampa was in the war – the war was when the Germans came, she's too small to catch it, yelling for help, stairs are muddy, car other side of the wall, she's in a parking space, it's raining, it's windy, she doesn't have much money, she hasn't got a mum or dad, she got lost because she didn't listen to her mum and dad, she's scared, waiting for her mum, the wind blew her balloon away.

WONDER Is she lost? Where did the balloon come from? Were her mum and dad in the army? Were her mum and dad killed? Where does she live? What year is it? Who is she? What's her name? Where is she from? Why doesn't she have a family? Is she alone? Does she have parents? Does she like Mario? Why did she choose red? Has she got a pet? Did she ever find the balloon? Is she homeless? Where did the balloon come from?

Laura felt that these responses were more detailed and mature than she would have expected, and provided an insight into the children's ideas and own experiences. The pupils talked about experiences that were personal and meaningful to themselves as well as starting to explore important issues. These could form the basis of further discussion and exploration about what love means.

Sarah Di Tomaso, from Oak Field Primary School in Barry, also introduced her children to See–Think–Wonder. Figure 4.2 features her unpublished blog about the experience of introducing this in her Reception class of 4–5-year-olds.

I just thought I would give you an initial update after Wednesday's introduction to thinking routines. I decided whilst it was still fresh in my mind to try it out with my reception class children. I used the same photo as we used as staff and was pleasantly surprised at their answers. It took a little time for them to grasp the differences between the see, think and wonder but by the end of the session I think they were getting it, although it was the more able offering the majority of the responses.

I then told them we would do another photo at the end of the day so we could practise using the columns, to which they were quite excited. At the end of day one I used a photo with a 'bullying theme' as I thought they may relate to this a bit more. Straightaway I could clearly see that more children were offering responses and some of those were children who would not normally speak out in a group discussion but were able to respond to the 'see' column with confidence. When responding to the other columns they related it to incidents that they had seen or had been involved in which opened up an emotional literacy discussion.

The highlight of this session was when my one pupil with ADHD said for the 'think' column … 'I think that the girl with the book is being tolerant!' … when I questioned what that meant and why he thought that, he replied, 'because she is walking away and ignoring the bullies'. We have just introduced the teaching of four values to our school and tolerance is one of them so for him to link the value with the photo was a real 'lightbulb' moment.

This morning the children asked during milk time if they could do another photo, it seems to be their new favourite thing to do during milk and snack time! I chose a 'food' photo as it links in with our food glorious food topic. As you can see from their responses they are really getting the idea of this and finding it much easier to focus given the three columns. They are enjoying the structure rather than a completely open questioning session. Their responses to 'wonder' are particularly pleasing.

Figure 4.2 A teacher's blog about the use of VTRs

3–2–1 Bridge

This routine is used to help pupils see changes in their thinking. For example, children in a Year 3 class were learning about 'flowers, fruits and seeds'. At the start of the topic they completed a 3, 2, 1 on seeds. They enjoyed individually writing their three words on sticky-notes and putting them onto group templates. Typically, the pupils described seeds as small, brown, round and hard. Questions included: 'Where do seeds come from?' and 'How do seeds grow?'. Analogies included: 'Seeds are like a ball'. The children then undertook sessions where they examined fruits, vegetables and flowers carefully to look at their seeds. They carried out some science experiments such as exploring wind-dispersed seeds (e.g. sycamore, thistle down or dandelion clocks) to see how they moved. They visited a local garden centre and looked at a wide variety of seeds, sorting and classifying these in various ways before designing seed packets. They watched a video that showed them about seed dispersal,[1] e.g. by wind (light seeds that spin, drift or glide), by water (seeds that float), by explosion (seeds that are flicked out from pods) and by animals (who will carry hooked or hairy seeds in their fur or eat fruits and carry the seeds away). They planted quick growing seeds such as cress and examined how these grew in different conditions, such as light, dark, warmth and cold.

After their activities, they returned to the 3, 2, 1 routine. This time their ideas were more varied, with one child commenting that it was 'hard to only think of three ideas 'cos seeds are really interesting and different'. Ideas for the three words included stripy, bumpy, hooked, light, tasty, poisonous and hard. They asked questions such as: 'What is the furthest a seed can travel on the wind?' and 'Why don't seeds start growing in animals' tummies?' They created analogies, including: 'A seed is like a tiny baby, waiting for the right time to be born'. The teacher felt that these responses were more detailed and imaginative than previously, and showed a depth of understanding about seeds that had clearly grown with the topic.

To encourage the children to reflect on their own learning journeys they were asked to compare their initial and final efforts. They enjoyed doing this – and could see how their initial ideas had bridged and developed. As one child put it: 'Well, I thought seeds were all tiny and round and brown, and now I know that some of them are, but there are way more types than that. My favourite are beetroot seeds 'cos they look like alien planets when you look at them – they are brown but they are also bumpy and cool'.

Zoom In

This routine requires pupils to pay close attention to detail and make inferences. Because it uses only sections of an image at one time, it is different from a See–Think–Wonder. As each section is revealed, pupils can make new inferences, and this helps them to realise that thinking is a process and minds can be changed based on new understandings. Teachers used this routine with pre-school children when the topic being explored was 'Houses and Homes'. The pupils were going to explore *The Three Little Pigs* story as a starting point for activities across the curriculum (such as building houses from different materials, learning about animal homes and role playing in the 'castle' home corner). In preparation for the Zoom In, the teacher printed a poster size picture from the story of *The Three Little Pigs*, and covered it with five numbered jigsaw pieces simply made from coloured paper. The aim of the activity was to look closely at each of the smaller pieces of the image that were subsequently revealed, and to share the thinking about what could be underneath. The teacher worked with a focused group of six pupils. Questions such

---

[1]www.bbc.co.uk/education/clips/znvfb9q (accessed 20 June 2018).

as 'What do you see?' were asked as the first piece of puzzle was removed. This generated talking and speculation among the pupils, who had no idea about the content of the picture. They considered colours, patterns and made guesses, for instance that it could be 'sky because it is 'blue'. Piece number two was removed and the pupils were asked questions such as 'What new things do you see?' and 'How does this change your thinking?'

The pupils were keen to talk about new things they could spot, and were interested about what made them change their minds. As more and more pieces were removed the pupils were asked 'What do you think this might be?' and they got more and more excited to find out what could be underneath. This encouraged them to use their observations and existing knowledge to make some predictions. The use of conditional language, 'what *might* this be', is important – as it suggests possibilities rather than absolutes (Langer and Piper, 1987), which encourages participation. The teacher noted the dialogue that ensued, and when this was reviewed after the session she found that all the pupils had participated and contributed ideas. They used increasingly complex vocabulary to explain and justify their ideas and were excited to see how their thinking was changing with revealed pieces.

Circle of Viewpoints

Students undertaking a Primary Post Graduate Certificate in Education (PGCE) at the University of Wales Trinity Saint David used this routine to examine different views on intelligence testing prior to completing an assignment. Students took the perspective of leading contributors in the field of intelligence and intelligence testing such as Binet, Terman, Spearman, Flynn, Gardner or Sternberg. They were given some study time in which they researched the background and theories of their allocated individual and then debated with one another 'their' view of intelligence and intelligence testing. In this way they considered perspectives of others, and were required to justify and elaborate on their own responses. After the session, the students were encouraged to reflect on the VTR. Megan felt that this was a useful routine to undertake:

> Looking at the theories from the perspectives of different researchers was really powerful. Even though my own personal opinion may not be in agreement with the researcher I was allocated, this process made me consider his perspective rather than just think 'no he's wrong'. That meant that my understanding of the whole topic was deeper – and I was able to see the complexities better than if I had just thought of my own view. It also made the research come alive – listening to my friends argue their perspective was really good. I'm definitely going to do this with my pupils in school – maybe when we think about characters in a story or in history.

Chalk Talk

This is a very inclusive routine as all participants are encouraged to consider others' viewpoints, and to justify and elaborate on their own. Typically, the class is arranged in groups of three to five people. This can be done as a class activity, with each group having their own paper, or with smaller groups at a time, depending on the teacher's preference and the age of the pupils. A stimulating topic is written in the centre of a large sheet of paper, or an image or artefact can be placed in the centre of the page (in one school, younger children had access to an electronic button which spoke the question aloud, ensuring that those who could not read the question had access to the activity). The question or prompt may reflect the theme of the training, topic or subject.

We often use Chalk Talk during professional learning events for teachers. It provides an opportunity for everyone to be heard. We have used prompts such as 'What are the main barriers to enjoyment of reading among our pupils?' Or the question may be designed as an icebreaker at the start of a session. We find that teachers at the start of a training course often like to consider 'What is your idea of a perfect weekend?'

Individuals have three to four minutes to note their own individual ideas and responses to the question on the paper, in silence. They are encouraged to reflect on their knowledge, experience and personal opinions. They are free to record their ideas in words, images or symbols (if each member of the group does this in a different coloured pen then at the end of the activity it is possible to see the record of individual contributions). Individuals then have time to respond to other people in their group. Still working in silence, they circulate the paper and 'comment' on the ideas that others have noted. This may be in the form of ticks, question marks or questions (so can be accessible for most pupils). Individuals look for connections between their ideas and those of others – circling these and connecting the ideas with visible lines on the paper. For example, when a group of teachers considered a perfect weekend, a common connection was the importance of 'relaxation' – many teachers noted this down, and included images of alarm clocks crossed out or words such as 'sleep'! Some mentioned food and drink – and were prompted to add to this: What sort of food? Where would they go to enjoy this? Some comments were more unusual – for the teacher who liked to spend time with their snakes some colleagues disagreed that this would be a good way to spend a weekend. The snake enthusiast then justified her opinion, and indicated that snakes get a bad press and are actually not at all slimy or scary. However, some others in the group indicated that it was the feeding of the snake that they felt sad about – and drew an image of a fluffy chick to illustrate their reasoning. All this conversation was done silently, and was captured on the paper.

Depending on contextual factors, such as age and numbers, pupils may then circulate to other groups, commenting on their responses, before returning to their own Chalk Talk and making any final additions or amendments. Emerging themes can be identified.

These may form the basis of future enquiry; for example, in our 'snake group' several individuals were interested in finding out more. If this was a class of pupils, we could use this 'learner voice' to support planning of future activities.

This 'silent conversation' provides pupils with time to follow through their thoughts and ideas without interruption. This means that pupils who tend to dominate oral class-room discussions are not the only voices being heard, and allows quieter or more reticent pupils opportunity to contribute equally. It highlights the notion of building understand-ing in a collaborative way through putting forward ideas, questioning one another, and developing the ideas further. If the Chalk Talk is done at the start of a piece of learning, it can be returned to at the end. This allows the opportunity for reflection and the chance to see how ideas have shifted and developed over time.

IMPACT

Much of the evidence about the use of VTRs comes from the USA and Europe. Therefore, we ran a research project involving six primary and early years' teachers in schools in Wales, in which several VTRs were introduced into their classes over the course of a year (Lewis, 2017c). At the end of the project the feedback from all the teachers and their support staff about the VTRs was positive. Each had embedded several VTRs into their classroom pedagogy during the project, and felt that, in terms of developing their chil-dren's thinking, they were highly effective materials. Comments made included:

> They are fun – and really easy to put into lots of different lessons. I like the fact that they have a very clear focus – like 'connect' – it helps me and the children remember the thinking focus.
>
> They are quick to pick up – children can engage with them. They are user friendly – and I am clear about what I am trying to teach.
>
> I like the clarity – you can use one which develops particular thinking when you need to, so can easily help with plans and the children enjoy them.
>
> They are clear and focused. They make me clear about the language to use, and the actual thinking skill we are trying to learn and so they help us reflect on the learning and thinking because everyone knows what is expected. (Lewis, 2017c: 244)

The teachers felt that the simple, clear and focused nature of the VTRs was beneficial. VTRs helped them to focus on developing specific thinking no matter the age or devel-opmental level of the children. The resources enabled them to plan activities that had clear thinking skills related to them – and this helped then to focus the discussion during the tasks. The resources were interesting to the children – and all the teachers said that the children enjoyed engaging in VTR activities. We also saw improvements in the amount of conversation that took place in the classrooms when VTRs were being used. It seems that the routines can help foster high quality classroom conversation possibly since they provide structure and make the thinking visible to the learner and the teacher (Salmon, 2008).

These findings are echoed in the literature about VTRs, which suggests that VTRs can help foster classroom conversation about thinking since they provide structure and make the thinking visible to the learner and the teacher (Ritchhart et al., 2011). The routines have been shown to develop positive attitudes to thinking, and to support quality interaction between adults and children, and between children themselves (Wolberg and Goff, 2012). Certainly, Laura Luxton feels that the routines are of benefit, indicating that the three-step process is supportive of the younger pupils:

> I've seen first-hand how 'See, Think, Wonder' can be used any time, any place, anywhere! The three-step process encouraged enriched answers from the children about what is in front of them. They were giving the most mature answers in a way I had never expected from 5 year olds.

Steve Lewis, the thinking skills lead in Tondu Primary School in Bridgend, shares this sentiment. He writes:

> See–Think–Wonder builds up the complexity of children's thinking, from being quite literal and low level in what they can see, to being incredibly open-ended and free in what they wonder. It is a challenging activity but allows all children to participate without fear of being wrong, as there is no wrong answer. We have used See–Think–Wonder as a starter activity across the curriculum. The greatest challenge with this strategy is to encourage all children to look more closely and to stick with the activity. At times some children will try to race through the activity, keeping their responses short and superficial. By giving them a time limit where they have to concentrate on each section at a time seems to help. For example, we will practise looking closely at the picture without responding for a minute before we do any form of writing. We then have a set time for each section. The time increases as the expected level of cognition increases from See, to Think and then Wonder. We also have discussion time between each section as this often encourages further insights.

The children that worked with us in our project all enjoyed using the VTRs. They said that they were fun, and made them 'think better'. They liked using 3–2–1 Bridge when they were looking at a topic on 'Fire and Ice', and enjoyed using See–Think–Wonder and

Circle of Viewpoints because of the practical nature of the tasks. VTRs also help pupils to become more aware of themselves as learners. For example, pupils in Vanguard High School, New York comment that, after using VTRs:

> I used to think that I couldn't do this because I was confused but now I think that I can do it. I used to think that writing was boring because it was a lot of work and confusion. But now I think it's fun because you learn a lot from your own writing. (Ritchhart et al., 2011: 160)

These statements illustrate that VTRs can help pupils develop confidence and positive attitudes towards learning. Pupils in Tondu Primary School also enjoy using the VTRs and suggest that, for example, using See–Think–Wonder to explore pictures 'gave you a structure to think about the picture. I enjoyed asking questions about the picture, usually you just have to answer questions. It seemed easy at first but you had to look really closely. It made me notice more detail. I was able to use my prior knowledge of the subject and link it to the picture'.

CHALLENGES

As Ritchhart et al. (2011: 30) indicate, 'Making thinking visible is not without challenges'. Even when teachers create opportunities for thinking to take place, because thinking is largely invisible it can be challenging to develop it effectively. VTRs need to be based upon the selection of an engaging stimulus that is worthy of pupils and teachers thinking in depth about it. This is not always straightforward, and teachers will need to monitor responses carefully. The success of these routines also depends on the interaction that is supported, both between the teacher and pupils, and between pupils themselves. This can take time to develop.

Ritchhart et al. (2011) suggest that when teachers use VTRs they must ensure that they question pupils effectively during the routine. This means showing a genuine interest in the ideas being explored. Questions should help pupils to see their own thinking processes develop. They need to be authentic so all participants are interested in the answers – in other words, teachers need to avoid asking the questions that they already know the answers to. Teachers also need to listen actively to what pupils say, thus providing 'an opening for students to make their thinking visible to us because there is a reason to do so' (Ritchhart et al., 2011: 37). It is also important to develop strategies to document the thinking – this helps monitor progress, helps participants to see the learning process and supports reflection.

As with other materials, there needs to be a balance between allowing pupils to become familiar enough with the routines so that they can use them independently and with confidence, and over-use, which can lead to disengagement. Here the teachers' role is again crucial in planning and assessing how and when the routines are appropriate to use in order to support development of key thinking processes.

SUMMARY

- VTRs are based on the premise that visible thinking should become part of the fabric of classroom activity.
- Teachers use many routines in their everyday classroom practice, and by extending these they can use them to develop thinking as well as behaviour.
- Routines are an important way to engage young minds to strengthen their intellectual dispositions.
- VTRs can help develop children's ability and inclination to think.
- VTRs provide a useful structure for teachers of all ages, and in all areas of the curriculum, who want to develop effective thinking in their settings.

THINKING HATS

INTRODUCTION

Most people who have listened to Edward de Bono speak, as we did at the 2013 International Conference on Thinking in Wellington (New Zealand), are struck by the simplicity of his presentation style. At the age of seventy, De Bono delivered his keynote speech in a very measured manner, recording his stick-figure illustrations onto acetate sheets displayed via an overhead projector. He did not need any other technological prop to convey his clear and powerful message about the importance of teaching children to think. De Bono has contributed substantially to the field of thinking through sixty-two books, games, conference talks and courses. In this chapter, we introduce perhaps his most famous legacy – Six Thinking Hats.

BACKGROUND

Edward Charles Francis Publius de Bono was born in St Julian's Bay, Malta on the 19 May 1933. His father was a doctor and his mother an Irish journalist. De Bono attended school and university in Malta, graduating in medicine in 1953. He then won a scholarship to Oxford University, where he studied psychology and physiology. De Bono pursued his medical training and research at Harvard Medical School, before setting up in New York a School of Thinking in 1980. The De Bono Institute was established in Australia in 1996 as a centre for new thinking. De Bono has since received many awards and nominations and in

2007 was ranked as one of the Top 50 Global Thinkers. His works are known and used all over the world, including Argentina, Venezuela, the USA, Canada, Singapore, Australia and New Zealand. *Six Thinking Hats* was first published in 1985 and has since become a multi-million best-selling book. One of the appealing features is that *Six Thinking Hats* can be used in all walks of life, from business to relationship counselling.

INTRODUCING THE RESOURCES

Six Thinking Hats is based on what De Bono calls Parallel Thinking, which simply means 'laying down ideas alongside each other' (De Bono, 1994: 44). He maintains that Parallel Thinking (Figure 5.1) is much more effective than argument to explore subjects. This is because in argument people withhold information that does not support their view. The goal of Parallel Thinking is to pool all ideas rather than a selected few. If there is disagreement, then both positions are put down in parallel and examined before later deciding upon the best option. If it is not possible to choose, De Bono maintains that any solution should try to cover both possibilities.

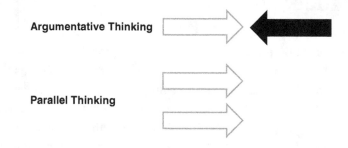

Figure 5.1 Argumentative and Parallel Thinking

Parallel Thinking is symbolised by wearing the same coloured hat at the same time. Each colour denotes a different direction of thinking. The colours were carefully chosen because of their associations in everyday life:

- White – paper (information)
- Black – judges' apparel (caution)
- Green – growth (creativity)
- Blue – sky (overview)
- Red – warmth (feelings)
- Yellow – sunshine (optimism).

The hats are not descriptions of thinkers but simply represent different types of thinking. Once a hat is worn, the mode of thinking represented by that hat is assumed.

Once it is removed and replaced by another hat, then its thinking mode is taken up. The De Bono Institute provides exact guidelines on how the hats should be used. An allocated time is provided when everyone 'puts on' the same hat. De Bono suggests one minute per person – so in a group discussion of four, then four minutes would be allocated. There is no need to follow a set sequence in using the hats although some schools prefer to do so to achieve a specific outcome. For instance, if they want to focus on the emotional side of thinking the Red and Yellow Hats may take priority. If they are looking to develop pupils' creativity, then the Green Hat assumes greater importance.

A fixed sequence of hats can be set ahead of discussions when the intention is to gain a definite result. A more flexible sequence can be used where the order of hats depends upon how pupils respond. Hence the Red Hat might result in strong support or opposition to an idea, e.g. the venue for a school party, funding priorities, testing products on animals, or plans to redesign the town centre. This could be followed up with a Black Hat to see how much logical basis there is to any opposition or the Yellow Hat to justify any potential benefits. A third approach is not to have any pre-set sequence after the first hat is chosen. This might apply when there are complicated issues to discuss and it is not possible to predict the outcomes.

Some teachers find it helpful to use the hats in pairs. For instance, the subjective Red Hat is used before or after the White Hat, which is meant to be objective, free of emotion and sticks to the known facts. This allows pupils to contrast feelings with facts. An individual cannot switch from one hat to the other during the time allocated for each specific hat. It is very much a group think approach to ensure that everyone is thinking in parallel, from the same perspective. Only the chairperson (teacher or lead pupil) signals a switch of hats. In any given session, the teacher and pupils may use one or more Thinking Hats. There is no stipulation that all hats need to be used on every occasion, although clearly to get a balanced picture most teachers will use each of the hats through the course of a project or unit of work.

These guidelines are important to follow because, despite the simplicity of Six Thinking Hats, they can be misinterpreted and misapplied. In the 1999 edition of *Six Thinking Hats* De Bono included a special note on the Black Hat, which had wrongly become known as 'the bad hat'. He regards it as the most valuable and used of all the hats, one that has dominated Western tradition with its emphasis on critical thinking. De Bono uses the Black Hat to signify caution, potential problems and dangers. It is important to display the vocabulary associated with the modes of thinking represented by each hat (Table 5.1).

WHITE HAT

The American author Samuel Langhorne Clemens (1835–1910), better known by his pen name Mark Twain, once said, 'Get your facts first, then you can distort them as you

Table 5.1 Language associated with Six Thinking Hats

Hat	Vocabulary
White	Facts, figures, information, data, questions, research
Black	Risk, problem, barrier, rules, laws, rights, negative, minus, bad, danger, care
Red	Feelings, emotions, anger, disgust, fear, happiness, sadness, surprise, disappointment
Green	New, novel, idea, different, unique, make, create, design, growth, possibilities, options
Yellow	Positive, plus, good, benefits, 'on the bright side'
Blue	Summary, process, control, manage, conclusion

please' (quoted by Kipling, 1889: 180). Establishing the facts of any matter and separating these from opinions is an important life skill for children to learn. The White Hat's function is to establish as far as possible the neutral facts and figures without recourse to judgement or interpretation. In a court of law, barristers are skilled at asking witnesses questions that seek to elicit only factual answers. However, they are seeking to build up a case for their client and therefore will ask questions that support their line of argument or destroy the other side. Impartial judges on the other hand will seek firstly to establish the known facts of the case. This is where White Hat thinking is useful.

But how does one know whether something is a fact or not? Facts are defined as things that are proven to be true, that exist or have happened. De Bono distinguishes between *believed* (unchecked) and *checked* facts, both of which are included under White Hat thinking. Something that is believed to be a fact is included because 'the tentative, the hypothetical and the provocative are essential for thinking' (De Bono, 1999: 34). Someone may say something like, 'I read that Apple mac computers never get viruses' and hold this as a genuine belief. This can be included under White Hat thinking as well as researched facts such as Macs are considered to be safe and secure but are not immune from malware. Personal opinions, however, are not expressed under the White Hat. The key point about White Hat thinking is framing the information. So, for example, where there is some uncertainty over the truthfulness of believed facts the participant is expected to say so with phrases like 'I believe this is the case', or use quantifying terms such as 'This often happens' or 'Sometimes this is true'.

BLACK HAT

There are many instances in life when holding back rather than rushing into decisions brings considerable benefits. The Black Hat offers a checkpoint when thinking: What are the risks and potential problems to overcome? How does this fit with our values and ethics? What care do we need to exercise here?

The Black Hat is essentially the mode of thinking that has ensured the survival of the human race. Hunters and gatherers had to decide which berries to pick and which animals to hunt. Military commanders had to weigh up the odds of going to battle or not. Governments ponder the consequences of their policies, albeit at times not very well. And families consider the pros and cons of decisions such as moving house. In short, the Black Hat represents critical thinking. De Bono points out that criticising and finding fault is easy. This can result in overusing the Black Hat or exaggerating its importance. For instance, suppose a school council is considering redesigning the playground so that children can make the most of their break time. If 95 per cent vote in favour of a proposal and 5 per cent disagree, the tendency may be to focus on the 5 per cent against the proposal.

RED HAT

Of all colours, red is perhaps the most provocative – it is the colour of love and anger, Cupid and the Devil. Under the Red Hat the thinker is encouraged to express feelings. There is no expectation that the feelings are explained or justified. Otherwise, if people think they must justify how they feel then they will only offer a limited range of feelings. Only the feelings held at the time should be shared even though these may change in twenty minutes' time or the following day. De Bono suggests that it can be useful to don a Red Hat at the beginning of a task or meeting and again at the end, to see how feelings have changed. As with all the hats, the Red Hat is applied on an individual basis. Even when an individual has no hard or fast feelings about a matter, then these should still be expressed. For instance, an individual can say that he or she is undecided, not particularly bothered or has mixed feelings.

The Red Hat gives legitimacy to expressing intuitions or 'gut feelings'. This is not to suggest that we should trust our instinctive feelings. The evidence is mixed on this. But wearing the Red Hat brings feelings out into the open and negates the need to second-guess what people feel. There is no need to justify feelings. Participants simply need to say, 'This is how I feel about this'. Such openness is not in keeping with the 'stiff upper lip' tradition, said to be the backbone of the British Empire. It represented strength and mental toughness in repressing feelings. And yet in recent years, prominent figures have spoken about the damage such a tradition can do to one's health. Prince Harry describes how he needed counselling following the death of his mother, Princess Diana, whose death marked a turning point in the nation's emotional journey (Khaleeli and Dowling, 2017). It is no longer seen as a sign of weakness for men to cry or to express their feelings openly.

In education, children's emotional wellbeing is now consistently associated with their academic success, attendance at school and criminal behaviour (Currie et al., 2010).

Ultimately, as noted in Chapter 1, the divide between emotions and thoughts is artificial. As neurobiologist Joseph LeDoux (1998: 25) observes in *The Emotional Brain*, 'Minds without emotions are not really minds at all … They are souls on ice – cold, lifeless creatures, devoid of any desires, fears, sorrows, pains or pleasures'. One of the myths about emotions is that they are irrational and do not depend upon reasoning and thinking. We know that emotions and intelligence go hand in hand which is why humans, highly intelligent beings, are also the most emotional creatures on earth (Lazarus and Lazarus, 1994). Cholle (2011) points out that the belief that our minds work in a hierarchical way, with reason directing feelings and instinct, does not match up with reality where feelings intertwine with thoughts in a chaotic rather than linear manner. As De Bono (1999: 53) puts it, emotions are 'a necessary part of the operation of the brain, not an intrusion or some relic of the age of animal survival'.

There have been various attempts to classify human emotions. Ekman (2004) identifies six basic emotions (anger, disgust, fear, happiness, sadness and surprise) while Plutchik (1980) suggests eight main emotions (grouped into four opposing pairs) and eight derivatives (Figure 5.2). Lararus and Lazarus (1994) distinguish between:

- three 'nasty' emotions (anger, envy and jealousy)
- existential emotions (anxiety-fright, guilt and shame), which reveal something about who we are and the quality of our existence
- emotions provoked by unfavourable life conditions (relief, hope, sadness and depression)
- emotions provoked by favourable life conditions (happiness, pride and love)
- empathetic emotions (gratitude, compassion, pride and love).

Under the Red Hat, there is a danger that children may refrain from expressing the 'nasty' emotions and respond as they feel the teacher wants. However, emotions such as anger can bring beneficial results. They signal clearly to others the intensity of feeling held and consequently can persuade people to change their minds, or simply enlighten those who may not have been aware of the depth of feelings. Righteous anger can also make someone feel good about themselves. When anger is directed at the achievement of a longer-term goal, say mastery of a skill, it can prove a constructive force. What is important, however, is understanding the motive that drives the feelings, being able to express emotions in a safe environment, recognising the impact emotional responses can have on others and learning to manage emotions. In the 1990s, American teenagers who attended a school in an exceptionally tough environment (the 'hood' of Long Beach, New York) were inspired by an inspirational teacher to work through their anger, hatred and sadness by keeping diaries (Gruwell, 2009). The Red Hat offers a similar channel for this to happen.

Burton (2015) examines over twenty-five emotions ranging from boredom to lust. He argues that emotions govern all the major decisions in our lives, from choosing a partner to religious and political beliefs. And yet in education, Burton (2015: ix) maintains that the emotions are 'utterly neglected … leading to millions of mislived lives'. His claim that schools focus on the 'cold and cognitive' is to downplay the important work of many teachers, support staff, leaders, councillors and educational psychologists who take the emotional wellbeing of children and young people seriously.

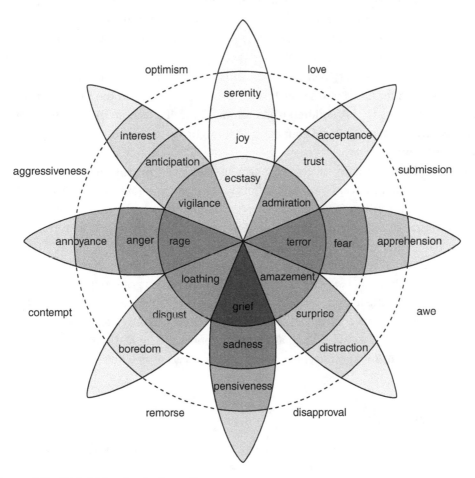

Figure 5.2 Plutchik's wheel of emotions

Source: Wikicommons

Nonetheless, statistics bear out the need to provide emotional support in school. In 2017, the government announced plans to invest £95 million to fund a senior lead for mental health in every school in England to help pupils access specialist therapies amidst reports of a mental health crisis in the classroom (Bloom, 2017).

Over recent decades, much has been made of the need to develop emotionally literate schools, i.e. where there is a commitment to provide secure, open and honest environments which focus on converting difficult emotions into productive energy (Antidote, 2003). Emotional literacy can be generated through curiosity, dialogue and reflection. The Red Hat is one tool to support this. One of the important considerations when using the Red Hat is to develop pupils' vocabulary so that they can describe precisely how they feel. Often when parents ask how their children's day went, the children respond in black-and-white terms such as 'fine', 'ok' or 'bad'. Few respond using a more sophisticated range of emotions: 'I was really amazed in the science lesson ...' 'The assembly was a moment of real serenity', or 'I was very pensive in RE'. This is not simply about building vocabulary. The curriculum itself has to offer such stimulating experiences in the first instance. And also, the questions we ask children when reframed can illicit more thoughtful, reflective answers. Rather than, 'How did your day go?' it might be better to ask, 'What was the best part of the day?'

It would be flippant to suggest that regular Red Hat thinking in classrooms would fully address the significant emotional strains many young people face. However, clearly providing opportunities for pupils to express their feelings in a non-judgemental manner on a range of issues would be welcome. What matters is that children recognise that feelings come and go. They are transitory moments. Unfortunately, there is a tendency for children to define themselves based on temporary experiences. Instead of saying 'I *feel* sad right now' they say 'I *am* sad'. As Siegel and Bryson (2012) point out, the failure to distinguish between the temporary 'feel' and the more permanent 'am' means that children conclude that they have fixed traits, which they can do little to change: 'I'm so stupid. I can't do this' or 'I'm not very good at ... so why bother?' The Red Hat then has merit in starting conversations about feelings but these must lead somewhere positive.

YELLOW HAT

The Yellow Hat is about positive thinking. It is different from the Green Hat because it does not focus on creating ideas. Someone may be very good at identifying positive aspects of a situation but not so good at suggesting changes, innovation or ways forward. Under the Yellow Hat there is no obligation to find new ways of working or different features to a product or service. Rather, the focus is on what has worked well, what is effective about existing arrangements or the potential value of something. Under the Red Hat, someone may express very positive feelings (joy or happiness) but it is the thinking associated with the Yellow Hat which articulates the benefits from such feelings.

There is now plenty of evidence to show that an optimistic outlook is good for one's health. In a survey of 70,000 women over an eight-year period, optimists were less likely to die from cancer, heart disease or infections than pessimists (Dillner, 2017). Those who hold the basic belief that life is likely to turn out well, are more likely to live longer, manage stress better and live more contended lives. Being positive is a matter of choice. It is something that we can all control. Yellow Hat thinking seeks out the value in any situation or idea, however unattractive on the surface. Sometimes it is very difficult to find anything positive to say. But De Bono maintains that it is all a matter of perception. The Yellow Hat facilitates positive thinking by asking questions beyond our egocentric state, e.g. 'Who (else) might this benefit?' Obviously, there is a danger of being overly optimistic and so a probability scale can be used as a reality check (Figure 5.3).

No chance   Unlikely   Even   Likely   Certain

Figure 5.3 Probability scale

Yellow Hat thinking allows for dreaming the impossible. Even potential benefits, which may appear to be very remote or have no chance of materialising, should be registered and not be discounted completely. The history of medicine has many examples of ideas that were initially ridiculed by the medical authorities, but were later widely adopted. For instance, the nineteenth-century Hungarian doctor Ignaz Semmelweis noticed that before doctors operated on new mothers they failed to wash their hands, even after performing autopsies. He urged his colleagues to disinfect their hands in between operations but his idea was widely rejected. Part of the reason was that it was considered an unorthodox idea, which ran contrary to the Christian belief that the dangers of childbirth were inherent to the lives of women. Sadly, Semmelweis became an isolated figure and was later admitted to an insane asylum against his will, where he was badly beaten and died after two weeks (Obenchain, 2016). The story also illustrates another point, namely that positives are sometimes ignored based on *who* as well as what is suggested. Semmelweis suffered from bipolar disorder and he was not an easy man to get along with.

GREEN HAT

The Green Hat is concerned with creative thinking. It signals the intention to generate new ideas or improvements on existing ones. The expectation is that all within a group should participate in suggesting ideas, which conveys the message that creativity is not confined to the few. By donning the Green Hat, individuals are permitted to put forward possibilities along the lines, 'We could try this, or maybe do that'. Green Hat thinking can be used to support creative thinking across the curriculum including persuasive writing in English (Figure 5.4), generating product refinements in design and technology, looking at alternative historical interpretations or creating fresh combinations in music, art or dance.

Magical Mexico

Relax and rest whilst looking at the spectacular sunset.

Where your dream holiday

begins!

Exclusive offer. Book now and get 20% off.

Don't lounge around, this offer will end soon!

Dive into the crystal-clear, calm sea.

SUPER SUNSHINE ALL YEAR ROUND.

What are you waiting for?

This is the one and only best hotel in the whole of Mexico.

Don't delay.

Call today:

543761

It's a perfect paradise. Sit under a tropical palm tree and sip on a refreshing cocktail.

Figure 5.4 Green Hat thinking used by a Year 6 pupil to generate ideas for advertising a holiday to Mexico

The main point is that the status quo is challenged and change embraced. If lots of ideas are suggested and there are too many to discuss, the Red Hat can be used to select those which 'feel' most appropriate, i.e. fit a specific brief such as 'low-cost ideas' or 'ideas which can be tested easily'.

Creative thinking takes time and energy. Hence it is important to give pupils the regular space to play with ideas or what De Bono calls 'thought experiments' (De Bono, 1999: 119). And with any experiment, there is no certainty as to what the outcomes will be. Living with risk, provocation and uncertainty is a necessary part of becoming a good thinker, although unfortunately many pupils are locked into a 'right–wrong', binary thinking process. While the Green Hat cannot make pupils more creative, it gives creative thinking necessary time and hence status. The most creative ideas take time and often emerge from a zig-zag process of false starts, sketches, and drips and drabs, rather than Eureka! moments (Sawyer, 2013).

Sometimes, pupils may find it difficult to come up with fresh ideas, perhaps because of fear of putting forward an idea that might be ridiculed, the timing may not be right, or they may hold back in a desire to offer the perfect solution. Green Hat thinking can be used in conjunction with specific techniques. The educationalist Bob Eberle (2008) suggests the SCAMPER tool to prompt students' imagination (Table 5.2).

Table 5.2 SCAMPER technique to generate creative ideas

	Element	Prompts
S	Substitute	• Who else? • What else? (e.g. materials or resources to swap) • Another place or time?
C	Combine	• Combine what? • Combine purpose? • Combine talents? • Combine colours, shapes, materials?
A	Adjust	• Reshape? • Use in another context? • What could be toned down?
M	Modify	• Change shape, colour, sound, look, feel, taste? • Enlarge? • Lighter? Slower? • Stronger? Thicker? • Reduce? Make smaller?
P	Put to another use	• Somewhere else? • Somebody else? Child? Elderly person? Young mum? Disabled person? • Recycle?
E	Eliminate	• Remove features? • Simplify? • What happens if you take this away?
R	Reverse	• Try the opposite? • Reverse the process? • Start at the end? • Which roles could you swap? Regroup? • Change the sequence?

Source: adapted from Eberle (2008)

Originally, SCAMPER was used in business and industry where it has proven successful in creating new products, improving methods and solving various problems. A teacher could place on the table several bottles of sports drink and set the challenge of designing a new one, say for a specific audience such as runners. Using the prompts in Table 5.2, the teacher might invite the group to think about changing one element. What happens if we make the bottle smaller – a mini bottle? What if we change the name, colour scheme or the shape?

BLUE HAT

The Blue Hat provides an overview of the thinking process. This should not be confused with the cliché 'Blue Sky Thinking', recently voted among 2,000 business travellers as one of the ten phrases likely to make you scream (Davidson, 2017). Blue Hat thinking is not about creating ideas free from preconceptions, but the control exercised in the thinking process itself or metacognitive awareness (Flavell, 1976). De Bono (1985; 1999) likens the Blue Hat to the conductor in an orchestra or a ringmaster in a circus who sees what needs to be done at the right time. It offers the thinker a means of managing his or her thinking. When the hats are used in a systematic way, the Blue Hat is used at the start and end of discussions. The Blue Hat represents the bookends of a meeting. At the beginning, the Blue Hat sets the agenda including the sequence of which hats are to be used. At the close, it provides a summary of progress. This might take the form of a short oral report, a few bullet points or a sketch. During the meeting, it provides structure and re-direction if necessary. So, for example, the chairperson may say: 'We're not making much progress here. Let's put our Red Hats on and say what we feel the problems are'. In the context of a meeting, typically, the Blue Hat is worn mainly by the chairperson, group leader or facilitator who directs others to wear the Blue Hat: 'I think we need to pause for a moment and do some Blue Hat thinking. How can we ensure that everyone has a turn?' For teachers, it is important to try and ensure that all pupils are included in discussions and their voices are heard. We know, for example, that very shy or quiet children tend to be overlooked or 'lost' in whole-class discussions (Coplan and Rudasill, 2016). Hence the Blue Hat is important in developing an inclusive ethos.

Essentially, the Blue Hat represents the planning aspects of thinking, like a computer program. Blue Hat thinking offers focus to discussions. It is designed to prevent drift and waffle. We have all been in staff meetings where individuals go off on a tangent or have plenty to say for themselves (and are permitted to do so). The Blue Hat seeks to define the purpose of any discussion, to keep participants on track. De Bono (1985; 1999) suggests this can be achieved by asking two types of questions. *Fishing* questions are exploratory (like putting bait on a hook but not knowing whether this will be taken) while *shooting* questions (like aiming at a bird and hitting or missing) are closed in nature, with yes or no answers. Hence Blue Hat thinking might remind the group: 'What is our objective?' or 'What are we trying to find out?' (shooting questions) while at another time the group might be asked: 'Why are we finding this difficult?' or 'Can we put another hat on. What ideas do you have to take this forward?' (exploratory questions).

THE THINKING HATS IN PRACTICE

In classrooms, Six Thinking Hats can take the form of a game with certain rules. Once pupils know the rules, they can play the game. If they break the rules, then their behaviour is considered uncooperative. So, for instance, once pupils know that the Yellow Hat is about positive thoughts and they have all been told to think in that direction, it would be 'unfair play' for someone to point out shortcomings (Black Hat) or express anger (Red Hat). Rather, the facilitator should sense the mood of the group and suggest a new hat, or stick to pre-arrangements, for example relating to how much time is spent on each hat (a timer is a useful resource). Once pupils know the set up and routine, Six Thinking Hats works smoothly.

One of the big advantages of Six Thinking Hats is their flexibility. They support any curriculum topic. Table 5.3, for instance, illustrates Black Hat thinking across a range of subjects.

Table 5.3 Examples of Black Hat thinking across the curriculum

Curriculum area	Examples of Black Hat (cautionary) thinking
English	• Checking spelling, grammar and tone is appropriate when writing a report • The negative aspects of publishing online • Stories that can be written within the bounds of decency
Mathematics	• The errors made in calculations • Making the most of a tight budget • The problems in using analogue or digital clocks
Science	• The health and safety considerations that must be followed when planning experiments and investigations • The ethical considerations of science experiments • The challenges in keeping animals in the class
Humanities	• The risks people faced in the past (e.g. as coal miners, explorers, railway navvies); the rules and regulations that governed society at the time (history) • The caution needed when carrying out fieldwork along a riverbank or near the sea (geography) • Commandments, codes of conduct and restrictions (Religious Education)
Technologies	• The e-safety rules to follow when using social media • The potential problems in spending too much time playing video games
The Arts	• Handling tools and other resources correctly • Assessing the risks if someone pulls out of a theatre performance • The potential problems if it rains heavily during the summer sports day

Another advantage of Six Thinking Hats is that they enable users to see the big picture. By considering all perspectives, pupils are more likely to reach a rounded and informed decision. For example, a Year 6 class familiar with Six Thinking Hats used the approach in their study of evacuees during World War Two (Photo 5.1; Figure 5.5). Each group was given a different photograph showing various scenes of children standing on railway station platforms about to be evacuated. Some of the photographs showed smiling, eager and well-supervised children in busy stations, while others showed more isolated and frightened figures clutching their favourite toys for emotional security. Using their Red Hats, the pupils discussed the photographs. A mixture of responses included: 'sad', 'lonely', 'worried', 'excited', 'nervous', 'angry', 'frightened' and 'tired'. The teacher asked the group to use an online thesaurus to extend their vocabulary looking for synonyms. 'Worried' became 'anxious', 'sad' became 'heavy-hearted', and 'angry' became 'resentful'. Each group was then asked to put on their Blue Hats and select three words they thought best summarised their photograph. These were then shared with the other groups and listed on the board. Wearing their Yellow Hats, they were then asked to think about how the children might benefit from evacuation. They were given copies of local newspaper reports and asked to use yellow highlighters to underline any benefits. These included a safe place to sleep, a good breakfast, making new friends, and even reforming London children from 'habits of thieving!'

In the next lesson, the groups put their Black Hats on and gathered evidence about the negative aspects of evacuation. These included missing family and home, and disturbing stories about mistreatment and abuse. The pupils used approved Internet sites to research stories. One group found oral history memories showing that evacuees 'didn't mix much with the locals, it was them and us. There was always mud fights and everything', while another reported that some evacuated children could not get to sleep because the village was too quiet. Donning their Black Hats, the pupils also discussed the regulations at the time (e.g. payments received) and the difficulties the authorities faced in checking up on the whereabouts and progress of each evacuee.

The groups, confident in the use of Six Thinking Hats, switched between the Yellow and Black Hats debating whether the evacuation did more harm than good. They could not agree and so (using their White Hats) decided to draw up a list of precise questions, e.g. 'Were there any evacuees in our area and what were their experiences?' 'Do our families know of any evacuees?' 'Would any evacuees be alive today?' 'How could we contact them if they were?' Their further research managed to establish contacts with a local history society and speakers were invited into class. Using their Blue Hats, the pupils discussed their roles during the interviews: who would welcome the guests, ask questions, check timing, take photographs, make notes and so forth. They considered what exactly they wanted to know, i.e. the focus for the interviews and whether it would be alright (ethically) to video record the interview. Towards the end of the project, the class discussed how they would present their findings. Using the Green Hat, suggestions included making a presentation to the local history society, adding to the school website

White

What do we know about evacuation?

What do we need to know?

How can we find out?

Apart from photographs, what other historical sources are there about evacuees?

If we could interview an evacuee, what would we ask?

Yellow

How was evacuation good for the children?

What's working well in our project?

Black

What were the risks of evacuation?

How was evacuation bad for the children?

What are we finding difficult to research?

What if we can't find any evacuees to interview?

Green

What if evacuation didn't happen?

Did evacuation happen in other countries, such as Germany?

How can we let people know about our project?

How can we present our findings?

Red

In three words, how did the evacuees feel?

How might their feelings have changed before, during and after evacuation?

How did their mothers feel?

What about the feelings of the hosts?

Blue

Who does what in the research project?

How can we improve how we work as a group?

What do I need to think about next time to improve my ... writing, reading, etc.?

Figure 5.5 Six Thinking Hats and questions about evacuees in World War Two

and holding a special assembly. For these pupils, the Six Thinking Hats were a familiar whole-school routine and part of their learning culture. They understood their value in helping them to think about subjects from a range of perspectives.

Photo 5.1 Using Thinking Hats in a study of evacuees during World War Two

In practice, it is important for learners to adopt the thinking role represented by each hat rather than focus too much on the hats themselves. In any event, older Key Stage 2 pupils may find it too 'childish' to wear the hats and younger ones may prefer a different symbol, such as Six Thinking Bears wearing different coloured T-shirts. While De Bono chose the hat metaphor carefully, because of its association with thinking, e.g. 'put your thinking caps on', other symbols have been used effectively. For instance, Yvonne Yorkshades, one of our ex-students, used six thinking badges that the pupils wore. These are labelled with the hat and a summary word, e.g. yellow = benefits; red = feelings; white = information. The pupils wear these badges during sessions to remind themselves of the type of thinking a task requires.

Six Thinking Hats can also be used to support assessment practices. At Marown Primary School on the Isle of Man, use of the Six Thinking Hats has led to noticeable improvements in self and peer assessment (see Chapter 11). Pupils can be asked to review their work individually, in pairs and in small groups using all or a selection of the hats. Pupils can suggest:

- a single word to sum up their feelings about the piece of work (Red Hat)
- a question or something they are unsure about (White Hat)

- two strengths (Yellow Hat)
- one main weakness (Black Hat)
- a suggestion to address the weakness (Green Hat)
- one priority target to move forward (Blue Hat).

The thinking behind the hats can also contribute to pastoral care, support and guidance. For instance, following an incident in the playground the hats might be used to work through a problem in a calm, measured manner, setting aside egocentric thinking. Individuals can be encouraged to use the hats when approaching personal problems such as handling relationship issues. At Barton Court Grammar School in Kent, the Six Thinking Hats are used in personal tutorial sessions and provide opportunities for students to listen to different perspectives.

IMPACT

Despite the widespread popularity of Six Thinking Hats, much of the evidence to support their use comes from small-scale research projects in a range of educational contexts including the training of nurses (Wang et al., 2002; Taie and El Kamel, 2013). Generally, these studies report positive findings in terms of improving students' skills including teamwork, creative thinking, writing, speaking and listening (Horsfall and Bennett, 2005; Tooley, 2009). In schools, Wells (2009: 7) suggests that Six Thinking Hats represents a deliberate and systematic approach that fosters a 'common language' across all subjects and enables pupils to create 'better ideas quicker'. Belfer (2001) reports that Six Thinking Hats is a useful metaphor to guide thinking when creating online learning environments and where teachers want to make greater use of technologies to facilitate the exchange of information. Thinking Hats then can prove beneficial for teachers' planning and instruction, although student perceptions of their value are not always positive (Dhanapal and Wern Ling, 1999). Fisher (2005: 80) cites research with junior-age children showing that unless the different Thinking Hats are used regularly they are soon forgotten. They need to be used for an extended period across a range of learning contexts.

SUMMARY

- ◌ Edward De Bono devised Six Thinking Hats as a metaphor for how we think.
- ◌ The White Hat is about facts and information we need.
- ◌ The Black Hat is about risks and difficulties.
- ◌ The Red Hat is about feelings and intuition.

⊘ The Yellow Hat is about benefits.
⊘ The Green Hat is about new ideas.
⊘ The Blue Hat is about managing the thinking process.
⊘ The Six Thinking Hats are very flexible resources and can be used in many contexts.
⊘ There is not a lot of empirical evidence about the effectiveness of Six Thinking Hats in schools, although there is strong testimonial support.

THINKING MAPS

INTRODUCTION

This chapter introduces a set of visual tools that help teachers and pupils make thinking visible and therefore explicit. These are known as Thinking Maps (Thinking Maps, Inc., 2011), and are flexible materials that can be used across the curriculum, with pupils of all ages and at all stages of development. Using visual images can be a powerful technique. Lynell Burmark, an education consultant, suggests:

> unless our words, concepts, ideas are hooked onto an image, they will go in one ear, sail through the brain, and go out the other ear. Words are processed by our short-term memory where we can only retain about seven bits of information (plus or minus 2) ... Images, on the other hand, go directly into long-term memory where they are indelibly etched. (Burmark, 2002).

BACKGROUND

Thinking Maps originated from the work of David Hyerle, in Northern California in the mid-1980s. They were born out of Hyerle's desire to integrate content learning, thinking process instruction, and collaborative leadership across whole schools. Hyerle's model has evolved into a set of materials, which contain eight specific Thinking Maps. The maps combine the use of key cognitive processes such as comparing and contrasting, with the concept of a visual organiser. This is based on findings from research (e.g. Marzano, 2001; Hattie, 2009), which show that approaches to teaching thinking have greater effectiveness when pupils represent ideas clearly and reflect on their thinking.

Thinking Maps align with what we know about how the brain works. Clark and Paivio (1991) developed a dual coding theory based on the premise that we can store information in the form of linguistic (words) and non-linguistic representations, including mental pictures, smells, tastes and other physical sensations. The more we use both of these dual codes in the classroom, the more powerful the learning opportunities can be, providing the information that is given will advance learning. So, for children who are learning about the phases of the moon, as well as reading and writing about this, teachers may provide children with cookies, which can be eaten in different amounts, creating a physical representation of the phases.

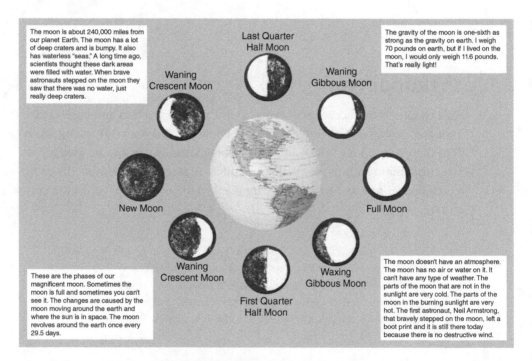

Figure 6.1 Cookies to represent the phases of the moon

Source: adapted from http://brendajohnston.blogspot.co.uk/2014/11/moon-phases-with-oreo-cookies.html (accessed 20 June 2018)

Other activities that can create non-linguistic representations include generating mental models, role-play, using graphic organisers and drawing pictures, sketch notes and diagrams. These activities allow pupils to elaborate on their knowledge in ways that are meaningful and accessible to them. In a similar manner, Thinking Maps encourage pupils to capture their ideas about thinking by using dual coding strategies in the form of words and images. The visual patterns that underpin Thinking Maps® are therefore powerful. They can act as a language for thinking (Hyerle and Alper, 2011).

Understanding about thinking and thinking processes is enhanced because the maps show these clearly and visually. The maps act as a scaffold, encouraging the pupils to recognise each thought process. Use of the maps helps pupils to become more conscious of their own thinking and that of others around them. Visual representation means that pupils can show each other their ideas and therefore allows for discussion and shared construction of understanding. Diagrammatic representations such as maps are useful aids to metacognition, since both pupils and teachers can look back at each stage of a learning activity and reflect upon it (McGuinness, 1999).

INTRODUCING THE RESOURCES

There are eight Thinking Maps, and each corresponds to a specific thinking process. Table 6.1 outlines these, together with key questions that could be used with the maps.

Table 6.1 The eight Thinking Maps

Map	Icon	Thinking process	Key questions and information
Circle		Defining in context	What do you know about this idea/topic/concept?
			In-the-moment assessment of prior knowledge, vocabulary, conceptions and misconceptions.
Bubble		Describing qualities	How would you describe this person/place/concept/feeling etc.?
			Use your senses to enrich your description, and use rich vocabulary to describe.
Double Bubble		Comparing and contrasting	What are the similarities and differences between these two things?
			Think critically about key information, characteristics and point and counterpoints.

(Continued)

Table 6.1 (Continued)

Map	Icon	Thinking process	Key questions and information
Tree		Classifying	How could you group, sort and categorise this information?
			What is the main idea and subcategories underpinning the information?
Brace		Part–whole relationships	What is the name of the whole object and what are the major (and minor) physical parts?
			All of the subparts are needed to make the whole. This is a map to use with concrete things – not concepts or ideas.
Flow		Sequencing	What are the names and stages of each event? What order did they happen in?
			Show what happened first, next and last in an event.
Multi-Flow		Cause and effect	Why did an event take place, and what happened as a result of this?
			Always start with the event (something that happened or happens) and work forwards and/or backwards from it.
Bridge		Seeing analogies	What is the relating factor between two things?
			This map needs to be spoken: 'This is to this as this is to this'.

Source: Adapted from *Thinking Maps®: A Language for Learning*, by David Hyerle, Ed. D. and Chris Yeager, M.Ed., ©2007, Thinking Maps, Inc. Used with permission

Underpinning all the maps are five common qualities, which support teachers in developing a common language of thinking in their classrooms. Firstly, the maps are **consistent** in format, and this format is a visual reflection of the thinking processes being used. This consistency supports pupils so that they can recognise specific thinking processes they are using. For example, consistency means that children in a Year 1 class could make independent decisions regarding the structure of their writing about how to make a sandwich for a picnic. They talked about how a Flow Map would be a useful way to show the sequence of events that making a sandwich entailed. They were familiar with the format of a Flow Map, and could then independently create their own representation of the sandwich making, using Post-it notes and large sheets of paper.

Secondly, the maps are **flexible**. They can be added to or amended during an activity or over time (such as a topic or unit of work), and so can grow in complexity as the thinking develops and becomes more complex. Although commercial map templates exist, these are not essential to use, and so teachers and pupils can have ownership of the maps, and can create their own. For example, while the Bubble Map template consists of a simple large circle with five smaller circles around it, when describing characters in C.S. Lewis's *The Lion, the Witch and the Wardrobe*, pupils in a Year 5 class found that they wanted to use more adjectives to describe Aslan the lion, they didn't want to stop at five. They added more adjectives to their Bubble Map, as illustrated by Figure 6.2.

Figure 6.2 Aslan the Lion Bubble Map

Similarly, when learning about bees, instead of using circles as the template icons, pupils in the early years created a flower with adjectives in petals as their map design. Pupils in Danescourt Primary School in Cardiff learnt about Jonah and the Whale in their Religious Education lessons. They created a large Circle Map display about this to document how they would feel and what they thought Jonah had done – but rather than use the circle as an icon, they created the map in the shape of a whale. The scaffolding that the map provides can be amended, but the underpinning thinking remains the same.

Photo 6.1 Jonah and the Whale Circle Map

Thirdly, the maps are **developmental**. They can be used with pupils of all ages and stages and they can be adapted to be completed using practical apparatus, on paper, on the computer, or for older and more experienced thinkers they can be internalised. For example, one undergraduate teaching student, Matthew Noyes, taught a topic about 'Myself' to a nursery class of children. One of the activities that he planned was intended to encourage pupils to think about how our needs change, as we grow older. When thinking about the needs of babies, the pupils talked to Matthew and to one another about the toys babies liked to play with. Matthew then worked with focused groups of around six children at a time. They sorted real toys into groups, such as 'soft toys' and 'hard toys', and they then arranged the toys in the layout of a Tree Map. The children could then talk about how they had sorted and classified the toys according to different criteria such as 'hard' and 'soft', and their friends could clearly see what they had done. Matthew could model and extend their vocabulary as they talked about the toys, and he encouraged them to explain their thinking to one another. The children then took photographs of their Tree Map so that they could return to this later in the topic.

The use of physical objects is not limited to the youngest learners. For example, when creating a Brace Map to learn more about the parts of a flower, pupils in Year 3 used a real flower and dissected this, arranging the parts into a physical representation of a Brace Map. They could move the parts about, and compare the real flower with images in reference books. They photographed their Brace Maps on a digital camera to create a lasting version of the map in their books.

Fourthly, the maps are **integrative** and so can be used alone, or can be used together during a lesson. For example, at the start of a lesson comparing a Celtic soldier with a Roman soldier, in one primary school, Year 4 pupils first used Circle Maps to capture their understanding of the topic. They then used a Double Bubble Map to compare the clothing and weaponry of the two before doing a piece of creative writing about the soldiers. They referred to their map throughout their writing so that they remembered key information to include. Pupils in Year 5 at Danescourt Primary School were learning about advertising.

They completed a Circle Map with their initial ideas about what makes a good advert, before comparing adverts in more detail, recording their ideas on a Double Bubble Map.

Finally, the maps are **reflective** – in other words they show what and how pupils are thinking about a particular situation or problem. This provides a visual stimulus that enables pupils to talk about, to explain and to justify their thinking to others. They also allow pupils to see their learning over time. For example, older pupils in a primary school started a topic on the Tudors. They used word processing software to create Circle Maps about Henry VIII (Figure 6.3), building on their prior knowledge. They returned to these Circle Maps at the end of topic sessions, reflecting on new knowledge and adding this in different fonts and colours to indicate their learning over time. They then returned to their maps at the end of the topic and reflected on the changes that they had made. This meant that they could identify shifts in their own understanding and knowledge. This also helped them talk about which sources of information had been most useful, and what gaps in their knowledge they would like to explore in the future.

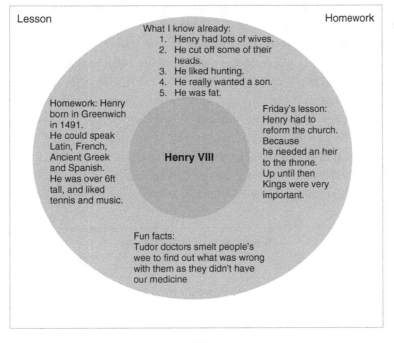

Figure 6.3 A Circle Map relating to Henry VIII

Source: http://primaryfacts.com/23 35/tudor-medicine-facts-and-information/

Thinking Maps are therefore versatile scaffolds to help make thinking visible and organised. One school that received an outstanding inspection report used Thinking Maps effectively, and the use of maps was seen to support pupils effectively:

'

Teachers' excellent questioning stimulates thinking skills and encourages them to organise their thoughts. They record their ideas onto 'Thinking Maps' when they are working in groups and this sets their work off to a flying start. (Ofsted, 2013)

'

THE FRAME OF REFERENCE

Creating a Thinking Map encourages pupils to use one of the eight cognitive processes outlined above. To become more reflective, a frame is created, surrounding each map (Figure 6.4). The purpose of this frame is to encourage pupils to consider, 'How do I know what I know?' For example, in the Henry VIII Circle Map above pupils were given different perspectives on Henry's character and motivation, depending on the evidence source they used. These sources can be noted in the Frame of Reference, allowing pupils to reflect on what has influenced them, whose perspective the information has come from, why the information is important, and whether there might be gaps in their knowledge that they need to address. This is particularly useful when considering how reliable information is – for example when gathering online information.

Children are often amazed by how different sources can report the same story. A good starting point to introduce pupils to the concept that sources may report differently, and to the idea of different perspectives and viewpoints, is to use familiar stories. For example, we may all be familiar with the 'Big, Bad Wolf' from stories such as *Little Red Riding Hood* or *The Three Little Pigs*. He is often portrayed as a cruel grandma or pig-munching villain. However, can we be sure that this familiar version of the story is accurate? We may be less familiar with the other side of the story as told from the wolf's perspective through stories such as *Honestly Red Riding Hood Was Rotten* (Shaskan, 2012), *The True Story of the Three Little Pigs* (Scieszka, 1989) and *The Wolf's Story: What Really Happened to Little Red Riding*

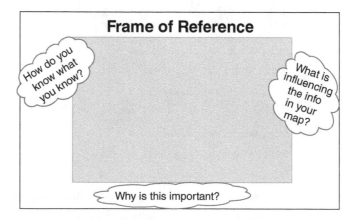

Figure 6.4 The Frame of Reference

Hood (Forward and Cohen, 2006). Different stories will retell events in different ways. By raising pupils' awareness of this, the Frame of Reference helps them to identify, evaluate and enhance their sources of information.

PRACTICAL EXAMPLES

How and when Thinking Maps are incorporated in lessons can vary greatly from school to school. Danescourt Primary School in Cardiff uses Thinking Maps among several thinking approaches (see also Chapter 11). Thinking Maps are used throughout the school from Nursery to Year 6, and Claire Lawton, the senior teacher responsible for developing thinking across the school, feels that they have a very positive impact on pupils. They are embedded across the curriculum in a variety of subjects and areas of learning. For example, maps are used to support learning and teaching processes in the school's English scheme of work. The maps are closely matched to genres where appropriate (see Appendix 1). For example, when writing poetry in Year 6, Bubble Maps are used to generate vocabulary to engage the reader. They are also used to support practical work. For instance, when pupils in Year 1 learn about sequences of movements in Physical Education sessions, they use Flow Maps to plan and design their sequences (Photo 6.2). They use cards that they have made with different movements on – for instance hop, jump, stretch and curl. They then arrange these cards on their Flow Map so that they can create a sequence of movements to perform to their peers.

Photo 6.2 Pupils creating a Flow Map in PE

Thinking Maps can also act as a starting point for other activities. In Deri View Primary School in Abergavenny, Thinking Maps are often used in the introduction to lessons to prepare pupils for the activities that follow. For example, Sharon Phillips, the thinking coordinator in the school, used a Circle Map to gather Year 3 pupils' ideas about 'heroes and villains' during the introduction of an English lesson. The pupils, arranged into small, mixed ability groups, each completed a Circle Map. A scribe for each group wrote 'heroes and villains' in the centre circle and then they worked together to fill the outer circle with what they knew – for instance, talking about common characteristics of superheroes and, in another colour, supervillains. Sharon extended children's thinking to 'real-life' heroes and villains, and included discussion around family members and the jobs people do. After the class discussion, the children worked in pairs to write a job description or used tablets to film a job advertisement for a hero. The Circle Map acted as a scaffold for the writing, reminding the children of key ideas. The job descriptions and adverts were then shared with other pairs, comparing ideas and noting ones they particularly liked. This lesson was followed by a Philosophy for Children session. Sharon read the book *You Are Special* by Max Lucado (1997) as the stimulus. The rest of the villagers dislike the story's main character, Punchinello. The story lends itself to discussion about how people's perceptions of the same individual vary and the question: 'Can heroes ever be villains and villains ever be heroes?' was discussed in depth (Grigg and Lewis, 2017).

Thinking Maps can also be used with older learners. In Castle School, Narberth (Pembrokeshire), teachers incorporate Thinking Maps into lesson plans alongside Thinking Hats and Thinking Dispositions. The school provides each child with a reminder of the maps to stick inside their books, and they are encouraged to use the maps as and when they are appropriate, with increasing autonomy. The maps are used across the curriculum. For example, a Circle Map is often used with Year 7 in their first Religious Education lesson of the term to see the pupils' prior knowledge of religions. The pupils use colours and images to record their thoughts and ideas. The teacher keeps the maps so that the pupils can repeat the activity at the start of Year 8 (after they have learnt about the major world religions). By comparing the Circle Maps, changes and developments in their knowledge and understanding can be discussed. The pupils then use a Bridge Map to consider religious symbols, so that they can look at how different world religions represented key ideas and concepts. The Bridge Map provides a visual summary of this.

Bridge Maps can also be used to show relationships between characters in books, mathematical relationships, or in the case of Figure 6.5, Year 2 pupils in Danescourt Primary School, studying a topic of 'Land Ahoy' considered the drivers of different vehicles.

Land ahoy year 2 cedar

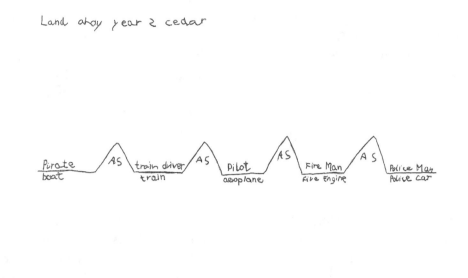

relating factor: drives

Figure 6.5 Bridge Map 'Land Ahoy'

In narrative form, this would be read: 'A pirate drives a boat, as a train driver drives a train, as a pilot drives an aeroplane, as a fireman drives a fire engine, as a policeman drives a police car'.

In mathematics, teachers have found a variety of uses for different maps. In Year 7 and 8 at Castle School, the 'problem-solving' flow chart is very helpful in supporting pupils' thinking about how to solve word problems, and gives them strategies to 'get started'. Double Bubble Maps were used to compare quadrilaterals in Year 7, while pupils in Years 10 and 11 used maps to support their independent exam revision. In English, Year 10 pupils found maps useful for helping to write for a variety of purposes and audiences more effectively. The teachers used a 'round the room' technique to help pupils gain confidence, ideas and focus for their work. Pupils around the room are collected in turn – sharing and discussing on a larger scale and contributing to whole class maps. The flexibility of the maps in allowing pupils to use images as well as keywords has proved useful in Castle School. One pupil with dyslexia articulated a very good GCSE answer when allowed to draw images in revision sessions rather than needing to write longer revision notes. Examples of planning from Castle School can be seen in Appendix 2.

Thinking Maps can also be used outside of traditional learning activities. Pupils from Rochester Grammar School visited local primary schools as part of transition arrangements, so that the primary school pupils could learn more about the secondary school. Secondary pupils buddied with the primary pupils to undertake a range of activities. The older pupils reported that the use of Thinking Maps made activities accessible and inclusive to Year 6 pupils of all abilities. Pupils in Year 10 and 11 also used Thinking Maps themselves, with increasing independence; 89 per cent of pupils taking GCSEs in the school used Thinking Maps to support their revision, and 84 per cent of pupils felt that the maps aided their achievement (Miller, no date). Moreover, 90 per cent of the pupils felt that they would continue to use the maps to support revision for 'A' level examinations.

IMPACT

Schools that use Thinking Maps report that they make valuable contributions to pupils' learning. For example, Claire Lawton is a senior teacher at Danescourt Primary School, which has achieved accreditation as a 'Thinking School'. Thinking Maps have been embedded into practice for over five years. Claire says that pupils have developed fluency of thought, and increased autonomy when using Thinking Maps. She finds that they are flexible visual tools, which support groups of pupils, including those with additional needs. The maps work well alongside other materials that the school uses to develop thinking (see Chapter 11). Claire also finds that Thinking Maps can be used as the basis for effective displays, which celebrate learning and challenge further thinking. The impact of the school's approach to developing thinking has been noted in the school's recent inspection report, which states:

> The school promotes the use of pupils' thinking skills very successfully. It uses a wide range of approaches to develop thinking skills consistently across the school. As a result, pupils have a range of very useful strategies to support their learning that they use to good effect, for example when analysing the impact of actions, such as whether their plans to improve playtimes are effective. (Estyn, 2016: 6)

Ruth Harris, a member of the senior management team at Castle School in Narberth, feels that when used well, the maps give pupils confidence and structure and the quality of work is improved. She suggests that this is because the maps give pupils an accessible focus to start a task, make information easier to digest and analyse, and provide structure and organisation to their approach. Being able to focus on a specific type of thinking which is made very explicit is valuable. Teachers at Castle School also feel that the benefits of the maps extend beyond the pupils. They can provide a quick reference point about their own teaching, as explained by the RE teacher, who stated that use of the maps 'gave them confidence, they were impressed with themselves and it also made me realise I hadn't done a bad job!'

The impact of Thinking Maps has also been reported at Whitchurch Primary School in Cardiff. Teachers promote thinking through a range of approaches. However, Thinking Maps contribute most to developing pupils' writing standards, with improvements noted year-on-year since their introduction in both the Foundation Phase and Key Stage 2. This has resulted in more children leaving the Foundation Phase in Year 2 with the higher outcome 6 (in 2013) than previously. The target for children attaining Level 4 at the end of Year 6 was 86 per cent, and 93 per cent of pupils in Whitchurch achieved this. It is thought by the teachers that a focus on using Thinking Maps within writing lessons has been a major factor in such improvements.

Steve Lewis, a teacher at Tondu Primary School in Bridgend, uses a variety of thinking materials in lessons. He finds that Thinking Maps provide useful structures to scaffold learning. He particularly likes their inclusive nature, allowing all children in his class the opportunity:

> to access the correct mode of thinking and to think more deeply. They are incredibly user-friendly and make the teaching of a particular thinking strategy much easier. The Double Bubble Map has been particularly useful when comparing and contrasting, and it is very versatile. We have used it when comparing different artists, when comparing localities in Geography and are currently using it to compare the experience of German soldiers to officers when they were held captive at Island Farm Prisoner of War camp in Bridgend.

Developing the use of Thinking Maps is not something that can be rushed if it is to be effective. It took two years to embed the maps across the curriculum in Christ the King Primary School in Cardiff. Patrick Affley, the headteacher at the time, feels that this was worthwhile, and comments:

> By far the most rewarding aspect is the impact on our pupils' attitudes towards learning, on their motivation and their growing sense of themselves as learners. We are constantly amazed by the way they share their thinking and we no longer make assumptions about pupils' capacities to learn. It is the pupils, more than any other members of our community, who ensure that we continue to develop our practice and understanding, so that together we continue to build an effective learning community. (Affley, 2012: 19)

Thinking Maps can also help children to understand more about the implications and impact of their behaviour on others. The visual nature of the maps can support this by making the causes and the effects of behaviour very clear. For example, in Kingsdown and Ringwould Church of England Primary School in Kent, headteacher Rose Cope says: 'The introduction of the Thinking Maps has had far reaching impact on academic standards and behaviour'. She gives an example of how using a Multi-Flow Map has empowered children of all ages in the school to identify patterns in their behaviours, and has helped them to identify triggers for non-desirable behaviours. This clarity has helped the children to recognise and take responsibility for their behaviour and the choices that they make. This has reduced incidents of poor behaviour across the school.

Using maps as a scaffold can also support pupils in their social development. In Ljan Skole School in Norway, Thinking Maps were introduced as part of a whole-school initiative. The use of these maps has supported pupils to think more deeply, and has also supported the development of social skills. Pupils have become better at sharing ideas and collaborating with one another. Teachers also report that pupils have become more reflective and organised in their work (Fiskaa, no date).

Many pupils generally feel positive about maps. For example, one Year 2 pupil at Tondu Primary School stated: 'We learn in lots of interesting ways. I love to use thinking maps – they make learning more interesting'. In a secondary school in England, 93 per cent of Year 7 pupils felt that Thinking Maps helped them to learn, and a quarter of pupils used them independently. One Third Grade student in America reflected: 'Thinking Maps are the paper of my mind', while a student in the first grade put it this way: 'My Thinking Maps have power. I have all these ideas and nowhere to put them. Thinking Maps let me get them out' (Hyerle and Apler, 2011: 62, 70).

Year 6 pupils at Burraton Primary School in Saltash (Cornwall) echo this, saying that the maps help them in planning and in recalling and remembering their work.[1] Pupils in Tondu Primary School enjoyed using Bubble Maps in particular. One pupil reported: 'Once I started seeing connections I found it easier to think of more'. For Olivia, a Year 6 pupil at Danescourt Primary, the use of maps is helpful across the different curriculum subjects. She found that using a Bubble Map was particularly helpful when writing poetry. The map provided her opportunity to reflect and reconsider her initial choice of vocabulary, giving time and space to refine and revisit her choices. She felt that thinking through the process of completing the map helped to make her finished poem better.

CHALLENGES

As with any strategies or resources, there are some challenges associated with using Thinking Maps effectively. McGuinness (1999: 2) points out that it can be challenging to infuse thinking skills across the curriculum – she comments that the thinking can become

---

[1]www.thinkingmatters.com (accessed 20 June 2018).

'watered down' or trivialised. Teachers at Castle School, for example, reflected on their approach to the use of Thinking Maps and concluded:

- I am trying to be too neat and controlling about the maps – I am imposing my organisational decisions on them.
- I keep forgetting to do the Frame of Reference.
- I am not encouraging them to actually think!
- I am trying to fit maps into my lessons rather than use maps effectively when they would enhance my lesson.
- Some pupils feel that they are 'over-mapped'. It gets too repetitive if they use them in all sessions.

To address this, teachers at the Castle School were encouraged to attend training events, regular staff meetings with a focus on thinking were held, and a whole-school approach was taken to planning. This enabled maps to be incorporated appropriately, allowed teachers and pupils time to reflect on the value of the maps, and to consider when and why they were using them. Guidance in the form of 'How to Think and Problem Solve' was produced by the Maths department – which included a flow chart of the process and lots of additional strategies to try. This was adapted by each department and displayed in all classrooms. Staff now only use or suggest Thinking Maps when the lesson or situation lends itself to them, rather than thinking that they should use them all the time. This was not an overnight process, and the school built the development of thinking into their School Development Plan over a three-year period.

SUMMARY

- Thinking Maps can be useful in supporting pupils to make their thinking visible, to develop a shared language of thinking and to organise their thoughts.
- Over time, pupils can start to select independently when and how to use these maps to support their thinking.
- Maps allow pupils to use dual codes to represent their thinking, and this can be a powerful strategy for learning.
- Pupils of all ages enjoy using the maps, and can see the value of them.
- Taking a whole-school approach to implementing and embedding maps is most effective.
- Care must be taken to identify appropriate opportunities to use the maps correctly, and to avoid 'over-mapping' or watering down their use.

Thinking Maps® is a registered trademark of Thinking Maps, Inc. Specific training and resources are needed to properly implement the Thinking Maps common visual language in the classroom. See www.thinkingmaps.com for more information.

THINKERS KEYS

INTRODUCTION

What do Brittanys, Lagottos, Spinone Italianos and Stabyhouns have in common? Well, apart from bright eyes, a wet nose and four legs, they are all members of the Gundog group. Far less familiar than other members such as Labradors, Cocker Spaniels and Golden Retrievers, they illustrate how many of the principles of creative thinking have been employed for centuries. For example, think about the Irish Setter. Tall, racy and red, in 1854 William Youatt, a veterinary surgeon, wrote: 'the setter is evidently the large spaniel improved to his particular size and beauty' (Hancock, 2013: 17). Over time, Gundog breeds have evolved to serve specific functions – so by making them bigger, smaller or exploring 'What if ...?', we have shaped and created a group of dogs who hunt, point, retrieve on land or in water, and who come in flat, curly or long coats of many colours. The basic idea of thinking creatively about change is illustrated through Tony Ryan's Thinkers Keys, which we review in this chapter.

BACKGROUND

Tony Ryan is a leading Australian educational consultant committed to environmental education. He established the EarthMovers Foundation[1] to support

---

[1]http://theearthmovers.org/ (accessed 20 June 2018).

young people in tackling local and global issues. Ryan (2017: 6) describes the world as 'a beautiful mess' but has faith in the younger generation to protect the environment if action is taken. He created Thinkers Keys after reading about the sixteen Thinker's Tools, which appear in *The Thinker's Toolbox* (Thornburg and Thornburg, 1989),[2] and the innovative ideas linked to thematic teaching highlighted by Dalton (1986) in *Adventures in Thinking*. He published *Thinkers Keys* in 1990 and there have been two further iterations since then, based on feedback from teachers around the world. The original edition had a strong focus on creative thinking whereas the updated Thinkers Keys cover both critical and creative thinking. They also consider the sequence of thinking strategies because Ryan suggests that quality thinking is more likely when relevant strategies are used in the right order and context.

INTRODUCING THE RESOURCES

This section provides an overview of the twenty original Thinkers Keys (Table 7.1) before briefly introducing the revisions.

There is an old saying that 'You can't add water to a full cup'. **The Reverse key** is designed to challenge commonly held assumptions and get pupils to move in an opposite direction. For instance, they may be asked to name five things that a computer cannot do as well as humans, three sounds they have never heard or ten things that cannot be cleaned. The Reverse illustrates the power of counterintuitive thinking. Cooper (2013) cites examples of counterintuitive advice from some of the world's leading entrepreneurs. Richard Branson, founder of Virgin, suggests 'go with your gut' when deciding whether an idea is worth pursuing, which runs contrary to established wisdom in gathering the evidence, and weighing up the costs and benefits. The Reverse key signals that thinking can change. For example, the latest advice of Leo Babauta (a leading blogger and author), is not to set *any* goals in life: 'It's absolutely liberating, and contrary to what you might have been taught, it absolutely doesn't mean you stop achieving things'. This marked a reverse in his thinking. He had suggested setting simple goals in his first book, *The Power of Less* (Babauta, 2009), which became an immediate bestseller with its emphasis on simplifying life and remains a popular motivation book for business.

The **What If ...? key** seeks to promote imaginative thinking and can be applied to any topic. This can be related directly to:

- curriculum subjects, e.g. 'What if Hitler had won the Second World War?' (history); 'What if we mix blue and green? (art)
- personal matters, e.g. 'What if you could change one thing about your life?'

---

[2]The Thinker's Tools are: Eliminate, Elaborate, Describe, Combine, Rearrange, Classify, Substitute, Associate, Exaggerate, Empathise, Compare, Reduce, Hypothesise, Symbolise, Separate and Reverse.

- local issues, e.g. 'What if a new shopping centre opened?'
- the future, e.g. 'What if we run out of oil?'

Table 7.1 Thinkers Keys

The Reverse	The What If?	The Disadvantages	The Combination	The Alphabet
Place words such as *cannot*, *never* and *not* in sentences which are commonly displayed in a listing format.	Ask the question on any topic and display responses in an ideas wheel.	Choose an object and list its disadvantages. Then list ways of correcting or eliminating these disadvantages.	List the attributes of two dissimilar objects, then combine the attributes into a single object.	Choose an object or category and compile a list of relevant words from A to Z. Then try to expand on some ideas that link with each of the words.
The BAR Use the acronym BAR (Bigger, Add, Replace) to reinvent or redesign objects.	**The Variations** How many ways can you ...?	**The Picture** Draw a picture that has no relevance to the topic and ask pupils to make links.	**The Prediction** Ask for a series of predictions regarding a given situation, product or circumstances.	**The Different Use** List widely different uses for a chosen object from an area of study.
The Ridiculous Make a ridiculous statement that would be *nearly* impossible to implement, and then try to substantiate it.	**The Commonality** Decide upon two objects that would generally have nothing in common and try to outline some commonalities.	**The Question** Start with the answer, and try to list five questions which could be linked with that answer only.	**The Brainstorming** State a problem that needs to be solved and brainstorm a list of solutions. Start the brainstorm statement with the words 'How to ...'.	**The Inventions** Encourage students to develop inventions that are constructed in an unusual manner.
The Interpretation Describe an unusual situation and then think of some different explanations for the existence of that situation.	**The Brick Wall** Make a statement that could not generally be questioned or disputed, and then try to break down the wall by outlining other ways of dealing with the situation.	**The Construction** Set up a wide variety of construction problem-solving tasks and use lots of readily available materials.	**The Forced Relationship** Develop a solution to a problem by employing a number of dissimilar objects.	**The Alternatives** List ways in which to complete a task without using the normal tools or implements.

Source: Tony Ryan (tonyryan.com.au) education futurist, author of the *Thinkers Keys, The Ripple Effect, Mindlinks, Brainstorms, Thinkfest,* and *The Next Generation*.

The Disadvantages key explores how to correct perceived weaknesses in an everyday product or service. For instance, one of the disadvantages of shopping online is that you are not sure when exactly the goods will arrive. Amazon has addressed this by providing safe lockers at Pickup venues where customers can collect goods at their convenience. In the United States, Amazon has introduced Instant Pickups where shoppers (mainly students) can collect certain items (e.g. snacks, drinks and phone chargers) on college campus sites within two minutes of making their purchase.

The Combination key works on the premise that many inventions originated when two dissimilar objects were combined. The disposable razor, for instance, was based on the concept of loading bullets into a rifle, combined with a normal razor. Similarly, the **BAR** (**B**igger, **A**dd, **R**eplace) **key** illustrates how altering a product, service or even animal (Photo 7.1) can result in a new creation. These changes involve making something bigger (e.g. food portions, cars, shops, schools), adding something (e.g. an ingredient to a dish, a free air freshener for a car wash, video technology in football games) or replacing an aspect (e.g. a name of a product, shop assistants with self-service counters, refinements in car design). Twenty-20 (T20) is a short form of cricket, introduced in 2002 as a means of boosting the game's popularity with the younger generation. The Indian Premier League, based on the T20 format, is now watched all over the world and has become a major commercial success. A good starting point for the BAR key is to consider with pupils how it can be applied to everyday, familiar objects, such as pencils, rubbers, books, water bottles, furniture, umbrellas, phones and televisions.

Photo 7.1   The BAR key applied by a Year 5 pupil to dogs

The Alphabet key is a means of sorting ideas. Pupils take an object or category (e.g. sport, food and drink, travel), which relates to an area of study, and compile an alphabetical list of associated objects. For instance, food and drink might prompt a simple list such as apple juice, bread, cake, dates and so forth. This seems simple, but the Alphabet key encourages research, creative thinking and problem-solving. **The Variations key** invites pupils to create a list of how many different ideas they can suggest for doing something, such as cutting the grass, making new friends or travelling from one place to another. **The Picture key** is a visualisation technique where someone draws a random sketch and others think about linking this to a given topic. In Figure 7.1, the sketch might suggest a frying pan (with an egg), dinner table or someone about to eat.

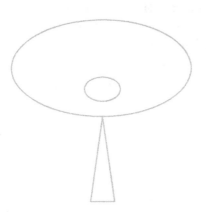

Figure 7.1 The Picture key: What does this sketch mean to you?

The Picture key is an adaption of a classic creativity test developed by E.P. Torrance in the 1960s when individuals were presented with an incomplete figure and invited to complete it in as many ways as possible. The adaption being that the suggested ideas link to a given theme. The importance of visual language should not be underestimated. Some of the most brilliant minds – Einstein, Marie Curie and Henry Ford – were all inveterate doodlers. Brown (2014) shows that doodling has led to breakthroughs in science, technology, medicine, architecture, literature and art. Within education, sketchnoting is increasingly used to allow learners to create a personal, visual story. Visual language is a powerful vehicle through which we make marks to help us think. A sketchnote is a quick way of stimulating the brain, releases creativity and can help us to see the big picture. The American author and illustrator Sunni Brown makes a strong case in her TED talk 'Doodlers, unite!' for harnessing the creativity of doodling (see also Brown, 2014).[3]

_____

[3]https://ed.ted.com/lessons/doodlers-unite-sunni-brown (accessed 20 June 2018).

The Different Uses key is another example of a well-known creativity test, introduced by Guilford (1967). Pupils are provided with an everyday object (e.g. paper clip, brick or coffee mug) and asked to suggest different uses. The test is designed to measure divergent thinking based on criteria such as fluency (how many ideas) and originality (how uncommon the uses are). It continues to be used widely by researchers. For instance, a recent American study asked office workers to think of alternative uses for ping-pong balls (Vohs et al., 2013; Young, 2017). The study aimed to establish whether those who worked in messy office environments were more creative than those who did not. The researchers report that while both sets of office workers generated the same number of ideas, those generated from messy desks were judged to be more interesting and creative. They put this down to disorderly environments producing fresh insights and breaking free of traditions and conventions. However, the problem with any such test is that none is wholly reliable and valid. The test may indicate potential, but this does not mean that individuals will in fact demonstrate creativity in the natural, real-life context.

The Prediction key asks pupils to predict the future related to a given topic or circumstances. For example, what might the school look like in fifty years? How might the game of football change by 2025? How will technology change our homes when the children are adults? Predicting is not random, futile guesswork as Future Studies is now a recognised field. Futurologists consider what is likely to happen based on current trends and state-of-the-art information. Among the significant mini trends identified by Watson (2012) is the growth of textual relationships where text is likely to overtake voice as the main means of communication among young people even though the happiest people tend to be those who engage in deep face-to-face conversation. Pupils might be asked: 'How do you think communication might change in the next ten years?' Technologies, environment change and fashion are a few examples of where applying foresight has huge political, economic and cultural significance.

Table 7.2 Five ridiculous ideas that have made people very rich

Basic idea	Creator	Estimated profit
Beanie babies – a sack full of beans with furry ears and cute names	H. Ty Warner	$3–6 billion
Yellow Smiley Face – accompanied by the saying 'Have a nice day!'	Bernard and Murray Spain	$500 million
Pet rock – a piece of rock on a bed of hay in a cardboard box that serves as a pet carrier	Gary Dahl	$15 million
Slinky – a tension spring that moves along the floor	Richard James	$250 million
Snuggie – a bathrobe put on backwards	Scott Boilen	$200 million

The Ridiculous key is designed to tackle negative thinking which puts roadblocks in the way of potentially strong ideas. Such thinking is characterised by sayings such as, 'That's not possible' or 'Don't be ridiculous'. Many ideas that have been dismissed out of hand have at some future point become a commercial success. Table 7.2 includes examples of ridiculous ideas that have made their creators a fortune.

Such ideas are reminiscent of the Grot Shop Empire created by Reginald Perrin (Leonard Rossiter), star of the 1970s BBC sitcom *The Return of Reginald Perrin*. Perrin opened a shop to sell junk with the promotional slogan: 'Every single thing in this shop is guaranteed absolutely useless'. He made a fortune from selling the likes of round dice and square hoops. As he told a customer: 'So much rubbish is sold these days under false pretences ... that I decided to be honest about it'.

The Commonality key also introduces pupils to unusual ideas. It is based on the premise that there are common links between things that on the surface appear very unrelated. In marketing, they call this 'dot' thinking – connecting the dots by bringing together words, pictures, logos, media channels and experiences to create a new market or expand the existing one. This is not a novel suggestion. Cambridge professor William Beveridge (1950: 7) in *The Art of Scientific Investigation* pointed out that 'originality often consists in linking up ideas whose connection was not previously suspected'. The cross-pollinating of ideas is central to creative thinking. Here are some examples:

- In 1448 Johannes Gutenberg combined the mechanisms from the wine press and punching coins to create the printing press, from which we get books.
- In 1987 Robert Plath, an airline pilot, combined a trolley and a suitcase together to create a suitcase with wheels (rollaboard).
- In 1990 visitors to an art exhibition in a Swedish village had nowhere to stay and so slept in an igloo on top of reindeer skins. This was the beginning of the first ice hotel with the snow and ice blocks rebuilt each year.

Sometimes the idea originates from simply bringing together two groups of people who have some common need. For instance, Travis Kalanick and Garrett Camp noticed that many taxi customers were frustrated hanging around for a taxi, while taxi drivers were under-used spending more time waiting for a job than doing one. Hence, in 2009 they launched Uber, which has transformed the taxi business.

These examples illustrate the original meaning of cognition (the process of knowing), which stems from the Latin verb *cognito* ('to shake together') while the term intelligence comes from *intelligo* meaning 'to choose, or select, from' (Rugg, 1963: 218). In short, acquiring, storing and processing knowledge involves the shaking together of ideas and selecting those that have potential. In his book *Scientific Genius*, the psychologist Dean Simonton (2009) suggests that geniuses stand out because they form more novel combinations than those who are merely talented. They imagine the impossible by focusing on 'what is' and 'what might be' rather than 'what is not'.

A variation on the commonality key, which we have used successfully with teachers, is an exercise we call Connect-4 (Figure 7.2). It aims to explore connections between ideas in an imaginative way. A random word is assigned to the corner of a box. The challenge is to connect each of the four words in as few steps as possible. The exercise can be varied, for example the teacher might stipulate that there must be exactly three steps. This is effective when pupils work in groups and share ideas. When the groups finish, they judge each other's work using two simple criteria: 'Have all the links been made?' and 'How imaginative do you think the link is?' Some teachers following a thematic or interdisciplinary approach have used Connect-4 as a planning tool at the start of a project, sharing with the class the key concepts they hope to cover and highlighting the links as they progress. These key concepts can be taken from the respective curriculum guidance documents. Connect-4 is deliberately designed to make pupils think about connections, however tenuous these may be.

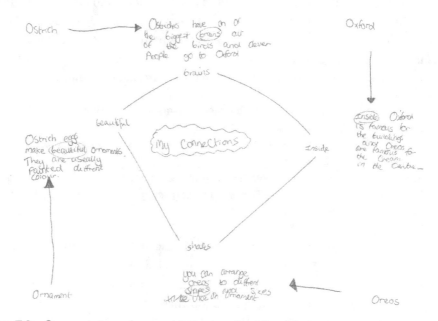

Figure 7.2 Connect-4 can be used to connect random ideas

The Question key seeks to encourage questioning by providing the answer first, thereby breaking the traditional pattern of interaction between teacher and pupils. It is a simple and flexible technique. In mathematics, for example, pupils can be routinely asked to generate questions to a given answer (e.g. '10', 'triangle' or 'midnight') placed on the board during registration. In geography, each day the teacher might write a new country or town on the whiteboard.

The Brainstorming key begins with the words 'How to …'. It aims to generate lots of ideas, irrespective of how silly they seem, without the anxiety of being criticised for getting things wrong. The ideas can be recorded in very creative ways beyond the flipchart or interactive whiteboard. Brainstorming does not have to take the form of words but can include symbols and pictures. Pupils can be given magazine pictures to cut out their responses for a visual collage or step outside and chalk the ideas on a wall. Colours can be used to denote different ideas, along the lines of De Bono's Six Thinking Hats (Chapter 5). Light blue, for example, might indicate calmness while bright red conveys passion.

The Inventions key encourages pupils to develop constructive ideas. Pupils can be given a specific brief, such as invent a machine that walks the dog or keeps you awake in lessons. These do not have to be as complicated as the famous illustrations of the cartoonist Heath Robinson. However, his wonderful cartoons may inspire pupils to invent their own contraptions. The Heath Robinson museum in London exhibits some of his wackiest ideas, such as the wart chair to remove warts from the top of the head. Pupils might more readily relate to the inventive genius of Wallace (from Aardman's animation *Wallace & Gromit*), creator of Techno Trousers and Knit-o-matic (Smith, 2013).

During the creative process, it is not uncommon to run into difficulties or barriers. **The Brick Wall key** encourages pupils not to give in too quickly. It focuses on thinking of alternatives to overcome 'the brick wall'. The teacher might issue a statement that is, on the surface, hard to refute and the pupils set about trying to dismantle the bricks. Ryan (1990) cites the example that governments need to collect taxes to provide public services. Alternative ideas could be for every government employee to be paid directly for a service as and when the customer needs it or reorganising services so that they are all provided locally by community groups of 500 people.

The Construction key is an example of practical creative thinking. The idea is to provide pupils with tools, materials and any other resources to solve a problem. This is quite common practice in early years' settings, such as building the tallest tower out of blocks (which can be counted), or more sophisticated challenges such as building the longest bridge using only ten straws and 1 cm of tape.

The Forced Relationship key encourages pupils to look for relationships between different objects, like the commonality key. However, the focus is on solving problems using one or more objects that are available. For instance, freeing a trapped cat from a tree using a kite, marble and rubber band or trapping a mouse using a piece of string, cheese and a can. **The Alternative key** is based on the adage that necessity is the mother of invention. The challenge is to complete tasks without using normal tools. For instance, cleaning your teeth without a toothbrush or cooking toast without a toaster. At its extreme, this is along Robinson Crusoe lines or, more recently, Bear Grylls' survival challenges. Dental floss or shoe laces can be used as fishing line, a dustbin liner can act as a rain jacket, socks can help collect and filter water while, at a push, a pair of glasses can be used to start a fire by concentrating the sun's rays on tinder.

Interpretations are central to the study of the humanities, arts, literature and citizenship. The **Interpretation key** seeks to build pupils' awareness of different explanations of events. These can be very imaginative because the point is to generate possibilities, however farfetched. The theme of not jumping too quickly to conclusions is behind the Interpretation key. Many years ago, a television commercial showed a bank manager wearing a pinstriped suit, carrying a briefcase walking down a high street. Behind him a young, scruffy punk rushed quickly towards him and pushed him aside. The viewer is left thinking that a mugging was in place, but as it transpired the young man saved the banker from falling debris. Similarly, there is a very funny series of adult television commercials (by the Ameriquest Mortgage Company), which carry the same strapline of not judging others.[4]

In 2005 Ryan developed further guidance in the form of Thinking Sequences that accompany a revised set of Thinkers Keys Cards. These are freely available to download on his website.[5] The Thinkers Keys are now arranged in two groups: supporting critical (Figure 7.3) and creative/innovative (Figure 7.4) thinking skills. Other changes include the dropping or replacement of certain keys although schools continue to use the original versions.

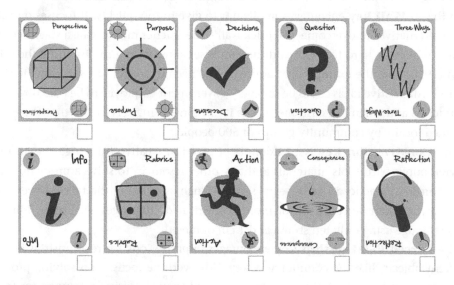

Figure 7.3 Critical Thinkers Keys

Source: Tony Ryan (tonyryan.com.au) education futurist, author of the *Thinkers Keys, The Ripple Effect, Mindlinks, Brainstorms, Thinkfest,* and *The Next Generation.*

---

[4]www.youtube.com/watch?v=NWQoxJA0xEw (accessed 20 June 2018).

[5]www.tonyryan.com.au/home/projects/ (accessed 20 June 2018)

Figure 7.4 Creative/innovative Thinkers Keys

Source: Tony Ryan (tonyryan.com.au) education futurist, author of the *Thinkers Keys, The Ripple Effect, Mindlinks, Brainstorms, Thinkfest,* and *The Next Generation*.

The sequences are left to the professional discretion of teachers, but as most learning involves critical and creative thinking then pupils are encouraged to use a combination of keys.

THE THINKERS KEYS IN PRACTICE

Ryan (1990) provides lots of examples of how the Thinkers Keys could be applied to popular themes, such as transport, communications, sport, the environment and Christmas. So, for instance, in a theme of food teachers might ask pupils to:

- list ten foods that you should never eat (The Reverse)
- list disadvantages of, and improvements to, chopsticks (The Disadvantages)
- find ten different uses for a pumpkin (The Different Uses)
- find common points between an apple and a saucepan (The Commonality).

There is no set sequence that must be followed and teachers are encouraged to experiment to see which best suits their purpose. For instance, to solve an issue pupils could use the question-brainstorm-decision sequence (Figure 7.5). Ryan provides guidance to help organise thinking but stresses that students should experiment with their own sequences to suit their needs.

Thinking is rarely a linear process. It is more organic and there is considerable toing and froing in reaching decisions. Hence the Thinkers Keys Cards can be cut up and arranged

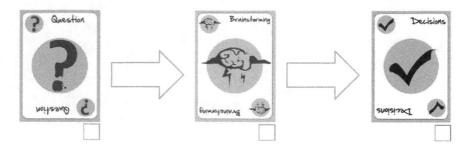

Figure 7.5 Possible Thinking Sequence for solving a problem

Source: Tony Ryan (tonyryan.com.au) education futurist, author of the *Thinkers Keys, The Ripple Effect, Mindlinks, Brainstorms, Thinkfest,* and *The Next Generation.*

in circles or other shapes to indicate the 'messy' nature of thinking. It is important to stress that as with all approaches to thinking, the Thinkers Keys should not be taught as an isolated set of exercises. Rather, they need an appropriate context. For example, if using the Perspectives key, reference could be made to topical news such as climate change, elections or sports results. Ryan's guidance on planning suggests that teachers should try to include:

- an explicit focus on an inquiry task that is intellectually rigorous
- a clarification of the core understandings linked to the topic
- use of key questions that directly refer to core understandings
- a list of the Thinkers Keys appearing near the front as reminders of the strategies to be taught.

The Thinkers Keys can be used during school visits. For example, pupils in Years 1 and 4 from Bynea Primary School in Llanelli visited a stately home as part of a local study. They worked alongside trainee teachers who were each briefed on the use of Thinkers Keys. Pairs of trainee teachers were situated in different parts of the house and given the task of developing the pupils' thinking skills. Year 1 pupils used the Alphabet key to find paintings and artefacts which featured animals. The trainees accompanied them as they went around the house and wrote the names of different animals on sticky-notes. So, for instance, they observed and recorded an **antelope** on a Victorian vase, a teddy **bear** in the bedroom, a **cow** in a painting of a farmyard and a wire-haired fox terrier (**dog**) on a push-along toy from the 1900s. This encouraged them to observe closely, cooperate and broaden their ideas. They struggled to find something for the letter 'y', for instance, until one pupil suggested that one of the animals in a painting was a 'yellow dog' – the trainees let him include this for thinking well.

Following an introductory tour around the house, pupils were left excited and impressed by the number of rooms, the lavish hallway, the ornamental staircase and the spacious grounds. The trainee teachers then introduced the Disadvantages key to Year 4 pupils with the aim of providing a more balanced view of life in a stately home. The pupils were encouraged to think about whether the size of rooms, which they initially thought was an advantage, could prove otherwise. They suggested that cleaning the rooms could take a lot of time and effort, while keeping it warm would also be costly. They then interviewed the owners of the house to gain further insight into the advantages and disadvantages.

Other groups of pupils used the Inventions key to create gadgets that would help the owners maintain their property. For instance, Finley (Figure 7.6) created a pulley system to help clean huge paintings that hung on the walls, whereas Kacie (Figure 7.7). invented the 'clutter cleaner' complete with extendable duster.

Figures 7.6 and 7.7 Pupil inventions to clean stately home paintings

Staff at Kingsdown and Ringwould Church of England Primary School in Deal wanted to enrich and extend pupils' learning through the Thinkers Keys, which were introduced from Year 2 onwards. In the story of *The Three Little Pigs*, pupils used the Inventions key to keep out the wolf. They used the Construction key to build the house with blocks, straw, fabric and other materials. The Interpretation key was used to consider the wolf's point of view. Staff at Portsmouth Academy for Girls used Thinkers Keys as a hook for learning to engage pupils at the start of lessons. What matters is being clear over the content that should be taught, deciding upon the kind of thinking skills and dispositions that pupils need to develop, framing learning intentions around these and then choosing the appropriate resources or techniques to support learning.

In the updated version of Thinkers Keys, Ryan suggests that teachers create Thinking Certificates and develop simple levels of attainment along the Novice, Competent and

Master Thinker lines. He relates these to pupils explaining and applying the Cards (Thinking) in context. So, for instance, a Novice Thinker might be expected to show understanding of Purpose, Info, Challenge and Improvement, a Competent Thinker might progress to applying ten Cards and a Master Thinker might grasp all twenty thinking strategies.

IMPACT

As with Six Thinking Hats, it is difficult to evaluate the impact of Thinkers Keys on pupils' learning because of the shortage of empirical research. A search on Google Scholar and other academic databases revealed few academic or professional articles that reference Thinkers Keys and those that do are largely within an Australasian context (Egan, 2007; Attard, 2012). However, they are clearly popular, particularly in Australia where they are referenced in the national curriculum.[6] Over the years they have been sold in at least twenty-eight countries.[7] Among the reasons for their popularity is their simplicity and flexibility. Moreover, the testimonies from schools using Thinkers Keys are very positive. For instance, senior leaders at Barton Court Grammar School in Kent attribute improvements in the quality of teaching and learning to the use of a range of approaches including Thinkers Keys. They are widely seen as straightforward, practical and flexible tools to enhance pupils' thinking.

SUMMARY

⌇ Thinkers keys are a set of twenty practical resources to support thinking, devised by Tony Ryan.

⌇ Thinkers Keys are used internationally, although they are particularly popular in New Zealand and Australia.

⌇ The revised Thinkers Keys are grouped to support critical and creative thinking.

⌇ There is not much empirical research associated with the impact of Thinkers Keys on learning. However, their flexible and practical nature appeals to many teachers.

---

[6]http://australiancurriculumf-6resources.blogspot.co.uk/2013/04/thinkers-keys-t-ryan.html (accessed 20 June 2018).

[7]Correspondence with Tony Ryan, January 2018.

PHILOSOPHICAL APPROACHES

INTRODUCTION

In 2016, a poll was conducted to find the world's greatest philosopher. One in four of the respondents suggested a toy bear (Sherwin, 2016). They were not kidding. When the author A.A. Milne created Winnie-the-Pooh in 1924, based on his son's favourite teddy bear, few would have anticipated his popularity and even fewer his academic prowess. While Winnie-the-Pooh acknowledges that he is 'a Bear of Very Little Brain', his sayings have been likened to some of philosophy's greatest minds. Catherine McCall, patron of the Philosophy Foundation, goes as far as to suggest that 'Poohisms encapsulate the thinking of many famous philosophers in beautiful, clear and memorable sayings that have inspired children and parents for generations' (Flood, 2016).

> 'If the string breaks, try another piece of string.'
>
> 'It isn't much good having anything exciting, if you can't share it with somebody.'
>
> 'Rivers know this: there is no hurry. We shall get there some day.'
>
> 'Never let things come to you, go out and fetch them.'
>
> 'It's best to know what you're looking for before you look for it.'[1]

---

[1] https://dcpi.disney.com/celebrate-winnie-poohs-90th-anniversary-favorite-poohisms/ (accessed 20 June 2018).

Such is the admiration for this bear's wisdom, that academics have written papers and books arguing that *Winnie-the-Pooh* is not simply a children's classic but a work of profound wisdom (Williams, 2003). His philosophy has been likened to the principles of Taoism, with Pooh, for example, personifying *wu wei* or non-action, going with the flow of nature and leading a simple life (Hoff, 2015). Winnie-the-Pooh serves as a good example of how philosophy can be made accessible to children.

Several children's writers have taken inspiration from Winnie-the-Pooh and developed stories and materials for schools using animals as a starting point. The 'But Why?' series of stories seeks to engage young children in deeper thinking using Philosophy Bear (Bowkett, 2004; Stanley and Bowkett, 2004) while a similar concept features in *Little Owl's Book of Thinking* (Gilbert, 2004) where Benny the owlet receives seven lessons in thinking from his wise old father. This chapter focuses mainly on Philosophy for Children (P4C), the most widely known approach. However, a philosophical mindset should not be limited to stand-alone P4C sessions and should permeate the life of the school.

Philosophy means 'a love of wisdom'. It sets out to engage with some of the fundamental questions about life: What is happiness? What is truth? What makes a good friend? Is it better to love and lose or never love? What happens after we die? By its nature, philosophy discusses abstract concepts such as freedom, peace, war, hope, generosity and mercy. The work of Piaget and other theorists suggests that young children struggle to handle abstract thought because they only think in 'concrete' terms at their respective stage of cognitive development. This has meant that philosophical approaches in the classroom have been traditionally treated with considerable scepticism.

Matthews (1980, 1994) was one of the early scholars who challenged the Piagetian view of child development. In *The Philosophy of Childhood* he makes the point that children are natural philosophers. Matthews cites many examples, beginning with the story of his 4-year-old daughter Sarah. She watched her father de-louse Fluffy, the family cat. She asked how the cat got fleas in the first place. He explained that the fleas must have jumped from another cat, which prompted Sarah to ask how *that* cat got fleas. When she was told that it must have been playing with yet another cat, Sarah concluded: 'it can't go on like that forever; the only thing that goes on and on like that forever is numbers!' (Matthews, 1994: 1). Here was a version of what philosophers call first cause or cosmological argument. Since the days of Aristotle, thinkers have debated whether the universe had a beginning or stretches back to infinity. In their own way, children naturally behave in a philosophical way by asking questions and trying to reason things through.

The notion of children as natural philosophers, however, is at odds with the Classical images of philosophers depicted in Raphael's great painting, *School of Athens*, showing grey-haired, bearded old men. From the days of Plato onwards, there has been a tendency to see philosophy as something to be pursued towards the end rather than the beginning of life because children lack the knowledge content upon which to philosophise. Those who support philosophical approaches in school (e.g. Wartenberg, 2014) adopt a very different view, arguing that children's natural inquisitiveness is the basis for cultivating independent, critical thinkers.

BACKGROUND

Philosophy for Children is the most prominent philosophical approach used in school. Professor Matthew Lipman (1923–2010) and his colleagues introduced P4C in 1970 with the establishment of the Institute for the Advancement of Philosophy for Children (IAPC) in New Jersey. They were dissatisfied with the state of American education at the time, specifically the lack of critical thinking among their university students. Lipman saw the potential of philosophy to address this and so began by writing 'novels' or short stories as a means of introducing philosophical questions. The first story *Harry Stottlemeier's Discovery* appeared in 1969 and formed the basis of the Philosophy for Children programme. Its continuing aim is to reconstruct and present major philosophical ideas in a manner that allows children to reason well in a self-correcting manner (Sharp and Reed, 1991). The stories followed the example set by Plato's *Dialogues* in featuring open-ended points for discussion and twists to interest both the young readers and teachers (Lipman et al., 1980). What also mattered was seeing philosophy as a joint venture involving both students *and* teachers.

Thus, Lipman (2003) built on the concept of 'community of inquiry'. This was a term first used by Charles Sanders Peirce (1839–1914). Peirce (pronounced 'purse') worked as a government scientist, but was also an astronomer, mathematician, inventor, administrator and writer. In one of his articles, Peirce discussed the difference between doubt and belief, concluding: 'the irritation of doubt causes a struggle to attain a state of belief. I shall term this struggle *Inquiry*' (Peirce, 1877: 99). Peirce reckoned that scientific inquiry would eventually satisfy all doubts. And he thought that the distinguishing feature of scientific inquiry was its collaborative, public nature. He illustrated the importance of the 'community' aspect of inquiry with a simple story of three blind men trying to describe an elephant. Each man offers a description of the elephant, but this was limited to the individual's perspective. It was only when the three compared and debated perspectives, tested new hypotheses and behaved like a community of scientific investigators that a more accurate description of the elephant emerged.

Lipman (2008) was impressed by Peirce's idea of a pragmatic, collaborative philosophy, with its emphasis on individuals working together to discuss and solve real-life problems. He broadened the notion of inquiry to non-scientific forms and, crucially, envisaged communities leading the field rather than being 'penned in by the boundary lines of existing disciplines' (Lipman et al., 1980: 15). For schools, this meant classrooms in which students and teachers followed their own lines of inquiry based on questions and interests.

Lipman and his colleagues, who included teacher educators, were mindful that philosophy needed to be made accessible to students. There was no point simply having communities of inquiry in classrooms without the teaching expertise. Lipman (2008: 130) put it more bluntly when he said he didn't want classrooms to become 'a dumping ground for unemployed and untrained philosophers' that had 'never been exposed to an hour of preparation for teaching'. Hence guidance for teachers was published and programmes for elementary and secondary schools were developed with age-appropriate materials. These were not designed to teach children how to win arguments but to develop clarity and accuracy in their thinking. Moreover, teachers should have the time and space within the curriculum to bring out issues, problems and tensions that engage students' attention and stimulate the formation of a community of inquiry.

In 1990, the BBC produced a television documentary, *Socrates for Six Year Olds*, which showed Lipman working in one of the most challenging schools in Merrick, New York. This sparked interest among UK academics, schools, education services and charities and led to the establishment of the Society for the Advancement of Philosophical Enquiry and Reflection in Education (SAPERE) in 1992. Today, SAPERE promotes P4C in UK schools and provides teacher training resources and materials. Unlike the original P4C, however, the SAPERE model also includes poems, images, films, picture books and artefacts, as well as novels. The focus is on promoting 4 Cs – critical, creative, caring and collaborative thinking.

INTRODUCING THE RESOURCES

One of the common aims of philosophical approaches is to teach children *how* to think based on the premise that it is not enough for pupils to learn subject content knowledge. They also need to learn how historians, scientists, geographers and others think in distinctive ways. Historians, for example, do not accept at face value what is recorded to have happened in the past. They dig deeper by asking questions about the context (e.g. who recorded what, when and why), comparing different accounts and reconstructions. At its highest level, thinking involves both critical and creative aspects; the critical is about reasoning and judgement while the creative involves artistry and imagination. The community of inquiry is the social context within which such higher-order thinking occurs, especially when there is a strong emphasis on dialogue. While the terms 'discussion' and 'dialogue' are often used interchangeably, dialogue seeks to explore, share meanings, challenge assumptions and reach agreement whereas the purpose of discussion is usually to tell, sell or persuade (Preskill and Torres, 1999). Wegerif (2010: 119) asserts that 'the quality of thinking is not found in individuals it is found in dialogues'. Fisher (2009) points out that dialogue forces children to translate their thoughts into words and expand their thinking into new areas.

P4C shares similarities with Alexander's model of dialogic teaching with its emphasis on the importance of promoting purposeful talk (with clear goals) as the foundation of learning (Alexander, 2008). He advocates moving away from the traditional question-and-answer routine, in which the teacher initiates the discussion, pupils respond and the teacher judges. Instead, class and group discussion becomes far more interactive, fluid and collective, i.e. teacher and pupils work together on learning tasks. Teachers establish a supportive environment in which pupils' views are expressed without fear of the embarrassment in giving 'wrong' answers. Such a shift in approach depends very much on the kind of values teachers uphold and the extent to which they value child-initiated conversations, the balance between teacher and pupil talk and whether children are confident enough to pose questions (Mercer and Dawes, 2008).

P4C is not the same as classroom debate or circle time. It differs from classroom debate because it assumes that individuals sincerely believe in the arguments they express. Those who engage in debate may not, necessarily, adhere to the points they make or want others to adopt. P4C is not about winning arguments but seeks to promote collaboration and mutual understanding. Circle time focuses on children's social and emotional development, and while emotional intelligence is an important element of P4C, the priority is to foster logical reasoning and the tools of philosophy, such as questioning. P4C seeks to encourage pupils to reflect on their own questions and those posed by their peers.

PHILOSOPHIES IN PRACTICE

Many schools run P4C sessions at regular slots, once a week for an hour. Duration and locations can vary although clearly pupils need enough time to share ideas and feel comfortable in their surroundings. This could be somewhere in the school grounds and linked to exploring the environment. At Deri View Primary School in Abergavenny, the children have P4C sessions outdoors as part of the Forest school programme with the skills of oracy developed around the school. P4C sessions usually follow a set structure (Table 8.1). The overriding principle is that pupils lead the discussion and work together as a community to engage in philosophical enquiry. Sessions typically begin with pupils forming a circle to symbolise the unity of the group. The children can also see each other and direct their comments anywhere within the circle. It is important to agree the talking or community rules negotiated between children and the facilitator. These might include reminders to:

- look at the person who is speaking
- wait until the person finishes talking before saying something
- say why you think this
- talk clearly and loudly so all can hear

- respect the right of people to think and share views
- not get upset if someone says something you disagree with.

At Deri View Primary School, children are also taught the importance of posture and how they sit to show that they are listening carefully. Less confident and articulate children form an outer circle where they listen and 'magpie' ideas to build on when they enter the inner circle. They are provided with starter sentences such as:

- I like your idea but have you considered ...
- I disagree with that idea. I think ...
- I agree with your idea because ...
- I don't think that is quite right because ...
- That's a good point but ...

The pupils learn that they are disagreeing with the idea and not the person. Encouraging genuine, respectful dialogue can be challenging because some children may be aggressive and dominant while others refuse to engage. Helpful strategies to build trust and rapport include the use of mini plenaries to sum up what has been said and what people think, visual displays of words such as 'perhaps' and 'maybe' to invite a range of possible views, posing questions for imagination (e.g. 'Suppose that ...? How would it look differently if ...? If we changed this how would you feel?), modelling uncertainties (e.g. 'I don't quite understand this', 'I haven't made my mind up yet because ...') and acknowledging different responses without passing judgement.

Table 8.1 The structure of a philosophy session

- Whole class sit in a circle
- Review the ground rules for discussion
- Optional warm-up (2 minutes)
- Show the stimulus for the session
- Provide independent thinking time (2 minutes)
- Provide small-group discussion and questioning time (5 minutes)
- Facilitator references concepts
- Facilitator scribes group responses on white board or flipchart
- Decide on the question to be discussed
- Whole class discussion following set rules (25 minutes)
- Plenary discussion including evaluation.

Sessions might begin with a warm-up, using a game such as 'Ask the Object a Question': a familiar object is placed in view of everyone and individuals take turns to ask it a question. The teacher may model the kinds of questions to ask, moving from concrete to more abstract subjects. For instance, if the object is a chair the pupils might ask: 'What are you made of?', 'Where were you born?' and 'Which do you prefer – tables or cushions?' The pupils need to enter into the spirit of the session and this means asking questions which may, on the surface, appear farfetched or plain silly. Maggie Jacobs, a character from the BBC comedy *Extras* (2005), had the habit of asking, 'Would you rather be …?' style questions. This can be used as a basis for philosophical discussions with pupils:

Would you rather …

- fly or be invisible?
- never eat your favourite food again or every day for the rest of your life?
- live in a place that was always very hot or always very cold?
- have just one arm or one leg?
- be an owl or a mouse?
- be character *x* or *y* in the story?

Folkman (2015) posed the first question to more than 7,000 business and professional leaders around the world and their responses revealed insights into their thinking and personality. Around three-quarters chose the ability to fly, on the basis that this meant being in the public light, centre stage and assuming a more powerful position. Folkman also found that those who admitted that they were less confident, less powerful or less in control tended to be more inclined to choose invisibility. So, a response to a hypothetical question can say something about personality traits and attitudes.

Stimulus

Following a mental warm-up, the teacher chooses and shows an interesting stimulus for the session. In the traditional (American) P4C sessions, this usually takes the form of a specifically written novel. However, any resource can be used which prompts children to raise questions: a film clip, piece of music, story extract, comic, poem, news headline, a quotation, fable or a painting. Stanley and Bowkett (2004) point out that the stimulus should have a high level of ambiguity to encourage pupils to generate questions. It should excite their imagination and contain strong elements of puzzlement. It is important that children are given independent thinking time before talking to a partner. This gives them the opportunity to rehearse in their minds what they would like to say. Some teachers provide pupils with thinking journals to record their emerging thoughts or questions.

Key concepts

Some teachers initially draw up a bank of big, abstract ideas for the pupils to refer to, alphabetically arranged. Here are 26 ideas generated by a group of teachers during an in-service training event:

A – art	I – injustice	Q – quality	Y – yesterday
B – beauty	J – joy	R – rights	Z – zeal
C – charity	K – karma	S – success	
D – darkness	L – love	T – truth	
E – eternity	M – mercy	U – united	
F – freedom	N – never	V – value	
G – generosity	O – objectivity	W – wrong	
H – hatred	P – peace	X – x factor	

These ideas can be displayed and added to during the school year. They become reference points when pupils discuss the stimulus. For instance, in the story *Emily's Art* (Catalanotto, 2006), Emily enters an art contest but her picture of a dog is rejected because the judge thinks it shows a rabbit and she hates dogs because one once attacked her. Emily loses heart and stops painting. The book raises questions about what art means, what criteria should be used when judging art and how different people interpret art. In the prologue to the story, the teacher's (Ms Fair) discussion with her class about an art contest raises lots of philosophical questions: who decides what the 'best' painting should be (the judge declares she is the judge because her cousin is married to an artist). The story introduces notions of subjectivity and objectivity. It illustrates differences between the artist's intention and the viewer's interpretation: Emily intended to paint a dog, which the judge interpreted as a rabbit. Once the judge understood the true nature of the painting, she disregarded it.[2] *Emily's Art* lends itself then to discussing a range of abstract concepts in an accessible format.

As a rough guide, teachers may benefit from grouping concepts as per subjects or areas of experience (Table 8.2). Some concepts can be explored across several curriculum areas, such as mathematics, history and science. The concept of change, for example, can be discussed in relation to personal growth, changes associated with the seasons of the year, and specific activities such as cooking (e.g. baking, whipping and dissolving) or studying historical change in the locality. A question such as, 'Should you ever talk to strangers?' raises issues relating to e-safety (technologies), neighbourliness (citizenship) and interdependence (geography). Children are generally brought up with the notion of 'stranger

---

[2]Ideas on using this story can be viewed at: www.teachingchildrenphilosophy.org/BookModule/EmilysArt (accessed 20 June 2018).

danger' and as adults we are fearful of breaking tacit, cultural codes around appropriate public behaviour. The author Kio Stark (2016) argues that as we live increasingly insular lives with our heads down and minds elsewhere, we rarely take time to talk to strangers. And yet, this can be a source of inspiration, adventure and fresh insight. The very notion of who should be regarded as a stranger opens rich potential for children's philosophical thinking.

Table 8.2 Key concepts useful for planning philosophical discussions

Subjects/area of experience	Key concepts for philosophical discussion
Language and literature	anger, argument, character, conversation, evil, fairness, forgiveness, good, justice, love, mercy, myth, poetry, power, revenge, romance, story
Mathematics	angle, calculation, error, infinite, length, line, money, number, one, order, pattern, shape, size, space, symmetry, symbol, set, time, two, weight, zero
Science and technology	animals, atmosphere, atom, control, darkness, design, electricity, energy, environment, ethics, evidence, experiment, extinct, fair test, force, genetics, gravity, light, magnetic, nature, star, theory
Humanities	*History*: cause, change, consequence, difference, Empire, evidence, interpretation, king, queen, nation, similarity, slavery, source, the past, truth
	Geography: climate change, cycle, economy, freedom, globalisation, habitat, industry, leisure, tourism, place, poverty, region, resource, rural, sustainability, soil, scale, urban, water
	Religious Education: assembly, awe, belief, death, faith, God, heaven, hope, prayer, spiritual, wonder, worship
Citizenship	belonging, charity, democracy, family, freedom, friendliness, home, honesty, humility, identity, leader, neighbour, politics, power, pride, right/wrong, war
ICT	communication, e-safety, fake news, games, knowledge, media, technology, virtual
Arts	art, beauty, copy, creativity, dance, design, elegance, fashion, image, look, meaning, mural, originality, performance, quality, real, reproduction, taste, sculpture, still-life, style, subjective
Health and wellbeing	appearance, body, confidence, energy, exercise, feelings, fitness, force, happiness, health, identity, joy, loneliness, medicine, mood, power, safety, sport, strength

Questioning

Philosophical discussions need a focal or anchor point. This can take the form of a big question. P4C sessions are led by pupils' questions linked to a stimulus. However, teachers themselves can take opportunities to pose questions to encourage deeper thinking (not necessarily related to P4C). The author Bernadette Russell (2016) suggests her top ten philosophical questions to use with children:

1. How should we treat animals?
2. What is love?
3. Is everything connected?
4. Can I think myself happy?
5. Can kindness change the world?
6. What is so great about the world anyway?
7. What's the difference between grown-ups and children?
8. What is friendship?
9. Are the best things in life free?
10. Can one person change the world?

To follow up on the fifth question, Russell started a project in response to the 2011 Tottenham riots, in which she tried to be kind to someone every day. Her website gives details of how the project unfolded.[3] It began when she paid for a young man to post his driving license at the local post office because he had forgotten his money. She felt an immediate glow and for the next 366 days she experienced an amazing journey. Her simple conclusion is that kindness to others, at work, in the community, to yourself and to those you disagree with, brings happiness (Russell, 2017).[4]

Teachers make effective use of questions when they first ascertain pupils' initial level of understanding, adjust their teaching accordingly and then use 'why' questions to get pupils to reason and reflect upon what they were thinking (Mercer and Littleton, 2007). While Table 8.3 gives a few examples of general questions that teachers can ask, the kinds of questions raised in philosophy sessions will obviously depend upon the topic.

Another way of viewing this is to consider questions that teachers should generally try and *avoid* if they want to promote philosophical thinking. These include:

- Rhetorical questions (when the answer is given), e.g. 'Can birds fly?', 'Can we do better next time?'
- Defensive questions (which seek self-preservation), e.g. 'Why didn't you answer me?'
- Agreement questions (which seek to persuade others), e.g. 'This is the best way to do it, yes?'
- Closed questions (which usually elicit limited single-word answers), e.g. 'What is the name of ...?'

---

[3]www.366daysofkindness.com/ (accessed 20 June 2018).

[4]Without wishing to spoil a good story, unfortunately this is not always the case. In 2015, the Wilkinson family offered hospitality to a young man sleeping rough. Tragically, Tracey Wilkinson and her son paid the ultimate price when they were brutally murdered by the stranger.

Table 8.3 General questions to ask during philosophical discussions

Questions	Thinking skills and dispositions
Who/what/where/why/how? So what? What if ...?	Questioning
What is the link between x and y? What is similar/different? What is the bigger issue here?	Connecting
How do we know? What evidence can you find to support this? Why do you think?	Justifying
What are the important points here? What are the key features? What are the funniest/saddest/scariest etc. moments?	Analysing
Do you agree with ...? What is another view of this? Is this *really* true? Who agrees/disagrees with ...?	Interpreting
How did ___ happen? How would you sort/classify ...? What would happen if ...?	Synthesising
How would you improve ...? What is your view of ...? What grade/mark would you give this?	Evaluating
What did we learn today? Who can remember what we said about ...?	Summarising

There are different ways of classifying questions (Bloom, 1956; Kerry, 1982). In terms of classroom application, there are three main types of question (Table 8.4) which teachers can model and encourage pupils to draw upon, depending upon their purpose. It is not the case that one question type is more important than the other. Much depends upon the topic of conversation and the answers being sought. If pupils, for example, want to find out the facts and figures behind an event, place or character, then closed questions are more likely to be appropriate. On the other hand, divergent questions help to explore people's motives, feelings, beliefs and opinions. Philosophical questions deal with bigger, more abstract issues. Any system of questioning is context-specific. A question that may demand considerable thinking by one student may simply be a matter of recall for another. The National Strategies for literacy and numeracy (1997–2011) provided schools with much useful practical guidance on questioning, such as the Pedagogy and Practice unit on Assessment for Learning.[5]

Table 8.4 Different types of questions

Question type	Purposes	Examples
Closed (convergent)	To elicit straightforward answers	What is the name of ...? Who ate the porridge? Where did the battle take place? What colour was the get-away car? How many agree/disagree?
Open-ended (divergent)	To seek viewpoints; to stimulate imaginative, creative thinking; to explore different ideas or alternative solutions; to investigate relationships	Why? Why do you think this happened? I wonder what might happen if ...? Are you saying that ...? How do you think x felt afterwards? What other ways are there of viewing this? Can you show us? Can you close your eyes and visualise? What if ...? Tell me how ...
Philosophical (provocative)	To prompt deep thinking, the answers to which are open to informed, rational and honest disagreement	How did life begin? Is there a God? What is truth? Is this always true? Is dishonesty always a bad thing?

At Maidstone Grammar School for Girls each week, all students in Years 7 and 8 have a timetabled session based on 'Big Questions' such as the following:

- Where does my language come from?
- Is there life elsewhere in the Universe?
- What in the world are we doing about waste?
- Why do we have countries?
- Does money make the world go around?
- Where do we come from?
- What makes a great thinker?

---

[5]Available on the National Archives website: www.nationalarchives.gov.uk/ (accessed 20 June 2018).

In P4C sessions, the questions generated by the pupils themselves are displayed for whole-class discussion. Questions can be collected after each session and kept in a question book or displayed on the wall, for future reference. To make the process of collecting questions manageable, teaching assistants might scribe questions, pupils could share questions in pairs or smaller groups. At Deri View Primary School, the pupils write down their questions and vote either secretly or using counters on which one they would like to discuss. Here are some of the questions they have discussed:

- Is it still important to study handwriting in school?
- What makes a good friend?
- Should we have a summer holiday?
- What is bravery?
- What would you change in the world?

Teachers should talk to children about their questions, encouraging them to think about their different *purposes*, e.g. to gain information ('What is the name of …?'), to seek opinions ('Do you agree with …?'), to exercise judgement ('What mark would you give?'), or to draw inferences ('What might have happened here?'). They should also discuss how changing one word in a question can significantly alter its meaning, e.g. 'Why do people travel to remote parts of the world?' is very different from 'How do people travel …?'

By providing the class with regular opportunities to ask questions, see good examples and learn from each other, pupils' questions should become sharper and more profound. For instance, questions that challenge assumptions and call for evidence should be more forthcoming, such as 'What evidence do you have?' or 'How do you know this is true?' (Davidson and Worsham, 1992: 61).

One of the key responsibilities of the teacher is to model questioning and dialogue, e.g. 'I agree with X because …', 'Can you give me an example to support what you say?', 'I don't quite understand. Are you saying …?' Pupils need to see the language of thinking modelled appropriately (Table 8.5).

Table 8.5 Prompts for discussion

To instruct	Give directions	'The first step is …'
		'Next …'
		'The last part is …'
To inquire	Ask questions	Who? What? When? Where? Why? How?
		'What do you think?'
To test	Decide if something makes sense	'I still have a question about …'
		'What I learned is …'

(Continued)

Table 8.5 (Continued)

To describe	Tell about something	Use descriptive words and details
To compare and contrast	Show how two things are alike and different	'Here is something they both have in common ...' 'These are different from each other because ...'
To explain	Give examples	'This is an example of ...' 'This is important because ...'
To analyse	Discuss the parts of a bigger idea	'The parts of this include ...' 'We can make a diagram of this'
To hypothesise	Make a prediction based on what is known	'I can predict that ...' 'I believe that _____ will happen because ...' 'What might happen if ...?'
To deduce	Draw a conclusion or arriving at an answer	'The answer is because ...'
To evaluate	Judge something	'I agree with this because ...' 'I disagree because ...' 'I recommend that ...' 'A better solution would be ...' 'The factors that are most important are ...'

Source: adapted from Fisher (2008)

Democratic principles for discussion should also be fostered, e.g. in decision-making, turn-taking and cooperation. Haynes asked a group of junior pupils for their advice to teachers starting off with P4C. They suggested: 'Give children more time to think, to explain things to the teacher and longer to say things', 'teach in different ways' and 'include everyone'. A shy boy told her that teachers should 'encourage quiet ones to join in. Ask them directly what they think' (Haynes, 2002: 16).

Community of inquiry

Central to P4C is the notion of a community of inquiry, which brings people together (sometimes from diverse backgrounds) with the common purpose of exploring issues and questions. Over the years, different community of inquiry models have been developed (see Gunter et al., 2007) but the basic features are noted in Table 8.6.

The success or otherwise often hinges on the quality of relationships and whether participants are willing to share their understanding even when disagreements arise. This suggests that teachers should focus on building trust between children and developing their own skills as facilitators (see Chapter 11) in responding appropriately to children's

Table 8.6 Key features of a community of inquiry

- Focuses on a common interest, puzzle, issue, question or problem

- Typically involves a small group (4–6)

- Based around discussion and critical reflection

- Includes research methods such as gathering information and synthesising ideas

- Teacher acts as a facilitator rather than instructor in providing support and guidance.

cues. Such 'relational pedagogy' (Sabol and Pianta, 2012) is not straightforward to master and requires skill, commitment and perseverance. Technically speaking, facilitators are not so much interested in the outcomes or the topic under discussion but the process. The 'true' facilitator's role is to ensure that the group has the best opportunity to explore relevant issues and reach informed conclusions (Bee and Bee, 1998).

High-quality facilitation means adopting a neutral position, providing factual and objective information as required by the group, questioning effectively to draw out views, behaving in a non-judgemental way and monitoring the group to encourage it to review its own performance and progress. Clearly the quality of interaction is governed largely by the climate of trust and relationships. Put another away, these are the kinds of behaviours to avoid when facilitating philosophical discussions:

- telling the pupils exactly what they should discuss and how to do it
- expressing set ideas about what is right and wrong
- directing the group to preconceived answers and solutions.

At times, difficult issues may arise, which call for sensitive handling. War and death are obvious examples, which may upset children, but anything in the news (e.g. a terrorist attack, a natural disaster, the closure of a local business resulting in family unemployment) might cause anxiety. While philosophical sessions should not double up as therapy or counselling services, it is unrealistic to assume that pupils are unaffected by what is happening at home, in the community and the wider world. Moreover, children do feel passionate about issues, such as animal welfare and the environment, and may feel a desire to express their feelings. A good facilitator will establish a climate where anyone at any time can opt out of a discussion if the content is causing distress. This is particularly the case with personal issues, which are inappropriate to discuss in a public forum. In such cases, the wise course of action is to explain that this is not something to be talked about here and now, but could be discussed in private later if necessary. It may be appropriate to agree with individuals that they can privately signal (e.g. code word) if there are personal issues that they would not want to discuss.

For communities of inquiry to flow well, participants need structure and support in working collaboratively. One of the challenges is ensuring that the kind of talk associated with a community of inquiry does not descend into mere chat or informal conversation. It should be focused and logical, while also allowing opportunities for more creative contributions. It should draw on multiple viewpoints rather than be dominated by one or two voices. The discussion should also occur within an appropriate ethical framework, where each participant feels valued, respected, safe and included. The facilitating skills then are demanding. Fortunately, there is plenty of guidance for teachers, based on the experience of effectively conducting group discussions and fostering cooperative learning (e.g. Baines et al., 2016).

Group work

Philosophical discussions can be held among groups as well as with the whole class. Effective group work in school can contribute to improving pupils' attainment when compared with pupils working alone (Johnson and Johnson, 1999). However, success depends on whether the group is set realistic and achievable goals that call for cooperation and if they respond positively to feedback – they sink or swim together. Merely arranging pupils in groups does not necessarily lead to learning and thinking interdependently. Some pupils may not participate because they are shy or uncooperative while others may dominate discussions.

It has been known for many years that effective collaborative learning and thinking does not necessarily follow when children are arranged in groups (Galton et al., 1980). As Richardson (1999) points out, children may work *in* groups but seldom work *as* groups. Findings from the SPRinG (Social Pedagogic Research into Groupwork) project show that group skills such as communication need to be directly taught (Blatchford et al., 2005). During group discussions, some teachers are concerned about off-task behaviour and increased disruption (Blatchford et al., 2005) while some pupils get frustrated or disappointed when they are not selected to answer a question. Others feel a sense of relief at being let 'off the hook'. The American educationalist Spencer Kagan maintains that children may feel secretly glad that their peers answer questions incorrectly because this gives them a chance for recognition. Since the 1970s, Kagan has developed more than 200 content-free strategies (known as Kagan Structures) to support more cooperative learning. He defines this as occurring when small, heterogeneous groups of students work together to achieve a common goal (Kagan, 1994). Examples of structures include:

- Timed Pair Share – one partner speaks for a set time while the other listens, before switching roles
- Round Robin – small teams take turns responding orally to a specific prompt, e.g. 'What makes a good speaker?'

- RallyCoach – partners take turns to solve a problem while the other coaches, then partners switch over
- Numbered Heads Together – pupils work within small teams, with individuals numbered 1 to 4. Individuals think about the issue or question with no talking. They then privately write their answers before putting their heads together to share and reach a consensus. The teacher or a 'spinner' then randomly selects a number from each team, who then writes the answer on the team response board or communicates this orally.

These strategies are effective in promoting strong interpersonal relationships (Slavin, 1991; Johnson et al., 2000) with the optimum group membership typically comprising one high, two middle and two low achieving pupils.

Similarly, inquiry skills also need to be modelled and cannot be taken for granted. Stanley and Bowkett (2004) suggest using 'building blocks' (a set of laminated cards that look like bricks) to erect a wall of skills. Each building block shows one skill such as:

- look for links between questions
- give reasons for our answers
- illustrate our thoughts and questions
- work together to sort out any problems
- ask others to clarify meaning
- recognise inconsistencies in arguments.

At the end of a session, the group discuss whether enough members used the skill on the card for it to be put up on the wall. The aim is to build a solid wall of interlinked bricks. What matters is the strength of the wall, i.e. the skills, rather than how long it takes to assemble.

Session plenary

Towards the end of a philosophical session, the class are brought together often in a circle to share a summary and evaluation. Those who have not contributed are invited to do so. In one school, the teacher compiles a 'Question of the week' book each week. These are then displayed in the foyer for parents and visitors to read and add their thoughts.

IMPACT

There is strong evidence that Philosophy for Children enhances pupils' thinking, literacy and mathematical skills (Sharp and Reed, 1991; Trickey and Topping, 2004; McCall, 2009). Naylor (2013), a practising primary teacher, believes that P4C has raised pupils' standards of speaking and listening, increased their vocabulary, self-confidence and enhanced problem-solving skills. Pupils at Deri View Primary School are in no doubt that P4C helps them learn: 'It allows you to find out what other people think and share your ideas without being judged'. In an independent evaluation of P4C based on forty-eight schools, Gorard et al. (2015) report that one-hour-per-week structured discussions have a marked positive impact on leaners in terms of cognitive skills, attainment in reading and mathematics, confidence to speak, listening skills and self-esteem. The teachers report that the programme's success depends on how well it is incorporated into the timetable on a regular basis. Haynes (2002: 12) is of the view that 'regular participation almost certainly contributes to the development of individual self-awareness and resilience'. Fisher (1998) cites positive teacher reflections on the use of stories for thinking. These include perceived improvements in children's self-esteem, listening skills, questioning, literacy and enjoyment of responding to challenges. McCall (2009) undertook a five-year research project with 5-year-olds to see how well they responded to philosophical reasoning. The Community of Philosophical Inquiry (CoPI) method generated lots of purposeful discussion and confirmation that young children can handle abstract ideas, contradictions and uncertainties, provided they learn in a supportive and challenging environment.

SUMMARY

◌ Philosophy means 'a love of wisdom'. It sets out to engage with some of life's fundamental questions.

◌ The traditional view was that philosophy was something best left to adults given they have the knowledge and experience to reflect upon. However, there is now a recognition that philosophy can be taught to children by building on their natural curiosity.

◌ Lipman introduced Philosophy for Children (P4C) using specifically written novels as a means of engaging children's interest and promoting purposeful discussion and inquiry.

◌ Given the central importance of language to thinking, P4C and other philosophical approaches strongly support the teaching of talk.

◌ A typical P4C session involves a mental warm-up, discussion around a story or some other stimulus and a summary.

◌ The facilitator plays an important role allowing and supporting participants to follow their own discussion based on the stimulus provided.

◌ A community of inquiry provides opportunities for pupils to think collaboratively.

◌ The Society for the Advancement of Philosophical Enquiry and Reflection in Education (SAPERE) provides useful resources and ideas to support teachers interested in developing philosophical approaches in the classroom.

◌ There is strong evidence that philosophical approaches such as P4C enhance a range of skills and dispositions.

COGNITIVE ACCELERATION

INTRODUCTION

The term 'acceleration' is associated with speeding up and moving faster. With this in mind, the term 'Cognitive Acceleration' (CA) refers to a teaching method that aims to promote and accelerate the development of pupils' cognitive abilities. Its underlying premise is that there is some form of general cognitive processing function in children, which develops with age and is influenced by the environment. The approach is grounded in constructionist theory drawn from Piaget and Vygotsky and supports the principle that learners, when in an environment which promotes challenge and collaboration, can improve their thinking. CA offers learners the chance to think deeply and reflect carefully on the process of learning that has happened in a lesson, and to consider ways to improve. This is done through peer interaction, which allows learning to happen because of pupils composing and colliding ideas with one another in a supportive context (Hu et al., 2013).

BACKGROUND

The first Cognitive Acceleration work was developed at King's College London in the early 1980s. The initial research focused on junior and secondary science students (aged 12–14 years old). This produced the Cognitive Acceleration through Science Education (CASE) (Adey et al., 1989) materials, followed by similar resources in mathematics (CAME) including PCAME (Adhami et al., 1995), a series of mathematics lessons for Years 5 and 6. Materials for developing thinking in primary science were also developed, as were materials for the youngest learners – for example through *Let's Think Early Years!* (Robertson, 2006), *Let's Think!* (Adey et al., 2001) and *Let's Think Through Maths!* (Adhami et al., 2004). The teaching of English (Key Stage 1–4) was supported through *Let's Think in English*. There are also materials to support teaching across the broader curriculum, for example in technology (Backwell and Hamaker, 2004) and junior/secondary music, drama and visual arts (Gouge and Yates, 2002). Each set of materials has an associated professional development course. These are 'intervention' programmes in two senses: they aim to intervene in the cognitive development of students, and the activities are interventions in the normal curriculum (Adey, 2005).

The CA approach to children's learning draws upon both Piagetian and Vygotskian perspectives. Piaget (1950) suggested that when learners encounter a new situation, they adapt their understanding of what is happening to make sense of the experience. They construct this meaning based on their experience. Piaget saw the child as an active participant in the learning process, bringing prior experiences with them into new learning situations. Each new experience means that the individual amends and adapts their existing understanding. Intellectual growth happens when the individual meets a new situation that conflicts with their existing understanding. This is what Piaget termed a state of disequilibrium – or cognitive conflict – and learning happens when the conflict is resolved. This 'construction' of meaning is something done by the individual, and happens in progressive steps as the learner matures biologically. These steps follow a hierarchical and predictable sequence based upon stages of cognitive development. Piaget's main focus was on the individual learner, but he did place value on social interactions, and he discussed the importance of argument and discussion in development (Piaget, 1924; 1928 in Muller et al., 2009).

Social constructivism is a closely associated learning theory, which owes much to the writing of the influential psychologist Lev Vygotsky (1978). He proposed that learning happens within a social context. Like Piaget, Vygotsky also believed that children constructed their own knowledge through interaction (Conkbayir and Pascal, 2015). However, he placed emphasis on the importance of the social context as well, and viewed language as an important tool in eliciting, transforming and shaping children's thoughts and ideas. This learning happens when a more knowledgeable other supports and extends the learning of an individual, which Vygotsky (1978: 86) describes as learning in the 'Zone of Proximal Development':

❛ The distance between the actual development level as determined by independent problem solving and the level of potential development as determined through problem solving under adult guidance, or in collaboration with more capable peers. ❜

Social constructivism has an emphasis on collaboration as a means of learning. While the individual has a crucial role in forming their own understanding of the world, they do not act alone in this process. As with constructivist learning theory, the view of the individual as active in the learning process is also one of the central tenets of the social constructivist view. Learners still have responsibility for constructing their own understanding of the world, but this happens because of their many and varied interactions. The CA approach builds on both theories so that pupils, in collaboration with peers, construct their learning through increasingly complex lessons in which the cognitive demands of activities are high.

INTRODUCING THE RESOURCES

Each set of materials includes teacher notes and resources. The number and detail of these varies – for example CASE and CAME provide one special activity to be used every two weeks instead of a regular science/mathematics lesson over two years, whereas *Let's Think!* provides one special half-hour activity to be fitted into lessons for Year 1 (5-year-olds) once a week for one year, and *Let's Think Through Science!* offers one activity every two weeks for one year for Year 3 children (7-year-olds). While some are designed for working with a small group of children (e.g. *Let's Think!*), others can be used with a whole class (e.g. PCAME). Irrespective of subject or intended age group, the materials all rest on the same five methodological pillars and all aim to promote general intellectual development (Figure 9.1). The five pillars are Concrete Preparation, Cognitive Conflict, Social Construction, Metacognition and Bridging. Although these are discussed sequentially here, in a CA lesson pillars may be revisited several times in an ongoing cycle.

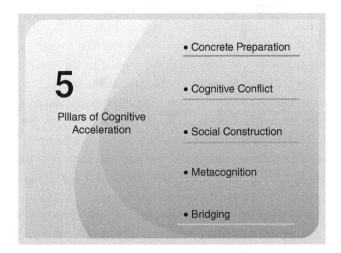

Figure 9.1 The five pillars of Cognitive Acceleration

The first pillar is that of **Concrete Preparation**. This part of the lesson typically lasts for five to ten minutes, and happens at the very start of the lesson. In this part of the session, a common language for the activities is negotiated between teacher and pupils and the teacher ensures that the pupils are familiar with the context and framing of the activity. These pillars can be illustrated through the first lesson in the PCAME mathematics materials.

This lesson is designed to develop mathematical ideas relating to multiplication and algebra, with a focus on number relations. The intended audience is a class of Year 5 (9–10-year-old) pupils. The lesson is entitled 'Sports League'. In one primary school in south Wales, the teacher planned the Concrete Preparation phase of this lesson to involve several short, focused activities. The teacher arranged the class into mixed-ability groups of three to four pupils. Firstly, they were encouraged to discuss in their group what good 'teamwork' means. They had three minutes to discuss this, before summarising three key elements they all agreed upon. These were then shared with the class, and key ideas noted on the interactive whiteboard. Typical responses included 'taking turns', 'listening and respecting other people's ideas', and 'sharing good ideas'. During this activity, the teacher observed carefully, looking at the group dynamics and encouraging participation. The pupils then were set a one-minute task – to think up as many sports as possible that are played in teams. This encouraged them to work together and provide ideas – the teacher noted that this allowed all pupils to join in and they were highly engaged. The final part of the Concrete Preparation phase involved the teacher spending a few minutes discussing with the pupils the notion of sports leagues – ensuring that all were familiar with the concept, and discussing matters such as home and away fixtures and league tables.

The second pillar is **Cognitive Conflict**. The teacher conceives of a situation that creates cognitive dissonance in the pupils' minds. In other words, their existing ideas are challenged by new information. While this could cause a sense of discomfort or even anxiety in pupils, the third pillar of the CA approach, Social Construction, minimises this. In other words, during a CA activity pupils work together to come up with a solution to what is a challenging question. They are not left alone to struggle, but are encouraged to discuss and try out solutions together. In the case of the Sports League lesson, pupils were asked to work in groups to find out how many fixtures would be played in a league where there are three teams (the sport being considered can vary, as can the names of the teams chosen). In this lesson, the teams were called 'Carlo's Champs', 'Penelope's Party' and 'Scarlet's Stars'. The children were given five minutes to discuss this and show on a large piece of paper how they had reached their decision about the number of matches that would be played by these three teams.

The teacher's use of language was important here, she did not say 'write' on the paper, the word 'show' was deliberately used so that pupils could use a variety of recording methods. This challenge created several strategies among the pupils to find the answer.

After five minutes these different ideas were discussed and shared among the whole class so that the **Social Construction** principle now extended beyond the individual group to include all the pupils. Everyone agreed that there would be six fixtures in total because of the home and away matches (Figure 9.2). The pupils were very interested to see that different groups had solved the problem in different ways. For example, some wrote out the fixtures in full sentences such as:

> Carlo's Champs play Scarlet's Stars at home.
>
> Penelope's Party play Carlo's Champs at home.

Others found that they could complete this challenge more quickly if they used some shorthand instead, for example by using initials and a 'v' for versus rather than writing 'plays' as in 'PP v CC'. They also decided that writing 'at home' was unnecessary since 'the first team is always the one at home – 'we don't need to say that'. One group had recorded the matches more systematically, using abbreviations and a diagram.

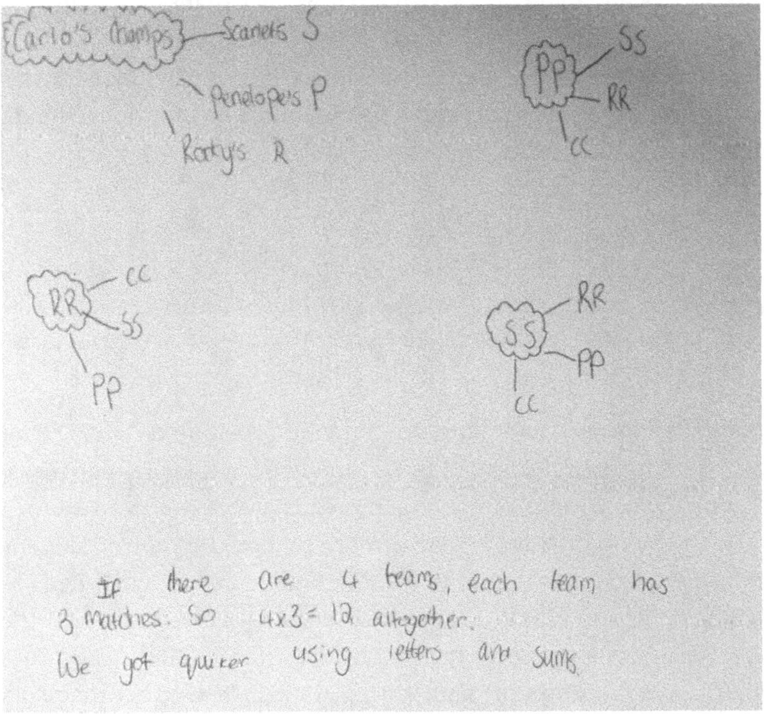

Figure 9.2 Diagrammatic representation of the matches played

The teacher encouraged the pupils to develop the fourth pillar of **Metacognition** throughout the activity, and particularly when discussing their emerging thinking. For example, as the pupils considered their own groups' strategy after the discussion and sharing, they were beginning to think about what had been successful, and what they might need to change. Metacognition is a key part of the CA process. Larkin (2010: 30) argues that if we want children to make 'thoughtful and wise life decisions', developing their metacognitive awareness is crucial. The pupils were encouraged to think about whether they could improve their strategy, and make it more efficient. Each group considered whether they would make changes to their strategy, and most said that they would. For example, some pupils had used images of players' shirts to illustrate the teams; however, they decided that while this 'looks nice, it takes a bit too long to do'. Their decisions were based on the discussions with their peers and on their reflections on their own strategies.

Further challenge was then added to the session – by introducing a fourth team. Pupils predicted how many matches would be played and then, using their amended strategies, worked out whether their prediction was accurate. Pupils devised strategies such as tables to help them work more efficiently. Figure 9.3 shows one group's responses during the lesson. This cycle was repeated for five teams, and then the teacher encouraged the pupils to begin to look for patterns and mathematical knowledge that might help them calculate the number of matches that could be played for larger leagues.

At this point in the session the teacher prompted the pupils to look for mathematical patterns. Some of the pupils could explain how they could use multiplication facts to help them calculate the number of matches, without the need to draw anything. For example, one pupil explained:

> If you have 20 teams, you can't play against yourself, but you can play all the others. So I would work it out by saying 20 x 19, because 19 is one less than the number of teams. You could say that for any number of teams – just times it by that number take away 1.

From this point, the teacher could introduce some simple algebra – talking about whether this could be true of 'any number' (n) of teams, and helping the pupils discuss and explain how the solution to the number of matches played could be expressed by the formula of 'n x (n–1)'. This part of the session provided a bridge, both to known mathematical facts and strategies, and to consideration of how to become more efficient when solving problems. Through bridging and reflection, pupils are encouraged to consider how the successful strategies they used help them solve the problems (metacognition), and secondly to use their imagination to explore how the same strategies might be used in other school learning contexts, or beyond. This is designed to increase the depth of insight the pupils have into the content of the activity, and helps them to identify transferrable learning opportunities.

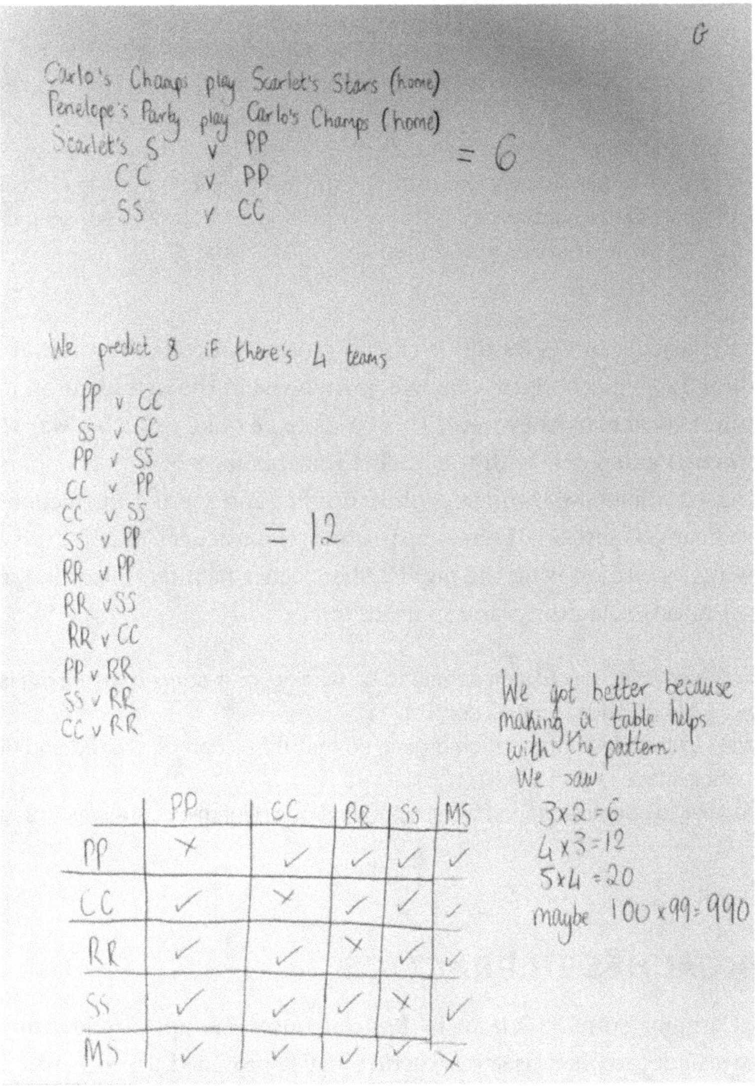

Figure 9.3 Progression in strategy during the Sports League lesson

The five pillars interweave during a lesson, and are revisited as new challenges are set, discussed and solved. Oliver and Venville (2017) suggest that the success of CA approaches is due to the cognitive challenges that are set, the pedagogy that drives the discussion and metacognition – they suggest that these strategies together improve student reasoning, supporting development through Piagetian levels. Adey and Shayer (2011: 18) suggest that the structure and principles (or pillars) of a CA lesson are interrelated:

'In practice, it is the cognitive conflict that generates the social construction and it is the process of exploring explanations through dialogue which maintains the cognitive conflict. Metacognition is another opportunity for social construction and it, too, brings its own quota of cognitive conflict. Interestingly it is sometimes the more able students, for whom it is difficult to generate cognitive conflict, who find difficulty with the process of explaining how they learned something, or how they solved a problem. 'I just did it', 'It's obvious' are typical responses.'

The role of the teacher in CA lessons is crucial. In the Concrete Preparation phase they must introduce the pupils both to what will be involved in the investigation to come and to any technical vocabulary they need. This needs to be done in such a way that most of the class can enter a dialogue with the teacher that creates a common understanding of the activity which will follow. During Cognitive Conflict and Social Construction phases, the teacher's role changes. Instead of direct instruction, the teacher's main task is to scan the class, observing and monitoring the pupils. The teacher facilitates learning, rather than instructing or directing learning, and so needs to:

- intervene when group discussion seems to be waning, or if some questioning is needed to create challenge and cognitive conflict
- remain alert to the ideas that are emerging, so that these can be shared and discussed with the whole class
- maximise peer to peer interaction by monitoring group dynamics carefully throughout the session.

CA APPROACHES IN PRACTICE

St Robert's Catholic Primary School in Bridgend uses CA approaches throughout all classes. CA was adopted because the teachers felt it provided a good structure for the development of problem-solving skills. They felt CA provided challenging scenarios and problems for the children to tackle, and enabled them to apply their mathematics to real world, authentic contexts. The focus on collaboration also fitted well with the school's teaching and learning strategy. Barbara Murphy, the school's deputy headteacher and Year 5/6 teacher, felt that the sessions enabled pupils to develop some of the higher-level skills such as algebra, essential for achieving a level 5 or above at the end of the Key Stage (at a time when level descriptors were used).

The school tailors the use of CA so that sessions are fitted in, as and when appropriate. If pupils have been focusing on number patterns, then a suitable lesson is chosen at the end of the unit for the class to apply their learning and see the relevance of the mathematics they are learning to the real world. Sometimes the CA approach is used if the context links to a class topic or unit of work, e.g. a sporting topic such as the World Cup might mean the class will do the league tables activity. This enables pupils to develop their use of numeracy across the curriculum.

Generally, pupils are grouped by ability in these sessions but Barbara notes that she has also carried out many sessions with mixed ability groupings, and finds that both organisational approaches work well. In an ability group setting, higher ability pupils can be fully challenged and lower ability pupils supported either by adaptation of the task or adult input. Likewise, in a mixed ability setting, the collaborative nature of the sessions means that pupils can support each other in completing tasks and finding solutions. Those who are confident in mathematical skills may in fact be supported in applying these by pupils who are good at thinking logically and strategically. This mixed grouping allows for social construction to occur, and can be very powerful.

Barbara says that children throughout the school enjoy the sessions and nearly all are engaged fully with the different activities. She feels that the scenarios are very accessible to the pupils and allow them to see the importance of mathematics in the world around us. In addition to enjoying the sessions and the collaborative nature of them, she has found the CAME approach to be an effective way of extending the knowledge and understanding of pupils.

The Appendix includes a lesson plan for a CA lesson, created by Barbara. The planning shows how Barbara could build practical elements, such as working outside the classroom, assessment for learning and mathematical content into a lesson called 'Beanbag PickUp' (Appendix 3).

IMPACT

There have been numerous extensive empirical studies that report promising results relating to the impact of CA on long-term achievement, as measured in standardised tests (e.g. Adey et al., 2002; Adey and Shayer, 2011). There is a significant evidence base relating to CA approaches. Meta-analysis shows an above average mean effect size of 0.61 (Trickey and Topping 2004, in Higgins et al., 2005), while Hattie reports effect sizes of 0.60+ for CA approaches (Hattie, 2012). Cognitive Acceleration programmes have also been successfully adapted to educational contexts in countries outside the UK such as Finland, Australia, China, Ireland, Finland and the USA (Oliver and Venville, 2017).

As well as internationally in different cultural contexts, CA approaches have had an impact across age groups and subjects (Adey et al., 2002; Adey and Shayer, 2011). Internationally recognised, peer reviewed research carried out over twenty-five years at King's College, London, has repeatedly shown that students who experience a Cognitive Acceleration programme score higher than matched control groups in several cognitive and attainment tests including GCSE examinations. These include:

- measures of cognitive development immediately at the end of the programme and subsequently
- the subject matter of the programme (e.g. science, mathematics) up to three years after the end of the programme
- subjects other than the initial subject context up to three years after the end of the programme. For example, students who followed the CASE programme over two years when they were 12–13 years old went on to score significantly higher grades in an English examination taken three years later.

Over 2,000 secondary mathematics, science and primary teachers from more than 1,000 schools have been trained to use Cognitive Acceleration concepts and techniques. CAME, for example, is the only research-based intervention cited in the two most recent Ofsted subject reports on calculation in primary mathematics and on school mathematics (Ofsted, 2011). In Western Australia, over thirty schools are currently using CASE and CAME in a replication intervention programme. Oliver and Venville (2017) report on the positive effects of this extension, with an effect size of 0.47 on a set of standardised science reasoning tasks for students whose teachers had been trained in the CASE approach. Moreover, students were overwhelmingly positive about the CA lessons. In China, CA techniques are used in over 300 schools, reaching more than 200,000 students. In addition to showing that the approach is effective at raising attainment even in the high attaining Chinese context, Cognitive Acceleration has also addressed a significant additional concern among Chinese educators and policy-makers: the need for a greater emphasis on the promotion of creativity in school education. In a two-year intervention study, Hu et al. (2013: 17) found that Cognitive Acceleration enhances scientific creativity, reporting that the approach established 'an open, democratic and positive activity atmosphere', and 'encourag[ed] students to spend more time discussing problems with partners, thinking independently, speaking out their own ideas bravely, and judging others' views'.

Sarah Cunningham is the Year 6 teacher at Berrywood Primary School, a three-form entry school, on the outskirts of Southampton. She has started to use *Let's Think in English* with her pupils, and feels positive about the results. Sarah writes:

Let's Think has acted as an intervention for the teaching of reading. With a greater emphasis having been placed on reasoning and the mastery approach to teaching seeking a depth of understanding, *Let's Think* provides a collaborative structure, which encourages the children to feed off each other's responses. As a result of this, a classroom culture has been established whereby children feel at ease to share their opinion and can respectfully agree and disagree with each other, ultimately leading to deeper thinking. The metacognitive aspects of the *Let's Think* lessons ensure children can identify how their thinking has changed and what caused the change. The pedagogies and approaches used in *Let's Think* lessons have also been used and adapted in other lessons such as mathematics, whereby children are reasoning with each other more. SAT's scores have risen in reading 71 per cent in 2016 to 81 per cent in 2017. Furthermore, there is also greater evidence of the children inferring and referring to the text in their written responses to texts.

Year 6 pupils at the school are also positive about the impact that *Let's Think* has had on their learning. They comment on improvements in creative thinking – for instance Jordan suggests that *Let's Think* has helped him to think 'outside the box'. Pupils also indicate that the approach has improved skills in reading – for example, Sophie says:

> The *Let's Think* lessons have helped me to read through the text more carefully and look for clues in words I wouldn't normally look at. Although sometimes I don't want to answer the question, it has boosted my confidence to try.

This is echoed by Ruth, who suggests that specific skills have been improved through the approach:

> *Let's Think* has helped me with my inference skills and my skills for backing up my opinion. I have also learnt how to link other ideas to the conversation and plan out what to say before saying it.

The approach has also impacted on their confidence – so that they are more willing to express their views, and enter into discussion about them, as explained by Zoe, who says that:

> I say my answers in better ways and have more confidence to disagree with others' opinions if my own are different.

Further examples of how CA approaches are implemented in a secondary school context, and of their impact, can be found in Chapter 11, where Dr Martina Lecky, the headteacher of Ruislip High School, discusses her experiences of the approach across the school.

CHALLENGES

One of the main challenges associated with CA approaches lies with the requirement of creating appropriate opportunities to discuss and develop understanding through social construction. Such opportunities may be challenging to achieve in practice, and numerous studies have commented upon the difficulties of developing exchanges that contain high quality adult–child interaction (e.g. Robson and Hargreaves, 2005). Certainly, Adey and Shayer (2011: 18) provide words of caution – CA materials are not simply 'a set of print and IT resources which can be bought as a package and implemented without thought'. As with any thinking approach or materials, the role of the teacher in understanding the principles underpinning the approach, and in promoting and extending the learning, is crucial.

SUMMARY

- CA is based largely on the learning theories of Piaget and Vygotsky.
- Challenging contexts and collaboration in learning can lead to gains for all participants in a task, if the teacher knows the concept of acceleration needs to be balanced by what is developmentally appropriate for a child at any given moment.
- The benefit of the CA materials is that they are designed to boost and accelerate pupils' thinking in a supportive manner – through careful teacher scaffolding, social interaction and appropriate challenge.

DISPOSITIONAL APPROACHES (HABITS OF MIND)

INTRODUCTION

What does it take to be excellent or perform consistently well, in any field? Over recent years much has been made of factors other than raw talent. A string of popular writers (Gladwell, 2009; Coyle, 2010; Syed, 2011; Duckworth, 2017) point to the 'myth' of talent and the importance of cultivating dispositions, hard work and a positive outlook to achieve success. In one study, the success of Olympic swimmers was explained not in terms of talent but wide-ranging factors such as: living in southern California where everyone swims and the sun shines all year; parents who are interested in sport; above-average family income to meet travel and coaching costs; the luck of having a good coach; and the physical attributes of the swimmer, i.e. height, weight and proportions – the amount of talent needed for athletic success was 'strikingly low' (Chambliss, 1989). The world's leading swimmers painstakingly apply themselves to learning dozens of small skills – how to place hands in the water so no air is cupped in them, streamlined push off from the wall, how to eat the right foods, wearing the best swimming suit for racing and so on. The 'little things' count in becoming a top athlete. What also really matters is the determination of most Olympic champions to overcome setbacks and difficulties such as physical injuries. Other research suggests that outstanding performance is largely the result of hard work or 'deliberate practice' (Ericsson, 1993; Colvin, 2008), incrementally developed habits, consistently and correctly applied over many years.

While studies of exceptional performance can prove instructive, for example in providing good role models, we should not ignore the fact that most people who aim for the top in any walk of life never get there and this is not due to a lack of effort. Of 9,000 boys who are members of leading football academies and schools of excellence, 90 per cent will fail to make the first team and very few will become professional footballers (Williams, 2009). This is despite huge investment in time and effort, by parents as well as the boys themselves. Football's biggest issue is said to be the psychological damage caused to those whose dreams are shattered at a young age (Conn, 2017). One of the greatest challenges for young people today is learning to handle setbacks. In this chapter, we focus on the kinds of dispositions that ordinary people, as well as the exceptional few, demonstrate successfully when they face problems, challenges and issues.

BACKGROUND

The contribution of Art Costa and Bena Kallick reflects, over recent years, a growing trend among educationalists and psychologists who see intelligence as more than simply how well we think as measured by narrow standardised tests. While these provide a politically significant snapshot of academic performance (focused largely on literacy and numeracy), intelligence has a broader and more fluid meaning (e.g. Lazear, 1991; Gardner, 1993; Feuerstein, 2003; Armstrong, 2017). Advances in our understanding of child development, neuroscience and educational practice, along with the demands of modern life, point to the need for schools to recognise and cater for the diverse needs and capabilities of learners.

Standardised cognitive tests do not assess how well students develop the qualities, skills and dispositions they need to succeed in life, e.g. getting along well with others, self-motivation, flexible thinking and teamwork (Caproni, 2017). In *Successful Intelligence*, Sternberg (1996) suggested that less than 25 per cent of someone's job success is determined by his or her intelligence quotient (IQ). School-leavers may gain a clutch of certificates but struggle to adjust to the demands of the workplace or life in general. This is not to undermine the importance of academic achievements, but to recognise that the educational system does not meet the needs of many young people. One survey of a thousand secondary school-leavers reports that 76 per cent said their schools train them just to get good grades rather than prepare them for the world of work (Ali, 2015), while employers regularly complain about a lack of work readiness among applicants. One report on behalf of McDonalds UK (2015) forecasts that by 2020 over half a million employees will be held back by deficits in what it calls 'soft skills clusters' such as teamwork skills (e.g. working with multiple approaches), self-management skills (e.g. working well under pressure), decision-making (e.g. engaging in life-long learning, creative and innovative solutions), and communicating skills (e.g. listening effectively and communicating accurately and concisely). These are essentially the kind of skills, qualities and dispositions that Costa and Kallick call Habits of Mind and which schools need to cultivate if youngsters are to lead fulfilling lives.

The actual phrase Habits of Mind has its roots in the writings of the philosopher John Dewey. In 1910, Dewey wrote *How We Think* in which he stated that the business of teaching was to 'transform natural tendencies into trained habits of thought' and 'fortify the mind against irrational tendencies' (Dewey, 1910: 26). Costa (1981: 29–32) first used the expression 'teaching for intelligent behaviour' and was later struck by a phrase used by the psychologist Lauren Resnick in which she suggested that 'one's intelligence is the sum of one's habits of mind' (Resnick, 1999: 38).

Typically, effective thinkers are alert to contextual cues and respond with certain intellectual behaviours that often enable them to achieve their goals. Over time, these behaviours are strengthened through reflecting on experience and modifications so that performance improves. For Costa, what matters is not so much the behaviour of learning to solve problems but the internalised habit of doing so effectively on a routine basis. He duly established the Institute for Habits of Mind with the mission 'to transform schools into learning communities where thinking and Habits of Mind are taught, practiced, valued and infused into the culture'.[1] Similarly, the Art Costa Centre for Thinking was set up to engage teachers, parents, students and businesses in making the Habits of Mind relevant to school, home and the workplace.[2]

Costa and Kallick, who started to work together in 1998, define Habits of Mind as patterns of thinking, intellectual behaviours or dispositions that empower creative and critical thinking. They identified sixteen of these habits (Photo 10.1), building on the work of other researchers in the field (Feuerstein, 1980; Ennis, 1985; Perkins, 1985; Sizer, 1992; Goleman, 1995):

1. Persisting
2. Thinking and communicating with clarity and precision
3. Managing Impulsivily
4. Gathering data through all senses
5. Listening with understanding and empathy
6. Creating, imagining, innovating
7. Thinking flexlbly
8. Responding with wonderment and awe

---

[1] www.habitsofmindinstitute.org/about-us/us/ (accessed 21 June 2018).
[2] www.artcostacentre.com (accessed 21 June 2018).

9. Thinking about thinking (metacognition)
10. Taking responsible risks
11. Striving for accuracy
12. Finding humour
13. Questioning and posing problems
14. Thinking interdependently
15. Applying past knowledge to new situations
16. Remaining open to continuous learning.

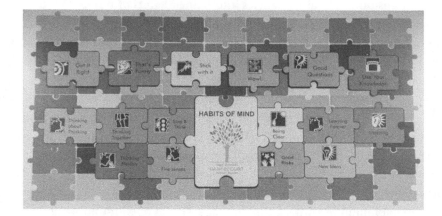

Photo 10.1 Habits of Mind wall display

Guy Claxton and colleagues developed a *Building Learning Power* programme based around seventeen dispositions, seen as the UK cousins of Habits of Mind (Claxton, 2002; Claxton et al, 2011). Other writers use different terms and fewer characteristics, but they essentially describe the same thing. Deakin Crick and Goldspink (2014) refer to seven 'learning power dimensions', such as critical curiosity (an orientation to want to 'get beneath the surface') and resilience (the readiness and openness to persevere in the face of challenge). Lilian Katz (1988: 30) was among the first scholars to discuss dispositions, which she defined as 'habits of the mind, tendencies to respond to situations in certain ways'. She later elaborated on this, referring to 'pattern of behavior exhibited frequently and in the absence of coercion and constituting a habit of mind under some conscious and voluntary control, and that is intentional and oriented to broad goals' (Katz, 1993: 16). Although Katz said little about how to develop dispositions, she thought that they were best acquired through modelling rather than instruction.

St John (2010) conducted interviews with more than 500 highly successful people, including the likes of Bill Gates, Richard Branson, Donald Trump and Oprah Winfrey, and found that they shared eight traits. These traits are not here referring to genetically determined characteristics but dispositions that can be cultivated. St John calls these the '8 to be great' and there is clear (though not exact) alignment with Costa and Kallick's Habits of Mind:

1. Successful people are passionate about what they do (*Responding with wonderment and awe*).
2. Successful people work hard while having fun (*Finding humour*).
3. Successful people have a specific focus (*Striving for accuracy*).
4. Successful people push themselves out of their comfort zones (*Take responsible risks*).
5. Successful people consistently come up with new ideas (*Creating, imagining and innovating*).
6. Successful people are constantly getting better (*Remaining open to continuous learning*).
7. Successful people provide value to others (*Thinking interdependently*).
8. Successful people are persistent through failure (*Persisting*).

In education, Costa and Kallick envisage Habits of Mind forming a bridge between different subjects and curriculum themes. They believe that schools can teach and cultivate these habits so that students can behave more intelligently. They highlight six dimensions that need to be incorporated within the Habits of Mind if they are to make a difference to the quality of learning.

- **Value**: Choosing to employ a pattern of intellectual behaviors rather than other, less productive patterns.
- **Inclination**: Feeling the tendency to employ a pattern of intellectual behaviors.
- **Sensitivity**: Perceiving opportunities for, and appropriateness of, employing the pattern of behaviors.
- **Capability**: Possessing the basic skills and capacities to carry through with the behaviors.
- **Commitment**: Constantly striving to reflect on and improve performance of the pattern of intellectual behaviors.
- **Policy**: Making it a policy to promote and incorporate the patterns of intellectual behaviors into actions, decisions, and resolutions of problematic situations. Costa and Kallick (2008: 17)

INTRODUCING THE RESOURCES

This section reviews the importance of the sixteen Habits of Mind, which represent the life skills and dispositions needed to work through challenges as evidenced by the experiences of those who have proven to be successful in life. These are explored at length because they complement the other approaches mentioned in previous chapters.

Persisting is the determination to stick at something especially when this is proving difficult. In a world of instant gratification and distraction, keeping at a task is demanding. One survey reports that 80 per cent of Americans break their New Year's resolution by the first week in February (Mulvey, 2017). Most teachers will have encountered pupils who say 'I can't do this' or 'this is too difficult'. They lack task persistence and tend to give up too soon. According to Kikas et al. (2014) when pupils struggle to keep going on tasks that are new, teacher-directed methods (e.g. modelling, explanation and drill) are likely to help pupils move forward more than child-centred approaches (e.g. play and open-ended exploration). On the other hand, pupils who have high levels of persistence generally respond better to child-centred teaching.

Language is central to thinking, although the exact relationship is a point of academic debate. Are words simply tools to express thoughts or does language shape what and how we think? What is less controversial is the importance of learning to **think and communicate with clarity and precision**. Unfortunately, this is something that many children and young people struggle to achieve. One recent study, based on an analysis of test data for cognitive abilities, suggests that each year around 30,000 GCSE pupils with 'hidden talents' underperform because they lack good communication skills required in examinations (GL Assessment, 2017). These children are regarded as spatial thinkers, those who think first in images and then convert thoughts into words. This is significant because many of these children have the potential to become scientists, technicians and engineers, which the UK desperately needs. Both Thomas Edison and Albert Einstein were regarded as spatial thinkers, who struggled with speech. Because standardised tests conducted in school do not typically include spatial measures, the argument runs that schools do not give enough attention to spatial thinking.

However, all young people need to learn how to communicate clearly and accurately irrespective of the field they wish to enter. Computer scientists, engineers and mathematicians need to learn how to communicate using correct names, labels and terms, just as much as historians, artists and writers. And yet many university students struggle to write clearly and resort to 'contract cheating' – tens of thousands of students buy professionally written essays for as much as £700 for an extended essay (Middleton, 2011; Yorke, 2017). The children's author Yvonne Coppard, who worked with university students, found that they struggled to follow a logical argument and the writing of many was sloppy, with 'sentences that draggle all over the place ... you can see whole pages without paragraphs, and as for speech punctuation – I don't know what's happened to that!' (Wilce, 2006).

Managing impulsivity is an important life skill. Impulsiveness can be productive when taking advantage of unexpected opportunities. This is known as functional impulsivity and it is particularly welcomed in fields such as advertising and public relations where quick thinking-on-your-feet is needed. However, impulsivity also has a negative side. Jumping into decisions without considering the consequences can have a detrimental impact in all aspects of life including health, relationships, finance, employment and education. Impulsivity can be a symptom of attention-deficit hyperactivity disorder (ADHD) although all children, at times, find it difficult to think before they act. Those who regularly struggle to control their impulses tend to be moody and are more likely to become involved in confrontation.

In the classroom, managing impulsivity is an important part of promoting behaviour for learning. Teachers are generally advised to focus on the impulsive act rather than the person so that impulsivity is not seen as a character flaw. Positive reinforcement when pupils control their impulses and instilling a sense of responsibility can also prove motivating. Visual reminders of how to resist impulsive behaviour and good role models also help. Specific techniques also have value, such as allocating pupils think or wait time ahead of answering questions and modelling pausing after a pupil asks a question. This is harder than one imagines. In a well-known study, Mary Budd Rowe (1986) found that the average teacher waits less than a second before calling on a student, asking another question or answering the question herself. By increasing this to three seconds, the quality of pupils' language and logical thinking improved, while the number of 'I don't know' responses decreased. Stahl (1990) introduced the term 'think time' as a distinct period of uninterrupted silence by the teacher and *all* pupils so that they both process information. Generations of educationalists have pointed out the importance of promoting young children's sensory development. Multisensory teaching is widely supported, particularly in the early years. Our brains **gather data through the senses**. To perform a role in a play requires movement, or to know the taste of marzipan, you have to eat it. When sensory pathways are alert and open, more information flows into the brain. Research reveals strong links between the senses (perception) and thinking (cognition) and the traditional separation of body, emotion and mind is widely challenged by academics. Claxton (2015) argues, for example, that it is misleading to think that the senses deliver information to the mind through one bodily door, with decisions then dispatched to the workhorses of the body through an opposite one. It is not simply a matter of seeing things, thinking about them, making decisions and finally doing things. Rather, the stomach, heart, senses and the brain are tightly bound together by chemical messages. The brain is the servant rather than the master of the body. A badly behaved bacterium in the gut, for instance, can quickly change the brain's decision. In short, it is one thinking eco system at work.

Listening with understanding and empathy is an active process of pausing, paraphrasing, interpreting and responding sensitively to messages. Pausing is necessary to take in what is said without interrupting. Paraphrasing or rewording the message enables the speaker to clarify intended meaning before the listener interprets what is said. Part of listening with empathy means knowing when to probe further for information if there is uncertainty in meaning. The pause-paraphrase-probe strategies can help pupils develop good listening skills so that they value and respect others. Such active, attentive listening goes beyond words to tune into feelings, body language and what is not said.

However, there are barriers at each stage of the listening process (Hargie, 2017). Noise can distort or block out incoming stimuli. Information may be too complex to understand. Our personal biases and prejudices can lead us to false assumptions. There are many competing distractions as the mind seeks to prioritise information. In-built filtering systems mean that at times we only pay attention to those ideas with which we agree or disagree or find relevant. Rather than focus attentively on what someone is saying it is easier to half-listen, jump in and give advice, or simply agree with whatever is being said to avoid argument. Discussing with pupils what makes a good listener (e.g. looking at someone, nodding, not interrupting, detecting emotional cues) and then providing opportunities to apply these signals in a range of contexts are steps teachers can take to improve pupils' listening skills. Creating an environment conducive to listening is also essential – classrooms that are too hot or cold, windows without blinds to keep out the bright sun, uncomfortable chairs, too many things going on, too much background noise – all of these factors hinder listening. Like other skills, learning to listen requires hard work and repeated practice.

As noted in Chapter 1, all humans have the capacity to think creatively in generating novel, valuable solutions. It is not the case that a few gifted individuals have a monopoly on creativity even though it is common to hear expressions such as 'I can't draw', 'I was never very good at art', 'I'm tone deaf' or 'I'm not very creative'. To strengthen **creating, imagining and innovating** as a Habit of Mind requires a commitment to see the world in different ways. Teaching pupils to observe carefully is a key skill – as St John (2010: 105) put it, 'Eye-Q can be more important than IQ'. Contrary to popular belief, being creative does not amount to 'anything goes' attitudes. The artist Michael Atavar (2011: 246) suggests that there are 'rules of creativity' including copying nature, using colour and doing the opposite. One of his rules is 'Converse with Blocks', which describes how artists overcome creativity blocks – by writing about it, drawing it, asking it questions, describing the block as an island, room or country, taking it to the supermarket, cutting a hole in it and looking through the other side and using words to make chinks in the armour of the block.

Pupils often believe that there is only one right way to solve a problem. But it is better for them to learn three ways to solve one problem than to learn one way to solve three problems. Therefore, prompting pupils to consider alternative strategies (e.g. 'How else might we do this?') is a useful way of promoting flexible thinking. **Thinking flexibly** occurs when we modify our perspective and see other points of view and ways of doing things according to the prevailing context. It relates to de Bono's (1970) concept of lateral thinking, when alternative viewpoints are considered simultaneously. Flexible thinkers shift between different viewpoints:

- egocentric – their own viewpoint
- allocentric – the viewpoint of others
- macrocentric –the big picture view
- microcentric – the close-up view.

As children develop they naturally move away from an egocentric stage towards understanding and empathising with others. A well-tried and effective classroom technique is to read stories from the viewpoint of different characters, which enables pupils to engage with various views. The macrocentric view is likened to looking down from a balcony or a hawk eye's view of the world. It is conceptual and holistic, considering the main issues and acknowledging that knowledge may be incomplete. It seeks to establish trends and patterns, skipping over the minor details so as not to be distracted. In contrast, a microcentric view examines the minutiae. It focuses on the parts that make up the whole and so requires attention to detail and precision. The Organisation for Economic Co-operation and Development (OECD, 2016) recognises the importance of teaching flexible thinking so that young people can handle feelings of 'culture shock' such as frustration, stress and alienation associated with new environments.

Responding with wonderment and awe is a core human experience, shared by artists, scientists, architects, poets, engineers, historians, geographers, theologians, mathematicians, athletes – indeed specialists from all walks of life marvel at the beauty in the world and human achievements. Wonder is a complex emotion. It involves elements of curiosity, surprise, joy and reflection. It is usually triggered by something rare, singularly beautiful or unexpected. Awe is like wonder but is directed at someone or something perceived to be much more powerful than we are. In 2017, the BBC's *Blue Planet II* was the most watched television show of the year – attracting more than 14 million viewers. The filming of the Bobbit worm (boasting a disputed etymology best kept from children) in action spooked many viewers but also left them in edge-of-the-seat wonderment. The sharp-daggered worm grows to 10 feet in length and waits buried in the ocean sand for passing fish, oblivious to its existence.

Teachers today are in a privileged position of having immediate access to stimulating resources that previous generations could only imagine. The annual editions of the *Guinness World Records* are an excellent source to astonish children with all kinds of bizarre achievements. The accompanying website includes a collection of free downloadable posters for classroom use on themes such as 'oldest', 'heaviest', 'longest', 'tallest' and 'superheroes'.[3] Many of these records can be used as a springboard for exploring concepts in an enjoyable manner. For instance, comparing the heights of children in the class with records of the tallest (Robert Wadlow, 2.72 metres) and shortest (Pauline Musters, 30 centimetres) people who have ever lived. Pupils can be asked to imagine a day in the life of these individuals and the challenges they must have faced.

Thinking about thinking (metacognition) involves developing a plan of action over time, maintaining the plan and evaluating whether the objectives have been met.

---

[3]www.guinnessworldrecords.com (accessed 20 June 2018).

It is a self-regulatory process. So, for instance, if pupils were asked to plan a family holiday abroad they would need to draw up plans that consider costs, location, timings, preferences and interests, seasonal demands, availability of hotel, climate, transport, food, insurance, health and safety and other factors. Much of this thinking is metacognitive in nature. It involves asking questions to check that the plan is working and reflecting on whether sufficient progress is being made towards achieving the desired goal. The ability to control one's actions, behaviour and thoughts is important in helping to achieve goals. Good self-control is related to many positive outcomes in life including improved health, wealth and safety (Moffitt et al., 2011).

Taking responsible risks means being willing to try something out which is different or new, without fear of failure. It is experiencing life on the edge, albeit momentarily. In many walks of life, the most successful people take responsible risks. Sometimes this goes badly wrong. The first hot air balloonist (Pilâtre de Rozier) died while crossing the English Channel, the man (James Fixx) credited with popularising jogging died from a heart attack during a morning jog, while Marie Curie (whose work led to the development of X-rays) was exposed to too much radiation and died of leukemia in 1934. However, fear of failure should not undermine the inventive spirit. Unforeseen occurrence can befall anyone. Where risks are taken irresponsibly, insufficient attention is given to health and safety concerns – in Russia, selfie deaths have become so common the government has issued guidance on how to avoid dying while taking a photograph (Horton, 2015).

Many argue that UK education and society at large is too risk averse. This means people are reluctant to take the initiative, even to show acts of kindness, because of how this may be misconstrued. The tragic case in 2006 of Abigail Rae, a 2-year-old who drowned in a pond after walking out of her nursery school in Warwickshire illustrates the point. A bricklayer passed her by as she wandered down the road but did not stop to help because he feared people would think he was trying to abduct her. Risk, of course, is essential to a balanced childhood. And yet since the 1970s, the distance children roam from home on their own has shrunk by 90 per cent (Henley, 2010). By being exposed to healthy risk, children experience fear and come to understand their own physical strengths and limits. In 2015, an All-Party Parliamentary Group called for policy-makers and those working with children to embrace the concept of 'benefit-risk assessment' (rather than risk-assessment) to promote a more rational evaluation of activities and situations.

Risk, by its nature, carries danger but also benefits. The balance between risk and safety is a tricky one and largely determined by cultural expectations – should young children learn to light fires and handle tools such as sharp knives? Children as young as six from the Masai tribe in north Kenya guard their flocks from lions while even younger children from the Piaroa tribe in Venezuela are taught to fend for themselves, including hunting the world's largest venomous spider for dinner. The BBC's *Human Planet* series is an excellent resource to stimulate class discussion about what is regarded as acceptable and non-acceptable risk and how this varies from one country to another.

Adventurous or 'dizzy' play motivates children to extend their boundaries, to develop persistence and recognise the joy as well as the fear of challenges. Constant adult refrains such as 'Don't do that' and 'Come down or you'll fall' undermine this. Taking responsible risks means learning skills such as testing the strength of a branch before climbing a tree or using a stick to measure the depth of water in a steam before paddling. Pupils should be encouraged to consider contingency planning *before* worst case scenarios may occur. If they try new food and don't like it, they can spit it out or drink water. If they are learning to ride a bicycle and fear falling off, they could cycle first on soft ground. Pupils need reassurance that fear is a natural response to risk and a valid emotion, but one that should not hold them back if they want to enjoy new experiences in life.

There are positive signs, especially among early years' practitioners, that attitudes are changing and responsible risk-taking is being encouraged by bodies such as Play England and the Health and Safety Executive (Tovey, 2014). In 2017 Amanda Spielman, Ofsted's chief inspector, called for schools to become less risk averse; despite the obvious irony that inspections bring considerable pressures on schools to ensure that they comply with safeguarding and follow due diligence in managing risk, or otherwise face the prospect of poor judgements or even prosecution.

Striving for accuracy is important in all aspects of life. Shoddy, slapdash workmanship is unattractive and, in fields such as medicine, architecture and transport, potentially dangerous. Moreover, billions of pounds are lost in the economy due to preventable errors. One analysis suggests that a single spelling error on a website can cut sales by 50 per cent (Coughlan, 2011). Insights from behavioural science, based on 'Nudge theory' (Thaler and Sunstein, 2009), show that many errors can be eliminated by going with the grain of how people behave but making very minor changes to policy and practice. For instance, ensuring people are reminded to do things (e.g. fill in forms) at key moments; personalising messages (e.g. using names in text messages) and highlighting the positive behaviour of others (e.g. '9 out of 10 people pay their tax on time', Cabinet Office, 2012). There is no reason why the same psychology cannot be applied in the classroom to improve pupils' accuracy when working (O'Reilly et al., 2017). Using simple 'If ... then ...' statements (known as implementation intentions) can support pupils in achieving goals by setting out when, where and how in advance. For example, '*If* I get my pencil, rubber and book ready on the table before the lesson starts, *then* I will be ready to write when asked'. Simple techniques such as using tally marks can help young children get into the habit of recording data accurately, while Zielinski et al. (2012) report the effectiveness of a 'cover, copy and compare' method for the accurate learning of spelling lists by secondary school students with learning disabilities.

While it is important to teach children the importance of attention to detail and accuracy, they also need to learn not to take life too seriously. Laughter brings many benefits. The neuroscientist Robert Provine (2001), who observed thousands of incidents of spontaneous laughter occurring in everyday life, found that laughter brought people closer together. He stresses that laughter is primarily about social relationships rather than humour *per se*. Men, for example, like women who laugh in their presence irrespective of how funny their jokes are. Provine goes as far as to suggest that female laughter is the critical index of a healthy relationship. **Finding humour** can include using jokes, riddles, puns, funny props, visual illustrations, spontaneous comments and actions, and funny stories. Some kinds are inappropriate, such as sarcasm, ridicule, mockery and offensive humour, e.g. racist or sexist jokes. Clearly a line should be drawn between laughing with and at pupils. In the context of teaching English, Tranter (2011) refers to a wide range of sources, including: the use of Church signs (e.g. 'God answers: 'Knee-mail!'), ambiguous small ads (e.g. 'Illiterate? Write today for free help'), and howlers in school examination papers (e.g. 'a coma is a punctual mark like a full stop'). Banas et al. (2011) had the joy of studying four decades of humour in the classroom and concluded that it improves teacher's credibility, classroom ethos and relationships, although there is little to suggest direct effects on attainment (examination results). While humour may not be considered an essential element of effective teaching, good relationships are; and if pupils can learn to find and use humour appropriately this can contribute to a relaxed learning environment.

Whatever the lesson content, there should be opportunities for pupils to **ask questions and pose problems**. Questioning is central to creative and critical thinking. Knowing what question to ask in any given situation can contribute to the speedy resolution of problems. There are general questions which pupils should be introduced to and encouraged to apply when testing the truthfulness of claims, e.g. 'How do you know?' and 'What evidence is there for this?' When carrying out research projects, pupils should learn that questions can act as anchor points when sifting through relevant information. All research begins with a question or hypothesis, whether in the humanities, arts or sciences. Pupils can be taught to capture questions and *find* problems, for example on nature walks, using writers' notepads, artist sketchbooks and science journals. By reflecting on their own everyday experiences, pupils can be encouraged to identify hang-ups and things that annoy them which they would like to remove. One girl hated washing up the cat food spoon and so invented an edible one made of pet food. Once the pet food was scooped out of the can, the spoon was thrown into the cat's bowl for it to eat (Starko, 1995).

Thinking interdependently is very much part of what makes us human as social animals. We are wired to connect with each other but some people are far better at relationships than others. They have developed what writers (Albrecht, 2006; Goleman, 2011) call 'social intelligence', which is essentially the ability to build relationships or get along well with others by gaining their cooperation. This has a darker side and can, in its extreme form, manifest itself in psychopathic tendencies. But most people have a built-in bias towards generosity, empathy, cooperation and interacting successfully with others. And yet in 2015 it was reported that almost seven million adults in the UK – more than one in eight of us – said that they had *no* close friends (Relate, 2015). Mental health charities have expressed concern over loneliness among young people as well as older ones. Loneliness is regarded as a 'silent plague' with Britain dubbed the loneliness capital of Europe (Gill, 2014).

Social intelligence aligns closely to thinking interdependently. This involves learning together by sharing ideas, listening attentively to others, and building on each other's strengths, interests and backgrounds. In academia, this often takes on a multidisciplinary nature. Employers consistently rank team-working skills as highly desirable among prospective employees. And yet there are still too many young people entering the workplace without the necessary interpersonal skills, which holds back productivity and damages the economy as well as their own relationships. A survey by the Confederation of British Industry found that one in four businesses report poor team-working skills among young people (CBI/Pearson, 2016).

The National Aeronautics and Space Administration (NASA), which employs more than 18,000 people, recognises the importance of thinking interdependently (teamwork is one of its core values). Scott Tannenbaum, an industrial organisational psychologist, advises NASA on the Science of Teamwork. His view is that team effectiveness means sustainable performance over time. He points out that teams vary across a continuum of interdependency. In sport, for instance, solo swimming calls for low levels of interdependency, cricket demands medium levels with team members coordinating some of the time while football demands high levels because most members must coordinate consistently. His research (Tannenbaum and Cerasoli, 2013) reveals that one of the key drivers for improving teamwork is regular debriefing (performance improved by 20–25 per cent). The nature of these debriefs can be kept short and simple: reviewing what's going well, what needs to improve and agreeing on next steps (e.g. who does what).

The most successful problem-solvers **apply past knowledge to new situations**. They learn from experience. Teachers can support pupils in bridging prior knowledge and new learning through questions and prompts such as:

- What do you remember about ...?
- When have you seen something similar to this?
- How is the story different from the story we read last week?
- Tell me what you already know about this.

There are many strategies to activate pupils' prior knowledge. One of the most popular is the Think-Pair-Share routine where individuals have time to think about a question related to the topic of study. They then pair up with a partner to share their thoughts. Finally, the pairs select one major idea to share with the whole class (Kagan, 1994). Another strategy is called Carousel Brainstorming. Questions about a topic are posted at different numbered 'stations' around the classroom and the class divided into groups of five to six pupils. Each group is allocated a different coloured pen and given two minutes to write their responses to the question. When time is called, each group moves in a clockwise direction to the next question station. Before leaving their final question station, each group chooses three ideas to share with the rest of the class (Lipton and Wellman, 1998). A third strategy is called Talking Drawings where pupils are asked to think about a topic and draw a picture of what it means to them. After a lesson on the topic, they draw another picture and talk about the differences and explain any changes. The social nature of thinking and learning is highlighted in another strategy called the Walk Around Survey. Pupils move around the class for the purpose of finding out what others remember about a topic. They record the thoughts of three informers on a simple survey sheet and then return to their seats to write a summary sentence. These summaries then inform a whole-class discussion.

The final Habit of Mind is **remaining open to continuous learning**. One of the goals of education should be developing a lifelong love of learning. This is particularly important given that the UK has a growing but ageing population, which is reducing the ratio of workers to retirees, so that productivity will need to rise to maintain standards of living. It is forecast that people will need to work longer and change jobs more frequently and so economic security is linked not to keeping a job for life but renewing the right skills through lifelong learning (Government Office for Science, 2017). And yet the UK has poor levels of literacy and numeracy skills among young people (aged 16–29), the third worst in OECD countries ahead only of Chile and Turkey (Government Office for Science, 2017: 30). This is not only about relatively poor performance in examinations. Around 30 per cent of young people in England with GCSE qualifications still have low literacy and numeracy skills. Moreover, one in four adults in the UK seldom pick up a book for pleasure (Flood, 2013).

One way forward suggested by research is to make greater use of 'contextualised learning', where skills are acquired while learning something else that interests young people (Vorhaus et al., 2011; House of Commons, 2014–15). Low-skilled learners who hold negative feelings about school literacy and numeracy lessons develop greater self-confidence and achieve higher qualifications when engaged with apprenticeship-style occupations and realistic work settings, such as hotels and beauty salons (Ofsted, 2014).

In every community, schools will find examples of good role models for pupils to illustrate the importance of lifelong learning. Grandparents are an obvious starting point with events such as Grandparents Day, while there are many intergenerational projects, which seek to bring young and old together to share learning experiences as well as promote greater understanding and respect. The Beth Johnson Foundation is a national charity, which aims to make the UK age-friendly and provides useful links and resources, which illustrate the importance of continuous learning. The TOY-PLUS project (Together Old and Young), for example, aims to provide online materials to develop skills across Europe. Similarly, Sugata Mitra and Suneeta Kulkarni developed the Granny Cloud so that grandparents all over the world could act as mentors to young people, sharing knowledge, skills and wisdom, but also to gain ideas so that all users give back as much as they can.[4]

HABITS OF MIND IN PRACTICE

Costa and Kallick have developed a range of materials to support teachers. The guidance is summarised in Table 10.1 below. Much of this will be familiar to teachers because it aligns with what is known about effective pedagogy. There is an emphasis upon education as a *process* of understanding rather than a product of recall and simply doing things in class. The starting point for implementing Habits of Mind should be developing a shared understanding of the kind of pupils that you want leaving your school. In other words, what successful learning means. Some schools convey this through mission statements (where the school is now) and visions (where it wants to be). St Anne's Church of England Lydgate Primary School in Oldham has the mission of 'A Family of Creative Thinkers Aspiring to Excellence', accompanied by the vision to 'develop outstanding citizens of the future who are innovative, resilient and committed to making a difference'. To become meaningful, such statements are always best devised through consensus. They then need to be translated into practice through the curriculum, classroom instruction and assessment practices. There is no point, for example, in talking up creating, imagining and innovating unless the selected teaching approaches and timetable allow pupils the space, time and independence to develop these skills and dispositions.

Similarly, senior leaders need to invest in professional development to ensure that teachers have the know-how and confidence to teach creatively and foster creativity. Key policies, such as behaviour and teaching and learning, need to reference the Habits of Mind so that staff, particularly new teachers, see the commitment of school leaders. If the Habits of Mind are to become normalised, they need to be an integral part of classroom and school culture. This means, for instance, teachers regularly modelling the habits and seizing opportunities to praise, discuss and reflect upon those shown by pupils and others. This should include reference to the inspirational stories of those

---

[4]www.grannycloud.org/ (accessed 20 June 2018).

who have shown remarkable dispositions. Those featured should not only be famous faces but those drawn from families and local communities, acknowledged by various awards around the country through organisations such as the Rotary Club. Engaging parents and the wider community (e.g. businesses, sports clubs, libraries, local media, other schools) can reinforce key messages to pupils that goals can be achieved, sometimes against considerable odds, with effort, support and persistence. Workshops, coffee mornings and joint projects in the locality, all afford opportunities for collaboration and raising awareness.

Table 10.1 Fostering Habits of Mind

- Have a clear shared vision of what successful learning looks like.
- Plan for professional development to ensure consistency of understanding.
- Feature Habits of Mind in key policies, such as teaching and learning.
- Review the curriculum requirements and map Habits of Mind.
- Work towards integrating the Habits of Mind across the curriculum.
- Develop a nurturing culture.
- Draw on pupils' prior knowledge.
- Use and display the vocabulary of Habits of Mind.
- Give pupils regular thinking time.
- Adopt the role of co-learner.
- Seize moments to highlight Habits of Mind among learners.
- Make reference to real-life stories of those demonstrating Habits of Mind.
- Seek the support of parents and the wider community.
- Gather data on the Habits of Mind and evaluate their impact.

One of the key elements behind the effective teaching of Habits of Mind is developing a common shared language in the classroom, school and wider community. This might take the form of posters, flash cards and other visuals. The important thing is to ensure that the language is accessible, precise and accurate (Table 10.2). Early years' practitioners in Notting Hill Preparatory School use Rabbits of Mind as an age-appropriate means of introducing the Habits of Mind. In some schools, each Habit of Mind is a teddy bear and children show their Habits of Mind in the way they care for the toy each day.

Table 10.2   Examples of language prompts for Habits of Mind

Habit of Mind	Useful phrases and words
1. Persisting	Keep going, stick at it, repeat, don't give up, try again, never give up, hang in there, drive
2. Thinking and communicating with clarity and precision	Be clear, explain, define, avoid slang, put simply, illustrate, use correct names, be specific, edit, review, choice of words
3. Managing impulsivity	Wait a minute, don't jump in, take your time, count to five, be patient, stay calm, be reflective, take a deep breath
4. Gathering data through all senses	Dance, engage, experience, hear, express, hands-on, listen, move, observe, sense, smell, study, taste, touch, watch closely
5. Listening with understanding and empathy	Consider other views, put yourself in his/her shoes, think before speaking, show care, be respectful, sum up, concentrate, tune in, be compassionate
6. Creating, imagining, innovating	Brainstorm, clever, explore, imagine, invent, investigate, productive, speculate, try a different way, new, novel
7. Thinking flexibly	Give and take, try this, be open-minded, fluent, change your mind, consider alternatives, What about ...?, What if ...?
8. Responding with wonderment and awe	Show curiosity, Aha!, appreciate, ask questions, astonished, excitement, fresh, gaze, mystery, puzzled, impressed, enjoy, surprise, shock, weird, wacky
9. Thinking about thinking	Think aloud, ask yourself questions, reflect, metacognition, ponder, be alert, inside your head, self-evaluate, inner thoughts
10. Taking responsible risks	Adventurous, dare, explore, gamble, venture, weigh up pros/cons
11. Striving for accuracy	Be exact, correct, no room for error, precise, measure twice cut once, double-check, review, accurate, re-read
12. Finding humour	Comedy, comedian, smile, giggle, jest, laugh, relax, enjoy, feel good, joke, laugh with not at someone, playful, riddle
13. Questioning and posing problems	Be curious, ask why, what, where, who, when, how, what if, so what, hypothesise, query, puzzled, investigate, enquire, seek, quest
14. Thinking interdependently	collaborate, cooperate, mutual help, share ideas, social, teamwork, work with others
15. Applying past knowledge to new situations	Make connections, recall, remember when, reminds me, use what you have learnt, reuse, recycle, transfer, translate, just like the time when you ...
16. Remaining open to continuous learning	Always learning, avoid complacency, inquisitive, failing forward, help yourself, learn from mistakes, lifelong learning

Source: adapted from Costa and Kallick (2009)

Habits of Mind are not a quick fix and do not lend themselves to direct instruction. The goal should be to infuse them across the curriculum and in practices such as behaviour management. Costa and Kallick (2009) suggest that in their experience in many schools, this can take between three and five years. Many teachers make explicit reference to the Habits of Mind as reminders and prompts to focus attention before lessons begin. For instance, they might ask the class: 'Which of the Habits of Mind will help us solve this mathematics problem?' or 'As I read the story, which Habit of Mind might help you understand?' They may also regularly encourage pupils to think about how the Habits of Mind might be applied in life *beyond* the classroom so that regular connections are made to real-world learning. For example, in areas such as football training, learning to play the piano, keeping their bedroom tidy, shopping or managing pocket money.

Habits of Mind can be easily incorporated into everyday classroom life. For example, when marking pupils' books teachers can move beyond corrective feedback to encouraging pupils to spot their own mistakes and those of others (striving for accuracy). By simply writing at the top of the page: 'Find three errors in this work' pupils soon get into the habit of self-correcting (metacognition). Hattie (2012) shows that self-regulatory feedback is the most effective in improving pupils' work.

Table 10.3 shows examples of practical strategies that teachers can use to foster Habits of Mind.

Table 10.3 Practical strategies for teaching Habits of Mind

Habit of Mind	Guidance and ideas for pupils in/outside the class
1. Persisting	Ask a classmate or an adult; re-read or review; break down the task; work with someone who doesn't give up easily; use checklists and tick off each task when completed; use reminders of what works well; take a mini break.
2. Thinking and communicating with clarity and precision	Try to learn and use phrases such as 'I think this ... because ...'; when explaining, give examples of what you mean; use words to help the listener follow what you say, e.g. when listing things use 'first, second, third' or 'next, then, to conclude'.
3. Managing impulsivity	Take a deep breath; count to five in your head; create your own calm-down kit (e.g. play dough, squishy ball, soothing music using headphones); allow your mind to take a 'time-out'; create a personal reward system for delayed gratification or pleasure.
4. Gathering data through all senses	Take opportunities to play outside in the fresh air; play listening games with friends; go on a sound walk around the school grounds; play 'I-spy' and other sight games with friends and family; find out about optical illusions; try 'spot the difference' challenges; experiment with scents and smells; make scratch and sniff games using flowers, spices or herbs that have a strong smell; find out about the story of Christy Brown, born with cerebral palsy, who learned to paint and write with his left foot, his only controllable limb, then try painting with your feet; plan blindfold taste and touch experiments for classmates; plan a sensory Olympics for the class or school.

Habit of Mind	Guidance and ideas for pupils in/outside the class
5. Listening with understanding and empathy	Ask for more information if necessary; try to sum up what someone has told you in a few words; if you were the other person consider how would you feel; be quiet when someone is speaking; don't feel you have to say something immediately; look at the person.
6. Creating, imagining, innovating	Sketch or paint an idea; act it out; doodle; daydream; mix with people who have good ideas; use the Internet to find out how others have tackled a problem; don't be afraid to borrow ideas from others (you may need to ask permission) – can you improve on these? Ask 'Why?' Read about great inventors and inventions; turn 'Can't' into 'Can if' and 'Not yet'; think the impossible.
7. Thinking flexibly	Consider the opposite of what you are thinking; what happens if you change one thing, e.g. timing, audience, size, colour, shape, type of resource, setting, people? Make a list of options – which is the best one and why? Try looking at things differently (reframing) – how might the other person feel? Who might help?
8. Responding with wonderment and awe	Share something awesome from the *Guinness World of Records*; read about how people with disabilities achieve amazing things; feed and watch birds collect the food; use a magnifying glass to explore a spider's web; think about the feelings of the first person to ... step on the moon, sail the world, run a marathon, climb Everest, etc.
9. Thinking about thinking	Talk to yourself, rehearsing what to say or do before a situation arises; draw a mind map of your thoughts; stop, read and think about information; use diagrams to connect ideas; look for patterns; read something new every day to feed your thinking; think about what you are trying to achieve; set small targets; use checklists to remind yourself of what important things need to be done; don't be afraid to 'think-aloud' when reading.
10. Taking responsible risks	Make a list of things for and against (pros and cons); ask yourself, 'What is the worse that could happen?' or 'How likely is this to happen?' and plan what to do if this occurs; try something that is not too scary to begin with and build up confidence; accept that everyone feels frightened in different ways and so repeat the saying, 'Feel the fear and do it anyway'.
11. Striving for accuracy	Double check; re-read, get into the habit of estimating; measure twice; use visual timers to keep on track; ask someone who you know is good at something to check your work; focus on something small and practise this daily; seek and act on feedback; try to beat your personal best; sometimes accept that this is 'good enough'.
12. Finding humour	Tell a joke a day; read a comic; look at YouTube and type in 'The funniest ...' (dance, animal, joke, baby, video, etc.); share with a friend; find weird words to amuse your friends, e.g. 'bumfuzzle', 'cattywampus', 'gardyloo'; search for unusual place-names, e.g. Beer in Devon, Boring in Scotland; find out how to become a comedian; do one thing to make someone smile each day; laugh at yourself for being silly.

(Continued)

Table 10.3 (Continued)

Habit of Mind	Guidance and ideas for pupils in/outside the class
13. Questioning and posing problems	Do crosswords and puzzles; ask the question, 'How do I know this?'; think about whether a problem could be solved another way; keep asking: 'what if ...?', 'what if ... not?' and 'what ... Is changed?'; use flow charts and other visuals to help work through problems; watch someone solve an everyday problem such as washing the car; Ask yourself do you have enough information to solve the problem; draw pictures to represent the problem; use 'first-then' approach (first you do ... then you can do ...').
14. Thinking interdependently	Write a story with a group of friends; build something together; ask questions if unsure; offer to help someone; use the words 'we' and 'us' rather than 'me' and 'I'; be willing to try different roles when working as a group; ask for feedback.
15. Applying past knowledge to new situations	Try listing what you already know about a topic beforehand using bullet points, charts or visual maps; share what you know with a classmate; make a list of questions that you would like to explore; ask yourself what have you learned today that you did not know yesterday; look back at a previous activity and think about how what you have learnt can help you today, and think about what you might need to improve this time.
16. Remaining open to continuous learning	Take up a new hobby; keep a 'to learn' list; make a note of ideas that interest you in a journal, jotter or scrapbook; try teaching someone something you are passionate about; join an afterschool club.

Source: adapted from Costa and Kallick (2009)

One of the challenges is assessing pupils' progress in developing Habits of Mind. Self-assessment rubrics can be used in which pupils record their perceptions of themselves as learners using a simple scale along the lines: 'most of the time', sometimes', 'not yet'. They can also record when they have demonstrated a particular Habit of Mind, when they may have seen it shown by others and what they could do to improve a particular habit in their learning. Teachers also use journals in which pupils are given prompts and questions related to the Habits of Mind and the projects they are undertaking. This can include seeking feedback from pupils on the Habits of Mind they think the teacher needs to improve upon.

IMPACT

The wide-ranging nature of Habits of Mind means that it is practically difficult to undertake research to gauge their collective impact on learning. However, Edwards provides a synthesis of research (Edwards, 2014) and a systematic literature review in relation to *individual* Habits of Mind (Edwards, 2016). Both were conducted on behalf of the Institute for Habits of Mind International. Edwards provides clear evidence that the Habits of Mind, albeit under different names, have attracted widespread interest among academics in different subject and phase contexts. Much of the cited research spanning thirty or so years is supportive of the intellectual, social and emotional gains associated with cultivating dispositions from elementary school through adulthood. What is less clear is how the Habits of Mind work together and their impact when taught collectively on teaching and learning at different stages of education.

We do know that as children move through schooling they become less positive about their experiences (Sammons et al., 2012). This may reflect growing demands placed on learners, the influence of peers, adolescent change or simply the pressures of life. One of the reasons why so many children and young people say they dislike school is because they perceive lessons as being far removed from the realities of life. While the concept of relevance is a contentious one, there is no doubt that many perceive schoolwork as being out of touch with what happens in the real world. One survey of a thousand teenagers found that more than four in ten found school boring or irrelevant (Paton, 2009). Robert Fried (2001: 58–59) observes:

> We have opted not to create schools as places where children's curiosity, sensory awareness, power, and communication can flourish, but rather to erect temples of knowledge where we sit them down, tell them a lot of stuff we think is important, try to control their restless curiosity, and test them to see how well they've listened to us.

Habits of Mind, based on the kinds of dispositions, qualities and skills that people have found essential to their success in life, offer schools the opportunity to bridge this school–real-world divide. The broad evidence suggests that successful learning depends upon developing dispositions alongside knowledge and skills (Tough, 2012; Duckworth, 2017). It makes sense therefore for schools to invest time in cultivating Habits of Mind.

SUMMARY

- Habits of Mind refer to the mix of dispositions and skills that characterise peak performance in all walks of life.
- Art Costa and Bena Kallick identify at least sixteen Habits of Mind: persisting; managing impulsivity; listening to others with understanding and empathy; thinking flexibly; gathering data through all senses; creating, imagining, innovating; thinking flexibly; responding with wonderment and awe; thinking about thinking (metacognition); taking responsible risks; striving for accuracy; finding humour; questioning and posing problems; thinking interdependently; applying past knowledge to new situations; and remaining open to continuous learning.
- There is considerable evidence to suggest that fostering the individual Habits of Mind improves attitudes to learning.

11

CASE STUDIES

In this chapter, we draw out key messages from case studies of schools that are successful in promoting pupils' creative and critical thinking. These case studies are based on first-hand experiences, drawn from networks such as Thinking Schools International and inspection reports that identify good practice. Although the case study schools vary in the contexts and use different approaches, they share common factors that contribute to their success: planning, practices, professional learning and partnerships (four Ps). Staff recognise the importance of strategic *planning* to ensure that developing pupils' thinking remains a priority. Their teaching *practices* reflect a pragmatic philosophy that values pupil-led investigations, while at the same time ensuring that pupils are taught the basic knowledge and skills to support such learning.

It is also clear that the schools are committed to providing a broad range of stimulating learning experiences. Leaders invest in the *professional learning* of staff, for example through supporting peer observation, action research, attendance at courses and membership of professional bodies. Finally, the case studies show that schools do not operate in isolation. They forge strategic *partnerships* with other schools to form networks to share practice, work closely with parents and the wider community, and are members of organisations such as Thinking Schools International and the Society for Advancing Philosophical Enquiry and Reflection in Education (SAPERE). These four areas are bound together by strong leadership that models the dispositions and values that the schools want pupils to develop. Figure 11.1 illustrates this with four dispositions, although many others are also shown in the life of the schools.

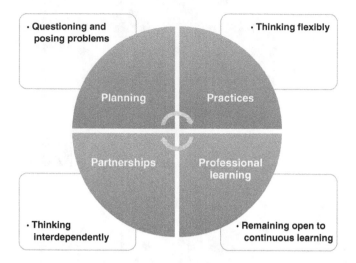

Figure 11.1 Core features of promoting thinking skills linked to dispositions

PLANNING

The successful implementation of any intervention requires clear strategic planning. School development or improvement plans need to identify appropriate priorities, key responsibilities, timescales, resources and success criteria. School leaders who identify promoting pupils' creative and critical thinking as a goal often align this with supporting improvements in areas of the curriculum, such as mathematical problem-solving, scientific enquiry, higher-order reading skills or independent learning. As Michael Barber notes, 'teaching thinking … is not an alternative to the standards agenda but a way of taking it forward' (cited by Claxton, 2002). Priorities are best identified as part of rigorous self-evaluation procedures and informed by evidence. Typically, schools draw upon a broad range of sources as part of their self-evaluation procedures including learning walks, lesson observations, questionnaires, focus group discussions, book reviews and data analysis.

Analysis of attainment data (usually in the core subjects of reading, writing, mathematics and science) provides a snapshot of pupil achievement but needs to be considered in a broader context of pupils' characteristics (e.g. how many are disadvantaged) and progress over time. Leaders in the case study schools apply the habit of questioning and posing problems when they interrogate data to identify the most pressing issues. For instance, if test data suggests that there is a gap in the performance of Year 6 boys and girls in mathematical reasoning, then questions need to be asked about the significance of the gap, how this compares to local and national data (if available), whether there is an established trend, what contextual factors (e.g. cohort size, change of teacher) might explain the performance differences and exactly which aspects of learning pupils found challenging. When used effectively, performance data can promote improved teaching and learning; for example, through more effective allocation of resources, challenging expectations, identifying pupils' achievements and the setting of appropriate targets (Kirkup et al., 2005).

However, data should be approached with an enquiring rather than an accepting mind. Comparing sources, such as the views of learners, parents and teachers, might reveal different conclusions. Tracking a 'day in the life' of volunteer pupils or teachers (e.g. by asking them to wear Point of View cameras), can reveal different perspectives and experiences in the school environment. Sometimes asking speculative questions such as 'What might happen if ...?' paves the way for small-scale practitioner research in selected classes to explore whether a planned intervention is worth rolling out through the school.

In the case studies, the promotion of pupils' thinking had a high priority in school development plans. This was expressed in different ways – some schools detailing specific skills and phases, such as improving problem-solving skills among low-attaining Key Stage 2 pupils in mathematics; while others provided a more general steer, for example to 'develop pupils' thinking skills and independence through learning in real-life contexts'. In their short-term plans (either on a daily or weekly basis), teachers should seek to implement the priorities identified at the strategic school level. And so, for example, the teachers in case study 3 plan to use thinking routines in their lessons so that they can understand what pupils feel, notice and think.

PRACTICES

Priorities set on paper only mean something if they are enacted on the ground. If a school genuinely wants pupils to develop as independent thinkers, then this should be self-evident when walking around the school. A learning walk with a focus on pupils' creative and critical thinking might pose the following questions:

- How visible is the support for thinking? For example, do the wall displays include key thinking vocabulary and prompts?
- Is the indoor and outdoor environment stimulating pupils' creativity?
- Are pupils routinely asking thoughtful questions?
- Are there examples of pupils using strategies independently to support their thinking?
- Are pupils regularly engaged in conducting their own enquiries?

Although this book is about teaching learners to become better at thinking, this does not mean that desired results will only be achieved if teachers adopt certain styles or approaches. In the case studies, staff undertook the role of facilitator, which is an important one in fostering talk that is central to thinking. There are times when teachers do need to take a step back and allow pupils the space and time to talk and think, practise, reflect and self-correct. But this is not suggesting that the teacher becomes redundant or, as the cliché says, a guide on the side. Orchestras who perform without a conductor, such as the Italian-based Spira Mirabilis, are exceptions. When teaching *new* content and skills, direct instruction is often more effective than guided discovery methods (Hollingsworth and Ybarra, 2018).

As teacher educators and school inspectors, we have observed several thousand lessons over the last twenty-five or so years. One of the things that stands out among the most effective practitioners is how adept they are in thinking-on-their-feet. They take cues from learners or the environment and quickly change something – they might introduce a new word, idea, challenge or resource, take a step back, offer some corrective feedback, focus on the needs of an individual, highlight good progress, introduce a mini plenary, re-direct the learning, set a new target and so forth. In these situations, teachers draw on their deeply embedded (and often difficult to articulate) tacit knowledge of students, pedagogy and the environment.

Hatano and Inagaki (1986) distinguished between routine and adaptive experts. While both could solve problems, they did so in different ways. When necessary, adaptive experts invented new strategies and procedures, whereas routine experts relied on tried-and-tested ideas that they had used before. Adaptive experts revealed greater understanding and flexibility in responding to changes in the environment. They could explain why they made decisions and evaluate which worked and which didn't and why. This kind of practical criticality aligns with what Schön (1991) calls reflection-in-action.

One way in which teachers demonstrate their flexible thinking is by adopting different roles, depending upon the needs of the learners. The case studies confirmed the important role of staff as facilitators of pupils' thinking. Facilitation is not a new concept. It is rooted in the ancient practices of spiritual and monastic guides (Gregory, 2006). It re-emerged in the twentieth century through new humanistic personal development approaches influenced by psychotherapists who saw learning as a means of recovering inner knowledge. From here, it transferred into adult education where experiential approaches to learning were preferred to direct instruction. Heron (1999: 1), one of the first modern writers in the field, points out that 'a facilitator is a person who has the role of empowering participants to learn in an experiential group'. Facilitation, which literally means 'easing', seeks to draw out learners' inner knowledge and help them realise their capacity to learn. High quality facilitators demonstrate the following skills and attributes:

- modelling – appropriate language and behaviour
- building and maintaining rapport – so that everyone feels at ease
- flexible thinking – using different techniques and resources
- questioning – drawing out and exploring ideas with the group

- active listening and observation – picking up verbal and non-verbal signals quickly, noticing the contribution of individuals
- pausing – to give the group time to reflect
- calmly maintaining order – to ensure that the purpose of the discussion is clear, all are kept on track and ground rules are followed
- managing and acting upon information – reflecting back and summarising ideas to check understanding of points, arguments or ideas
- eliciting feedback – gathering suggestions on what has been achieved and next steps.

Modelling is not simply the instructional type of showing pupils how to do something. It is modelling thinking and learning, which means being curious, asking questions aloud, taking risks, reflecting on when things go wrong, applying oneself in research and all the other intelligent actions associated with problem-solving. Ron Ritchhart (2002; 2015) says modelling is one of eight cultural forces that define thinking classrooms (see Chapter 4).

Lemov (2015: 66), in his observations of great teachers, reports that they create 'a culture of error' where learners feel safe to struggle and fail. They encourage self-correction, temporarily withhold answers, praise risk-taking, and use errors as teaching points. In philosophical discussions, there is often disagreement and pupils can be put at ease with phrases such as, 'People have been debating this issue for centuries and reached different answers. What's important is that you're thinking about the issue'.

Facilitation is not the only set of skills that good teachers demonstrate. At times, teachers in the case studies report that they take on a more directive role in explaining ideas or introducing new material. Direct instruction, which is a largely misunderstood term, is not incompatible with promoting creative and critical thinking. Lessons that run along direct instruction lines follow a typical sequence: sharing learning objectives, activating pupils' prior knowledge, presenting new material, offering guidance for learning (e.g. modelling using worked examples), providing time for independent practice, checking understanding and providing feedback. Teachers fully explain concepts and skills *before* pupils have opportunities to practise. They walk through an approach to solving a problem and then invite pupils to have a go themselves. Group discussion is possible, provided it focuses on the relevant concepts and skills.

One area that can prove challenging is assessing the quality of pupils' thinking. Teachers in the case studies typically gather information about thinking behaviours from observations, book reviews and the views of pupils themselves. Developing a classroom pedagogy that supports thinking, and particularly metacognition, has considerable overlap with the principles of Assessment for Learning (AfL) since AfL is concerned with finding out where pupils are, where they need to go and how they will get there. AfL and thinking development require pupils to recognise and talk about the process of learning. They need to discuss, reflect, monitor and evaluate their own progress and that of others through self and peer assessment.

The Welsh Assembly Government (2009) published optional skills assessment materials alongside its Skills Framework and although these have now been superseded by changes in the curriculum, the suggestions on how pupils progress in their thinking remain useful. Similarly, the Council for the Curriculum, Examinations and Assessment in Northern Ireland provides guidance on assessing thinking skills and personal capabilities on its website.[1] Swartz and McGuinness (2014), two leading figures in the field, review the literature in relation to assessing thinking skills as part of the International Baccalaureate. They draw attention to key assessment for learning (thinking) principles that should inform practice, such as aligning the kind of thinking to be assessed to the thinking-related learning objectives of the lesson or unit. They also stress the importance of activating pupils as owners of their own thinking. They recommend the use of visual prompts, explicit thinking criteria, standards, rubrics to assess pupils' work. Standards are necessary to determine the *level* of thinking revealed in the pupils' work, such as evaluating evidence. Viewed along a continuum, pupils might begin to understand that some things are facts, then recognise that there are differences between facts, beliefs and opinions, before identifying bias in accounts. Finally, pupils might evaluate sources to judge their reliability and validity (Welsh Assembly Government, 2009). Such progress can be described in simple terms such as 'bronze', 'silver' and 'gold' level thinking.

PROFESSIONAL LEARNING

One of the core dimensions of successful leadership is enhancing teaching through professional learning (National College for Leadership of Schools and Children's Services, 2010). In the case studies, staff undertook various forms of professional development to increase their knowledge and understanding of the theory and practice of promoting pupils' thinking. Most were members of organisations such as Thinking Schools International or the Society for Advancing Philosophical Enquiry and Reflection in Education (SAPERE). Both offer accredited courses. In the case of Thinking Schools International, schools can become accredited Thinking Schools. The criteria include an expectation that in time most (at least 80 per cent) of the school staff, including learning support assistants, will demonstrate a clear understanding of what is meant by 'a cognitive curriculum, why it has been undertaken and how they can best contribute to it' (Burden, 2006: 4).

At the Barbara Priestman Academy staff demonstrate the habit of remaining open to continuous improvement. They are all involved in research projects as part of their professional development. The outcomes have included publication of newsletters, professional

---

[1]http://ccea.org.uk/curriculum/assess_progress/assessment_practice/assessing_tspc (accessed 21 June 2018).

articles, a book chapter on engaging with families and parents, leading professional learning in other schools and among social workers and contributions to national conferences. The school leaders are continually looking out for professional learning opportunities that enhance the quality of teaching and pupils' *learning*. So, for instance, alongside P4C training, staff were introduced to Dramatic Enquiry which fuses philosophy with drama in education. The approach requires all participants to take on a role and to see things from a different perspective. Many of the school's students with Autism Spectrum Disorder (ASD) find it challenging to argue, debate, reason and justify their opinions and these were skills staff hoped Dramatic Enquiry would support.

Over the years, Dramatic Enquiry at the school has evolved. Staff experimented with different ways of grouping students and how Dramatic Enquiry could support the integration of students with ASD into mainstream classes. This presents challenges – a new environment, unfamiliar faces, busier corridors – and so staff invited a group of students from the local secondary school to come and participate in one of the Enquiry sessions. Students from the Barbara Priestman Academy took on the role of 'experts' to build their confidence in talking to others that they had not met before. Despite staff apprehension, the session worked so well that it became a regular feature. Reflecting upon the impact of the professional learning, one school leader acknowledges the challenge of evidencing student outcomes in relation to thinking skills. Through observations and discussions with students, they reported learning gains in speaking and listening skills, as well as self-confidence, risk-taking and seeing things from different perspectives. These were endorsed by comments from external observers, such as accreditors for the National Autistic Society and the Speaking and Listening Moderator for GCSE English. Some students gained the confidence and skills to participate in the Shakespeare Schools Festival and National Theatre Connections. Ofsted (2015) confirmed that in the view of its inspectors, the teachers effectively used questioning and other strategies to help students become more independent thinkers who had acquired enough confidence to engage in discussions of current issues such as forced marriage and 'science versus religion' (Ofsted, 2015).

Although budgets are tight for most schools, there is a range of low-cost opportunities for professional learning (Table 11.1). To sustain the impetus of interventions, senior leaders and staff need to be committed to updating their professional knowledge and skills. This is a feature of those successful schools promoting pupils' creative and critical thinking.

PARTNERSHIPS

The importance of schools working with strategic partners has been increasingly recognised over the last twenty or so years with the growth in England of sponsored academy chains, federations and multiple academy trusts, as well as concepts such as Teaching Schools where since 2011 those judged to be outstanding by inspectors support other

Table 11.1 Checklist: opportunities for professional learning and sharing practice

	Internal	External
Where?	Within the class/year group	Across local schools
	Within the phase	Within the authority
	Through the school	Nationally
		Internationally
Who?	Learners	Staff from other schools
	Teachers	Local authority
	Teaching assistants	Universities
	Parents	Media
	Governors	Publishers
		Community groups
How?	Assemblies	Courses
	Staff meetings	Conferences
	Observing colleagues	Visits to other schools
	Workshops run by colleagues	Local professional networks
	Focus groups	Thinking skills organisations
	Action/practitioner research	Higher degrees/qualifications

schools through Teaching School Alliances. Estelle Morris, former education secretary (2001–2002), once said that 'interdependence is as important as independence and we need a national community of schools rather that tens of thousands of independent institutions' (Morris, 2013). She was speaking about the growth of academy schools in England and a report (Academies Commission, 2013) that had called for Ofsted to recognise school leadership as outstanding only if there was an evidenced contribution to system-wide improvement. The concept of executive headteachers, National Leaders of Education (NLEs) and other 'system leaders' is designed to bring about a self-improving system (Hargreaves, 2012; NCSL, 2012). For this to happen, thinking interdependently is a key disposition.

Such shared thinking calls for an openness to collaborate and the commitment and support of key stakeholders such as governors, parents, the wider community and local authority (Armstrong, 2015). Clear, frequent and open communication through meetings, newsletters, workshops, fund-raising events and so forth can build trust to the extent that there is a critical friendship among the key stakeholders. This is supported through distributed leadership, which seeks to develop the skills and responsibilities of others across the network.

Subject associations, higher education institutions and bodies such as the National Foundation for Educational Research, the Chartered College of Teaching and the Education Endowment Foundation provide means by which teachers can broaden their knowledge and challenge taken-for-granted assumptions. The growth of grassroots organisations, such as researchED (founded by Tom Bennett), suggests that there is an appetite among teachers to improve their research literacy skills. Each of the case studies established strategic partnerships to support the development of pupils' thinking. For example, Alona (case study 4) joined with other teachers who share her passion for promoting pupils' thinking to form a network committed to making learning and thinking visible.[2]

In practice, research has a relatively small impact on informing teachers' decision-making, compared to sources such as ideas from other teachers and continuing professional development (Nelson and Sharples, 2017). The British Educational Research Association (BERA, 2014: 6) acknowledges the challenges:

> The expectation that teachers might ordinarily engage *with*, and where appropriate, *in* research and enquiry need not, and *must* not, become a burden on a profession that sometimes struggles with the weight of the various demands rightly or wrongly placed upon it.

Nonetheless, when teachers and schools undertake their own research, coupled with professional reflection, this can empower them so that they can better understand their own practices and their impact in the classroom and beyond. Moves to narrow the gap between research and practice can be seen in the discourse around 'evidence-informed practice' and concrete actions such as in-ear coaching schemes providing live commentary on lessons (Vaughan, 2016), and the setting up of in-school 'learning laboratories'. One example of the latter is run by Carnegie Mellon University (Pittsburgh, Pennsylvania), where teachers view their students working on online materials through mixed-reality glasses that show icons hovering over the students' heads. While some icons indicate that students are doing well, others suggest they are struggling or are stuck. Teachers are immediately guided to those pupils in need, whereas in traditional classroom interactions, the pupils who ask for help are not sometimes the ones who most need it (Weir, 2018). Technologies can certainly support both teachers and learners in their thinking habits.

The notion of school leadership is shifting from the traditional role of leading a single school to a much broader range of responsibilities across multiple sites. While notable

---

[2] www.visiblyengagedteachers.org (accessed 20 June 2018).

challenges exist relating to perceived power imbalances between schools (Lindsay et al., 2007) and additional workload (Aiston et al., 2002), the overall picture is positive. Armstrong's (2015) review suggests that collaboration has brought benefits in terms of teachers' professional learning and career advancement, sharing good practice and efficiencies in finance and organisation. The increasing mobilisation of knowledge and the shift towards learning-oriented and enquiry-based cultures are welcome developments.

The most powerful partnership in school is between the teacher and pupil. When teachers begin to see learning through the eyes of their students, they recognise the challenges they face, the fears and uncertainties, as well as their interests and creative energies. Making learning and thinking visible is one of the central themes behind the thinking approaches reviewed in this book. It involves a new kind of learning partnership where teachers are co-learners themselves and when pupils, at times, take on the role of teachers. The power of this is encapsulated in a scene from Ken Loach's drama *Kes*, based on the novel *A Kestrel for a Knave* (Hines, 1969). Fifteen-year-old Billy Casper has a terrible life of abuse but finds hope by rearing a kestrel. His English teacher and classmates are spellbound when he delivers an impromptu talk on how to care for the bird.[3]

CASE STUDY 1A – DISPOSITIONAL APPROACHES: HABITS OF MIND

Danescourt Primary School in Cardiff has more than 400 pupils (aged between 3 and 11 years). The school has a relatively low proportion of pupils (less than 10 per cent) from low-income families, as indicated by those eligible for free school meals, which is a common proxy for poverty. Around 20 per cent of pupils have additional learning needs, which is slightly below the national average. Around 19 per cent of pupils come from ethnic minority backgrounds and around 16 per cent speak English as an additional language.

The spur for taking an interest in developing pupils' thinking skills followed on from a school inspection report (Estyn, 2010), which highlighted the need to give pupils a greater say in their learning, to develop positive relationships and pupils' emotional resilience. The school sees Habits of Mind as a means of addressing these recommendations guided by the headteacher, appointed in 2013. The school leaders and staff worked towards becoming an accredited Thinking School. Training was provided in Habits of Mind as well as Thinking Maps and Thinking Hats. The main challenges faced by the school included ensuring a cohesive and consistent approach by all staff and maintaining their professional development, particularly for new colleagues.

---

[3]The scene can be viewed on YouTube at: www.youtube.com/watch?v=iRINyU7rvNg (accessed 22 June 2018).

The school links Habits of Mind to its Emotional Literacy Programme (ELP), which runs from Nursery to Year 6 over a two-year cycle. The ELP themes for each half-term are aligned to specific dispositions. Hence during the first half of the autumn term, all classes follow the theme of 'Getting Started!' and teachers focus on cultivating the habits of listening, thinking together and that's funny. During the second half of the term, the theme switches to 'Confidence' and staff concentrate on improving learning through 'Stop and think', 'Get it right' (striving for accuracy) and 'Use your knowledge'. Habits of Mind are also integrated across the curriculum and introduced in age-appropriate ways. For example, early years' practitioners use puppets such as 'Connie Confidence', 'Pete Persistence', 'Gabby Get-a-long', 'Oscar Organisation' and 'Ricky Resilience' to engage young children (Photo 11.1)

Photo 11.1 Puppets used with young children to model Habits of Mind

Lessons in ELP, with specific Habits of Mind intertwined in each lesson, are taught on a weekly basis by skilled teaching assistants supported and monitored by teaching staff. Habits of Mind run through all stages of the bespoke Treetops behaviour management system in school. For example, pupils are rewarded for actively demonstrating habits such as asking good questions, as they move up the tree. Similarly, they moved down the tree if they break rules, which are linked to the habit of thinking together (interdependently).

Staff use various tools to collect evidence of impact. These include:

- rubrics completed by the children from Year 3 to 6 to measure how well they are acquiring Habits of Mind (e.g. see Table 11.2)
- questionnaires to capture pupils' perceptions – since the introduction of thinking skills strategies, these questionnaires indicate a perceived improvement in pupils' emotional wellbeing
- inspection evidence – the most recent report (Estyn, 2016) highlights that the way in which the school promotes thinking skills is one of its strengths
- feedback from parents – workshops are held when thinking strategies are introduced to pupils. The uptake is good, with the number of parents ranging up to twenty plus at any given time. Parental responses, via questionnaires, are very positive and typically rate well above 95 per cent satisfaction. In particular, parents appreciate that the school is seeking to prepare their children for life by developing dispositions, attitudes and skills for their social and emotional, as well as academic progress.

Table 11.2 Rubric to assess pupils' progress in perseverance

Stick with it! How am I doing?
Name _____ Boy/Girl Y 3 4 5 6

Expert ☐	I stay on task no matter how difficult it is to find the answer to solutions. I am able to evaluate and use various strategies and ways to solve the problem. I search for and draw on a wide range of resources.
Practitioner ☐	I stay on task when trying to find answers or solutions to problems and things that I find difficult. I use the resources available.
Apprentice ☐	I try to complete tasks when the answers or solutions are not readily available, but I give up when the task is too difficult. I get easily distracted. I use a limited range of resources available.
Novice ☐	I give up easily and quickly when completing difficult tasks. I don't use resources that are around me to help.

Quantitative data, from the National Reading and Numeracy Tests in Wales, is also referred to although given the variables it is not possible to attribute progress recorded in these test scores specifically to the thinking skills interventions. However, school leaders strongly believe that the introduction of thinking strategies has led to academic as well as social and emotional learning gains and this is supported by independent inspection (Estyn, 2016). As part of their methodology, inspectors interview staff, examine pupils' books, observe lessons and speak to a range of learners. These included pupils who form learning forums (for Years 2 to 6), which meet twice a term. Their unanimous view is that Habits of Mind and other dispositional approaches help them learn.

The school's Think Tank Team, comprising a range of senior leaders, teachers and teaching assistants, meet at least once a term to evaluate current priorities linked to the school improvement plan. Through such professional dialogue, the school drives the implementation of its priorities, procedures and aspects of thinking pertinent at the time. Findings have been shared with other schools within the locality[4] and further afield, for instance at the annual Thinking Schools International conferences.

CASE STUDY 1B – DISPOSITIONAL TOOLKIT

Marown Primary School is a single form school in Douglas on the Isle of Man. There are seven classes of children aged from 4 to 11 years, with approximately 190 pupils on roll. The focus on developing pupils' thinking skills started in 2012 when the headteacher, Ian Longshaw, decided to make a move from 'what we teach' and 'what children learn' to 'how we teach' and 'how children learn'. The teachers spent the first year enquiring into existing practices in the school, carrying out action research to evaluate this provision. They then undertook whole-school training in approaches including P4C, Thinking Hats and Thinking Maps and considered concepts such as 'growth mindset' (Dweck, 2017), the 'Learning Pit' (Nottingham, 2013) and the implications of the United Nations Convention on the Rights of the Child. From this, the school developed a bespoke toolkit known as the 'Marown Learning Jungle' with the aim of supporting inquisitive, independent, resilient, positive lifelong learners.

The 'Jungle' has six animals (Figure 11.2), each of which is linked to one of the school's values. The toolkit comprises assembly stories, lesson plans, puppets, posters and awards that link to each animal. Lessons begin with a ten-minute starter activity related to one of the six learning dispositions (six Rs) that frame the Isle of Man curriculum:

- Readiness
- Relationships
- Resourcefulness
- Resilience
- Remembering skills
- Reflectiveness.

---

[4]www.danescourtprm.cardiff.sch.uk/

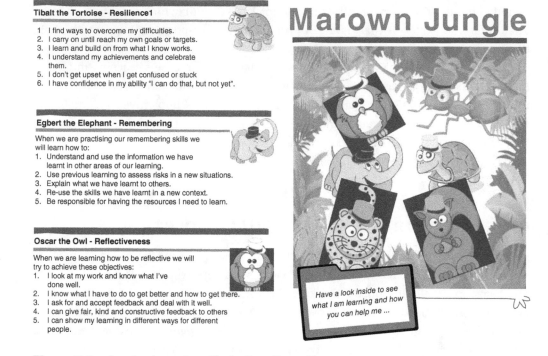

Tibalt the Tortoise - Resilience1

1. I find ways to overcome my difficulties.
2. I carry on until reach my own goals or targets.
3. I learn and build on from what I know works.
4. I understand my achievements and celebrate them.
5. I don't get upset when I get confused or stuck
6. I have confidence in my ability "I can do that, but not yet".

Egbert the Elephant - Remembering

When we are practising our remembering skills we will learn how to:
1. Understand and use the information we have learnt in other areas of our learning.
2. Use previous learning to assess risks in a new situations.
3. Explain what we have learnt to others.
4. Re-use the skills we have learnt in a new context.
5. Be responsible for having the resources I need to learn.

Oscar the Owl - Reflectiveness

When we are learning how to be reflective we will try to achieve these objectives:
1. I look at my work and know what I've done well.
2. I know what I have to do to get better and how to get there.
3. I ask for and accept feedback and deal with it well.
4. I can give fair, kind and constructive feedback to others
5. I can show my learning in different ways for different people.

Marown Jungle

Have a look inside to see what I am learning and how you can help me ...

Figure 11.2 Jungle characters illustrating dispositions

Displays have 'working walls' showing key vocabulary and reminders of the six Rs.

Reflecting on the dispositional toolkit, Ian points out that it has been challenging to maintain a whole-school consistent approach. But by linking the approaches to the school improvement plan and targets for teachers, it was possible to retain a strong focus on thinking skills. Whole-school training and a dedicated week at the start of the year focuses on 'learning to learn' strategies and offers valuable opportunities to refresh and recap on previous learning. A 'Drive team' and Cognitive Development lead oversee the work. Parents and governors are kept informed through newsletters, wiki posts and meetings, while evidence of impact is gathered through learning walks, observations, book reviews and pupil surveys. This collective evidence suggests that the toolkit contributes to high levels of pupil engagement, confidence and reflection in lessons.

CASE STUDY 2 – P4C

Barbara Priestman Academy is a special needs secondary school in Sunderland, which caters for 130 students from 11 to 19 years who have a diagnosis of Autism Spectrum Disorder (ASD) and/or complex needs. All students are unique with their own interests, likes and dislikes. The severity of their condition varies, but common features include the challenge of interacting with others in a social context and a love of order and routine. The school is one of five special schools in a multi-academy trust all based in the north-east of England. The school has achieved the National Foundation for Educational Research (NFER) Mark at extended level, which provides accreditation for schools or colleges engaging with research. It is also an Advanced Thinking School, currently the only special school to have achieved this recognition. In 2017, it formed part of a Thinking School Hub to share ideas and create resources.

The initial interest in thinking skills followed a review of provision by school leaders. They concluded that students were too passive in their learning, while the curriculum model was one of 'delivery' with the aim of giving information to pass examinations. There was little opportunity for learners to discover things for themselves and there was insufficient challenge in the teaching. Given that more than nine in every ten of the students are diagnosed with ASD, staff faced an additional barrier in that most of the students like things to be right or wrong and find it difficult when there isn't a definitive answer. One senior school leader points out:

> They [the students] have a fear of failure and were often reticent to volunteer an answer in case they were deemed incorrect. The majority of our students see subjects as very separate entities and compartmentalise skills, and as such were unable to transfer skills between curriculum subjects.

The school successfully applied to become 'a change school' through the Creative Partnerships. Leaders used the three-year grant to introduce thinking skills programmes and approaches to address the learning challenges. They began with Thinking Maps and Thinking Hats because these approaches offered students the opportunity to *show* their thinking, rather than having to *articulate* it, something that a lot of the students find challenging due to language difficulties often associated with ASD. The school appointed one member of staff, Judith Stephenson, to be coordinator of thinking in the school. All staff were trained in the use of Thinking Maps and key staff were trained as trainers for the delivery of Thinking Maps and Thinking Hats; this enabled staff to be self-sufficient and ensured sustainability when new staff joined the academy. In addition to providing something concrete for students to use, the school also introduced Philosophy for Children (P4C) and Dramatic Enquiry[5] as means of developing empathy and seeing things from other people's perspectives.

---

[5]Dramatic Enquiry combines P4C with drama to foster creative and transferable thinking skills.

The school's approach is underpinned by three core principles:

1. model the skills of enquiry
2. foster students' ownership of learning
3. develop students' skills in reflection.

Staff model the importance of asking questions to seek clarification. This gives students the confidence to handle uncertainty, illustrated in this extract that followed the reading of the story *The Heart and the Bottle* (Jeffers, 2011):

> Student 1 – What happened to her Grandfather?
>
> Facilitator – What do you think happened?
>
> Student 1 – He died?
>
> Student 2 – Did she really cut her heart out?
>
> Facilitator – Do you really think she cut her heart out?
>
> Student 2 – Nooo ... because she wouldn't be alive ... Was it about love and feeling emotion? She was trying to keep her feelings safe 'cos she couldn't cope with feeling sad.

The teacher, acting as facilitator, reflected that it would have been easier to simply tell the students that the grandfather had died or to just say 'no' to the student's question. However, she wanted to encourage them to think independently, and turning the question back to the student meant that she had to interpret the text and work out the answer for herself. In reflecting upon providing challenging learning for pupils with ASD, the teacher acknowledges:

> I think this is sometimes where we underestimate our students; we assume because of their ASD and their language difficulties that they are unable to think deeply and express their feelings. However throughout this process I realised that they are able to think at a much higher level if given the right environment, the time to think at their own pace and the encouragement and support to articulate their thinking.

The school's second important principle is to encourage students to take increasing ownership of their learning. This is achieved by framing lessons around democratic ideas, such as choosing a question from among the class to explore further in P4C lessons. One of the boys told the teacher how P4C had helped his learning:

> Staff just let us talk – it doesn't feel like there are staff in the room; they will ask questions that help us generate more opinions and to keep the talk flowing but it feels like

a friendship. It gets us thinking about stuff we've never thought about before and we support each other through it. You can disagree with someone but you don't say you're wrong because everyone's opinions are valuable; it's about respect and trust.

This student also learnt the importance of having a 'good' question to drive the enquiry. And a good question was one when 'you're still thinking and talking about it later in the day'.

Such a comment illustrates the third principle, namely fostering students' reflective skills. Teachers create an emotionally secure climate in which students voice their feelings and thoughts, free of ridicule or harsh judgement. One student who had previously been teased in his last school for having a stutter (which made him want to hurt someone) and as a result he talked very little – his friends talked on his behalf. Although anxious about P4C sessions, after six weeks this student grew in confidence and gained courage to participate in sessions. Another student, quiet by nature, reflected on the value of P4C in helping her to express views: 'I no longer just accept things – I challenge and have learnt to say why I think things'.

In Figure 11.3 students considered the question, 'Is there a difference between justice and revenge?' The teacher used a musical video as a stimulus ('Where Is the Love?' by the American hip hop group, Black Eyed Peas). Their award-winning song, composed in 2003, addresses many issues including terrorism, racism, pollution, war, crime and intolerance. The discussion is quoted at length to illustrate the role of the teacher as facilitator and how students discuss abstract concepts in a supportive, reflective and mature manner.

Student 1	Justice is when you do something right. Revenge is getting back at someone for something. Justice is about something being over with; revenge can continue.
Student 2	Revenge can be very bad. In the movies it never ends well.
Student 3	Revenge is a personal matter, e.g. if someone kills a family member you want revenge. Justice is for everyone's sake. Justice is for the greater good.
Student 4	Revenge, hate, emotion – leads to anger. Hate can spread. You may become someone you despise?
Facilitator	*So is revenge driven by emotion?*
Student 3	Revenge may be driven by jealousy.
Student 2	Countries take revenge then it causes war.
Student 4	Yes, but countries like ours don't look for revenge; they look for justice. We help out other countries. We stick up for other countries who couldn't help themselves. It isn't revenge that they want it's justice. It takes a bigger man to look for justice than revenge.

(Continued)

(Continued)

Facilitator	*So where does that justice come from?*
Student 5	Justice can come from the police, the courts – a jury and a judge.
Student 4	If you stand up to someone who wants revenge that may turn nasty.
Student 6	Revenge is driven by hate, jealousy, racism.
Student 1	It's not seeing the bigger picture. You can protest for justice in a peaceful way … The American football player knelt during the National anthem as a form of protest.
Student 7	In the Shakespeare play, Hamlet got revenge on his uncle who killed his father. The revenge continued and Hamlet was killed.
Student 4	Yes, revenge continues – people feel guilty, angry, frustrated, suicidal and then realise justice would be better.
Student 6	Justice is an outsider – a judge and jury making a decision on whether someone is guilty.
Facilitator	*Why is that?*
Student 2	Because they're not involved in the situation.
Student 5	They can be more fair.
Student 4	Sometimes, even though justice is done, hatred can still drive revenge.
Student 6	People should concentrate on their own lives and not on other people's. I can't understand why people can't just be nice to each other.

Figure 11.3 Discussion with Y10 students about justice and revenge

Following the discussion, the students summed up their thoughts in 'thought bubbles' and put them on the wall for others to read and add their own thoughts.

CASE STUDY 3 – THINKING ROUTINES

The International IB School in Ankara (Turkey) has more than a thousand students from Pre-Kindergarten to Grade 12 (4–19-year-olds). Alona Yildirim, the assistant principal, has worked as an early years' educator for seventeen years. She noticed that her young learners found it challenging to express themselves when asked quite simple question such as, 'Why do you like this picture?', to which a typical response would be, 'Because it is pink!' Having visited Reggio Emilia in Italy, famous for its experiential approach to learning, she reflected on the culture of thinking that she witnessed. This inspired her to find out more about thinking and in 2013, along with three of her colleagues, she formed a study group and signed up for an online course, 'Making Thinking Visible' at Harvard Graduate School of Education. The group learned about thinking routines, cultural forces and using artefacts, among other things.

Thinking skills now forms part of the skills-based school curriculum alongside research, self-management, communication and social skills. Thinking routines support cross-curricular units of inquiry. For example, one unit is on storytelling. It has three inquiry lines: stories have a form, stories can be told in many ways and everyone is a storyteller. In one lesson, pupils used the 'Zoom In' routine to focus on a picture from the traditional story of the *Three Little Pigs*. The teacher printed out a poster size picture from the story and covered it with puzzle pieces marked with numbers. The intention was for pupils to look closely at a small bit of the image and discuss their thinking. The teacher prepared the following questions:

After the first puzzle piece is removed:

- What do you see?
- What do you notice?

After two, three and four subsequent pieces are removed:

- What new things do you see?
- How does this change your thinking?
- Has the new information changed your previous ideas?
- What do you wonder about?

Both the pupils and teacher notice how their thinking changes after each puzzle piece is removed. As part of the same unit, the teacher also uses the 'Step Inside' thinking routine to help the pupils imagine things, events and problems from the viewpoints of characters inside the story. So, for example, with the story of *Snow White and the Seven Dwarfs* the routine helped the pupils see life from the viewpoint of the Queen. These are the planning questions used by the school:

- How would you feel if you were Snow White/the King?
- What would you do if you were Snow White/the King?
- If you were a fairy with a magic wand, what would you change in this story?

Through using the thinking routine, the pupils learnt about different perspectives.

They were upset with the King that he did not even attempt to go to the forest and look for his daughter the day she was lost. Two boys added that if they were in the story they would go and search for her, saying, 'I am sure I can find her!' They were curious about why the Queen so longed for the death of Snow White. They could not understand why the Queen was not happy, the children found her beautiful enough. They decided that the Mirror was mean. The responses to the question, 'If you were a fairy with a magic wand, what would you change in this story?' were: 'I would make the Queen beautiful, so she does not need to poison Snow White'; 'I would make the heart of the Queen kind, so she did not hurt anyone'; and 'I would use a LASER magic wand and wish for a good heart for the Queen'. In another unit of inquiry, called 'My Future Job', the pupils used the 'I Used to Think … Now I Think' routine. The teacher invited in a parent who worked as a cardiologist to speak to the class. Before the visit, the children were asked to draw a heart on sticky-notes. They explained their pictures. During the visit, the parent told stories of operations and showed pictures and a model of a real heart. The children were amazed at the size of the real heart compared to their pictures and they began to use the phrase 'I used to think … now I think …'. After the visit, the pupils drew pictures of their hearts on sticky-notes and put them alongside their original drawings. The drawings were more detailed, for instance showing arteries and veins.

Alona and her colleagues report on how thinking routines have helped them develop as learners themselves. Alona, for example, has created her own thinking routine, 'Read, Think, Wonder', to provoke thinking during book reading sessions. After sharing her work at a national conference about intelligence, other schools have also approached her and now use thinking routines in their settings forming a study group. As for the students, Alona has noticed that they participate willingly with some viewing the routines as games. She has seen an improvement in students' language development, for example more expansive vocabulary and clear sentence structures, alongside greater confidence in explaining and reasoning things through. Alona used the See Think Wonder routine with 5-year-olds who looked at Vladimir Kush's surrealistic *Departure of the Winged Ship*. This helped them to make connections from small objects to big ideas. For example, one child first said that he saw 'water', then he clarified that it might be 'a sea' and in a few seconds he added that he saw 'rocks that might be a land'. She used sticky-notes to record the pupils' suggestions such as 'little people', 'beautiful butterflies', 'net', 'catch', 'boat' and 'flag'. Another child suggested that there was a story in the picture and so Alona used the Beginning, Middle, End routine to explore possible stories. Here are three of the stories:

> I think people in this story are bad people. They catch butterflies. I think butterflies want to travel to a butterfly land. They all sit on a ship that will take them to the Butterfly Land. The butterflies were very big and the ship became heavy and it got broken. Here it is … this part of the ship is broken. So … the butterfly could not go to the land of the Butterflies and they stopped here where the bad people were waiting for them. How can we rescue butterflies? (Kaan)
>
> I think this boat is broken and butterflies help carrying the boat. What happened before … I think the ship cracked on the rock and these people were catching fish. I think the butterflies will bring the ship to the land and after rescuing that ship they will return to their homes. (Boran)
>
> I see water … boat … This ship is floating on water. I see clouds … this is evening. I see butterflies … They will fall asleep. Waterfall … the butterflies are looking for the

waterfall. People ... bad people ... they want to catch butterflies ... they want to fry them and eat them. I see a butterfly (on the left) ... it is not on the ship ... this butterfly can swim ... The bad people can't catch this butterfly. (Atahan)

It is clear from these accounts how thinking routines support pupils as they move from seeing into thinking and writing. The school has found that pupils develop greater confidence in suggesting and sharing their own ideas.

CASE STUDY 4 – COGNITIVE ACCELERATION

Ruislip High School is a mixed comprehensive school situated in the London Borough of Hillingdon. It opened as a new school in 2006 because of the demand for secondary school places in the Ruislip area.

Dr Martina Lecky joined the school as its second headteacher in September 2011. Her doctoral work involved research into teachers' professional development, as they became effective practitioners of the CASE (Cognitive Acceleration through Science Education) methodology. She introduced the CA programmes to Key Stage 3 in English, mathematics and science during the academic year 2011–2012. These programmes are often referred to as *Let's Think* (LT) and the overarching education charity is called the Let's Think Forum (LTF). As a member of the LTF council and trustees, Dr Lecky could use support from LTF tutors in English and mathematics as part of teachers' professional development with the intervention approaches.

Ruislip High School is currently the only known state secondary school in the country to be involved in the *Let's Think* programme in English, mathematics and science with Year 7 and 8 students (and Year 9 for some lessons). To embed the approach across the curriculum, the school has supported champions in each subject and there are clear expectations for how and when the lessons are delivered. In English, the lessons have been planned into schemes of work so that themes, genres or reasoning patterns work with the schemes. The science department conducts the Science Reasoning Test (SRT II) at the beginning of Year 7. This test was used in the original CASE research conducted in the 1980s by Professors Michael Shayer and Philip Adey; this provides teachers with Piagetian scores for students, which give an indication of their respective cognitive levels. The school finds that this data is very useful when delivering LT lessons as it allows practitioners to consider the cognitive demand of the activities on students. For example, in CASE lessons, the students are grouped using the Piagetian scores and teachers can focus their questions and support students' reasoning based on their group's social construction of the reasoning pattern. While the school has not conducted any post-test tests to measure the impact of the LT programmes, there is a range of teacher and student attitudinal feedback that supports the use of the approach at Key Stage 3. For example, the following quotations reflect how good students recognise the importance of discussing their ideas and enjoy the freedom of not having to get the 'right' answer.

> We like discussing ideas and if you don't know the answer, you can discuss it with your table and they can help you understand it. (Callum, 7D)
>
> I like *Let's Think* lessons better than normal lessons because they let you properly interact with the class, and you can learn from other pupils. (Natasha, 7C)
>
> I enjoy the *Let's Think* lessons a lot. The lessons make you really think and I wish we had more of them. Sometimes I leave the room still thinking. (Ben, 7A)

Teacher comments reflect how well they believe students respond to the constructivist approach as well as noting improvements to their teaching. The LT lessons are a reminder of the importance of oracy. For example, Ms Keenan who teaches LT English within the school, highlights that the paired and class discussion that takes place during the lessons raises pupil confidence, particularly when encountering new texts. This confidence is transferrable to other lesson contexts. The reasons for this may be because of the critical thinking skills that are developed during lessons. Ms Kidd, another English teacher in the school, suggests:

> *Let's Think* challenges students to think critically about texts and trains them in the practice of supporting their interpretations with evidence. The quick pace of the discussions means they become focused on reaching their conclusions without becoming distracted. Focusing on short stories means they also have experience in commenting on 'whole texts'. I've found that teaching *Let's Think* lessons has informed and improved the rest of my teaching: it's made me reconsider my questioning, assess how I choose students for feedback and how I respond to student opinion.

Creative thinking is also fostered through the lessons, and in mathematics this is frequently evident. Furthermore, teachers themselves have seen benefits in terms of how using the approach has impacted on their own teaching. Teachers feel that their understanding of the pedagogical principles underpinning the approach has improved. For example, Mr Pritchard from the science department feels:

> Teaching CASE has improved my understanding of science education pedagogy and my teaching practice. Instead of wanting the correct answer I now want to know why they think their answer is correct and allow students to show if they understand.

This sentiment is echoed by Mr Maclean, another of the school's science teachers, who says:

> CASE lessons improve your teaching skills by making you more aware of the underlying principles of learning. My lesson planning has improved since I started teaching CASE as I tend to provide more opportunities for peer discussion and debate between students.

The sustainability of LT programmes relies on teachers' ownership of the approach and their development through regular feedback about their practice. It has been important to identify LT subject champions and allow them to observe lessons in a coaching model to provide feedback about teachers' development with the classroom methodology. This has been more challenging in recent years with the focus on the curriculum and assessment reforms at Key Stage 4 and Key Stage 5. LT teachers are reminded, however, from feedback in the classroom as well as student focus groups and surveys that LT lessons have a profound effect on students and they are aware of the pedagogical benefits to their own professional development; therefore, they and school leaders remain committed to promoting LT programmes at Ruislip High School.

CONCLUSION

These case studies and others give a hint of what is possible when schools take the teaching of thinking seriously. Despite the prescriptive nature of the curriculum, particularly in England, teachers can exercise reasonable autonomy at the local classroom level. The approaches reviewed in this and previous chapters do not suggest that teachers need to introduce radical change to their practices. For example, thinking routines can easily be incorporated into lessons irrespective of the content. Only by making thinking more visible in and around the classroom, which is the shared aim of the approaches discussed in this book, are pupils likely to gain confidence in expressing views and interact more effectively with others and the environment.

SUMMARY

- The effective implementation of programmes to promote pupils' thinking depends on strategic planning, effective classroom practices, the right kind of professional learning and productive partnerships. Good leadership brings these elements together.
- Schools can promote pupils' creative and critical thinking in many ways. This chapter has reviewed case studies that are successfully using approaches that focus on dispositions,

P4C, thinking routines and Cognitive Acceleration. However, in many cases, schools use a variety of approaches and tools to suit their needs.

As teachers commit themselves to promoting pupils' thinking, they inevitably demonstrate and model Habits of Mind such as asking questions and posing problems, thinking flexibly, remaining open to continuous learning and thinking interdependently.

12

SOME CONCLUDING THOUGHTS

On the next appropriate occasion, ask colleagues what they want the children they teach to be like when they leave school. If part of a workshop, you might want to use a Chalk Talk routine (Chapter 4) to record their responses. The likelihood is that most colleagues will mention qualities, dispositions and skills such as independence, confidence, creativity, curiosity, problem-solving, digital competence, communication, teamwork, empathy, concern for the environment, caring and so forth. It is less likely that traditional academic skills such as reading comprehension, writing and arithmetic will feature so prominently. It is not that these skills are unimportant. It is simply that they are not sufficient to equip young people with what they need to join the workforce, establish good relationships, enjoy fulfilling lives and make a meaningful contribution to society as informed, responsible citizens. Take reading as an example: it is no longer enough for primary children to learn to read at a functional level, because the demands of modern-day literacy call for the skills of reading to learn, and being able to critique information from a range of sources. In this final chapter, we discuss how the book's key messages relate to existing knowledge of good teaching and learning and the likely future trends in education.

WHAT WE KNOW ABOUT HIGH QUALITY TEACHING AND LEARNING

There is a strong body of evidence associated with the most effective teaching practices in general (Hattie, 2009; Hattie, 2012; Husbands and Pearce, 2012; Coe et al., 2014) and teaching pupils to improve their thinking in particular (Higgins et al., 2004; Fisher, 2005; Lucas and Spencer, 2017). The most effective teaching:

- builds on pupils' prior knowledge, experience and views
- models correct procedures and techniques
- scaffolds pupils' learning, e.g. through prompts and questions
- uses a range of techniques and resources to stimulate interest
- communicates content clearly and accurately
- develops pupils' self-awareness and self-control (metacognition)
- encourages independence and responsibility
- provides timely and constructive feedback.

Effective pedagogy also rests on a teacher's secure content knowledge and building supportive relationships, underpinned by a strong moral purpose.

The question of whether one teaching style is more impactful than another has long occupied educational researchers (e.g. Bennett, 1976; Li, 2012). Turner (1979) asserted that strong school systems expose learners to different teaching styles. He deplored the idea that there was a single best style of teaching that teachers should adopt. Far better, he argued, for teachers to be skilled in several styles. More recent research suggests that once teachers adopt a certain teaching style, they generally stick to it day after day, year after year without giving it too much thought (Hollingsworth and Ybarra, 2018). Of course, teachers are not a homogenous group and are at various stages of professional development, working in a range of different contexts.

In discussing the development of student teachers, Twiselton (2006) suggests there are three 'types' on a sliding scale. 'Task managers' are those who are mostly concerned with organisation: keeping pupils busy, noise levels low, ensuring worksheets are filled in and 'getting through' tasks on time. They see themselves as in control. 'Curriculum deliverers' are conscious of meeting objectives, gathering evidence of pupils' progress and ensuring that lesson plans include what's expected. Their identity is wrapped up in compliance and coverage. Finally, 'concept/skills builders' are more interested in the learning itself and how pupils can transfer and apply concepts and skills in their everyday lives beyond the lesson. It is the latter type of teacher that is most likely to promote pupils' creative and critical thinking.

Tochon and Munby (1993) compared the difference between how novice and expert teachers used their time. They found that novice teachers adopted a 'diachronic' view where time was planned and scripted, lessons pursued in a linear manner and pupils allocated closed tasks. In contrast, expert teachers viewed time as 'synchronic', they were more open-minded and they adapted their actions depending on how pupils responded. Other studies show that expert teachers think on their feet rapidly, reframe problems to reach effective solutions and build on pupils' questions rather than curtail discussion (Elliot, 2015). In short, expert teachers demonstrate the very Habits of Mind that we reviewed in Chapter 10 as important for learners.

The mindset of teachers (their attitudes, values and beliefs), as much as the quality of their instruction, are the most important school-based factors that impact on learning (Hay McBer, 2000; Attfield, 2012; Coe et al., 2014). It is noteworthy that the main argument in a recent book by the research guru John Hattie is that how teachers *think* matters as much as what they do (Hattie and Zierer, 2018). He contends that the best teachers can answer not only what they are doing, but *how* and *why* they are doing what they are doing. They not only have the necessary knowledge and skills (competences), but also the will and judgement (mind frames) to exercise these appropriately. So, for instance, expert teachers ask themselves how they can evaluate the impact of their teaching, how they engage in dialogue as much as monologue, their role in building relationships and trust so that learners feel safe to make mistakes, and how they focus on the language of learning. If such mind frames are so critical for effective teaching, then they are surely even more significant for learners.

Carol Dweck's (2006; 2017) pioneering research on growth and fixed mindsets would suggest so. She and her colleagues claim that about 40 per cent of children hold a damaging fixed mindset, believing that intelligence is something you are born with – and so you are either good at something like mathematics or not. Another 40 per cent hold a growth mindset, which is forward-looking and sees potential, while the remaining 20 per cent waver between the two mindsets (Dweck, 2006). These figures should not be taken too rigidly. It's possible to have a fixed *and* growth mindset within the same subject area (e.g. a more positive attitude towards swimming than dance in physical education). Moreover, studies seeking to replicate Dweck's original research have not reached similar conclusions. For example, Li and Bates (2017) found no support for mindset effects on cognitive ability. Didau (2016: 311) suggests that getting too excited by growth mindset is 'dangerous wishful thinking' and he argues that growth is possible only when some things are settled, i.e. a fixed mindset is beneficial in some circumstances, such as learning times tables and grammatical rules.

Nonetheless, there is no doubt that seeing intelligence and abilities as areas that can grow is a positive development (Blackwell et al., 2007). The value of plain hard work has also been long recognised – as the ancient Biblical proverb put it, 'Go to the ant, you sluggard' (King James Bible, Proverbs 6:6). This is supported by modern neuroscience, which reveals that neuron networks are created and strengthened through effort and practice (Goldberg, 2009). A combination of effort and positive outlook is, of course, not sufficient to secure good progress in learning. Many other factors come into play including the quality of teaching.

In mathematics, Jo Boaler (2016) has applied Dweck's concept to show how students can move from feelings of self-doubt to strong self-confidence. Essentially, such a transformation is attributed to good teaching – the group arrangements, nature of tasks, questioning, feedback and so forth. But it is also about the 'hidden' messages that pupils absorb about mathematics and the resulting attitudes they adopt to the subject. If pupils are asked what their role is in mathematics lessons, many will say it is to answer questions correctly. As John Holt (1995 [1964]: 242) pointed out, 'How can we foster a joyous, alert, wholehearted participation in life if we build all our schooling around the holiness of getting "right answers"?' Rarely do pupils see their contribution as one of posing problems or finding situations in life where mathematics could help them. Thinking creatively is not something they associate with the subject and herein lies one of the fundamental reasons why many pupils are put off mathematics. If more children and young people were encouraged to approach mathematics as a field to investigate without fear of failing to answer a string of questions on calculations, then engagement would increase. For this to happen, teachers need to focus more on the subject's visual and creative potential, as well as its logical, abstract nature.

The potential of children as learners should certainly not be underestimated. In 2013, 7-year-old Zora Ball in Philadelphia became the youngest person to create a profit-making mobile video game. She designed the game in one of her lessons at the Harambee Institute of Science and Technology Charter School. In very different circumstances, Kelvin Doe from Sierra Leone taught himself engineering at the age of 13 using scraps of material picked up from rubbish bins. He invented a battery to light up homes in the district and now runs his own radio station under the name DJ Focus because he believes 'if you focus, you can do an invention perfectly' (Hudson, 2012). We know that young children can learn at a phenomenal rate when motivated to do so, when supported, by having a go, through trial and error, when they receive and respond to good feedback and when they take ownership of their learning.

Sugata Mitra has demonstrated this most powerfully through his famous hole-in-the-wall experiments in the slums of New Delhi, India. Children of mixed ages, living in desperate poverty, learnt sophisticated concepts by teaching themselves through a networked computer installed in a wall (Mitra and Negroponte, 2012). Interestingly, the children invented their own words for what they saw on the screen. For example, the hourglass symbol that appears when a program is 'thinking' was called *damru*, which is the name of a small wooden drum shaped like an hourglass that is a symbol of the Hindu god Shiva. The mouse cursor was called *sui*, a Hindi word for needle, or *teer*, which means arrow. Mitra describes how through this discovery-based learning (which he calls Minimally Invasive Education) children learn from each other, willingly share information and create vocabulary to describe their experiences, which helps them to generalise. After a while a stage is reached when no further discoveries are made and an adult prompt is needed, such as 'Did you know the computer plays music?' In the hole-in-the-wall experiments, the prompts were provided by passing adults or through accidental discovery. And so, another cycle of self-instruction began. After three months, what skills had the children acquired? Starting from a blank slate, they could navigate, load and save files, send and receive emails, use social media, download files, run software and troubleshoot. Field observers and local teachers reported improvements in attendance and performance in school examinations, English vocabulary, problem-solving, concentration, teamwork and self-regulation.

This field research seems to contradict those who claim that discovery-based learning is not as effective as direct instruction in promoting learning. For Mitra, what matters is giving children the opportunity to work within self-organised environments, making the traditional instructional role of teachers largely unnecessary. The debate over enquiry-based learning models and direct instruction is likely to continue with scholars debating research findings on a regular basis (Leat, 2017). In terms of our central theme, teachers can use a variety of approaches to promote creative and critical thinking, but clearly pupils need time and space to practise these skills regularly and in real-life contexts.

The key pedagogical messages from this book are summarised below. Most cover familiar territory in terms of the essential teaching skills that good teachers demonstrate such as drawing on prior knowledge, questioning, modelling, managing effective group work and providing feedback. There are also specific points relating to the teaching of thinking, such as making thinking explicit, using tools, maps and other visual organisers, and cultivating the thinking dispositions without which pupils will struggle to develop the necessary skills. This is often best achieved through social contexts in which pupils have regular opportunities to talk and share their ideas. To foster the skills of thinking, teachers should:

- prioritise the teaching of thinking
- plan for the teaching of thinking across the curriculum
- facilitate regular opportunities for pupils to talk about and engage in real-world problems and issues
- model the language of thinking
- provide classroom displays that are rich in visual images, thinking quotes, puzzles, challenges, prompts and questions
- invest in professional development
- evaluate the impact of thinking interventions.

Thinking has always had a strong social context since hunter-gatherers first collaborated to solve common problems. Nowadays, the benefits of thinking collaboratively are well illustrated in digital technologies such as Google and Facebook. These would not have developed if they had been left to individual inventors (Garrison, 2015). Having an audience also stimulates thinking. This is illustrated by research in which several dozen 4–5-year-olds were shown patterns of coloured bugs and asked to predict which would appear next in the sequence (Rittle-Johnson et al., 2008). One group worked alone quietly to solve the problems. Another group was asked to explain to a tape recorder how they were solving each puzzle, while a third group explained their reasoning to their mothers, who sat near them, listening but not offering any help. The groups were then given more complicated patterns, which were harder to predict. The results showed that the children who worked alone did worst of all. The ones who talked to the tape recorder fared better, with researchers suggesting that the act of talking aloud and sharing ideas helped their thinking. But the ones who talked to a meaningful audience did best of all, solving twice as many puzzles as those who worked silently. Similar findings have been reported with older students and adults (Thompson, 2013).

THE FUTURE

In 2017 at a roundtable discussion hosted by the OECD over three days, leading educationalists from around the world considered what schools need to do to prepare children for the world in 2030. By then, children now entering nursery school will become citizens. Thirty-five relevant, measurable, impactful and malleable 'key constructs' were identified as the future core business of schools. Many of these have been featured in this book. They include creative thinking, curiosity and persistence. These constructs are effectively more detailed elements of learning (knowledge, skills, attitudes and values). But, metaphorically speaking, rather than just talking about the brass section of the mental orchestra, these experts are beginning to describe the French horn, trumpet and tuba. They are comparing these instruments with those in the string, percussion and woodwind sections. Orchestras were once limited to a handful of musicians using a few wooden, stringed instruments. Today the typical orchestra, of a hundred or so permanent musicians, has had to keep pace with technological and social changes (e.g. electronic keyboards, new musical styles and the demands of diverse audiences). The OECD recognises, as many others do, that the orchestra of children's minds cannot be left behind if education is to help meet the demands placed on the future generation.

The OECD group maintains that if children and young people are to be well equipped to meet the challenges ahead, they must have a much greater say in their learning. For the OECD, the central idea that should bind everything together is learner agency or enabling children to create change in their own lives. This goes much deeper than child-centred practices and is not about children 'doing their own thing' because it involves pupils thinking interdependently, taking responsibility, demonstrating initiative and recognising the consequences of decisions. In the classroom, this means pupils actively discussing problems and issues, asking questions, justifying viewpoints, listening empathetically to others, offering suggestions for improvement, reflecting on their actions, self-regulating their thinking and caring for others and the environment. Again, these things have been discussed in this book.

Traditionalists who believe in teacher-led instruction are likely to balk at the sentiments expressed by the OECD. But a greater emphasis on learner agency should not diminish the skillset of teachers. Rather, teachers need to be more skilled if they are to focus on the needs of individual learners and less on a stand-and-deliver model. In *Building Learning Power* (BLP), Guy Claxton (2002) uses the term 'orchestration' to describe the way in which teachers might organise classroom activities and the environment. In a literal sense, teachers can learn much from modern-day conductors. Tom Service (2012) the journalist and broadcaster, likens conducting to alchemy. He points out that the best conductors 'become a lightning rod of listening; a focus so that the players and the conductor can become something bigger than all of them – than all of us – at the same time as feeling fully realised as individuals' (Burton-Hill, 2014). How can someone who does not make a sound, inspire others to jaw-dropping heights of musical creativity? The best conductors listen, act as bridges between what the audience sees and hears, show leadership skills and are fully committed to their own professional learning. Contrary to popular perception, in conductor competitions it is not the most flamboyant candidates who usually win. The panel of judges see through their energetic movements as a pointless Pony show. Richard Straus, one of the greatest twentieth-century composers, barely moved his hands. He once said that 'only amateur conductors get sweaty' (Almila, 2016).

Similar sentiments have been expressed about what teachers need to do to get the most from learners. Titles such as *Talk-Less Teaching: Practice, Participation and Progress* (Wallace and Kirkman, 2014) and *The Lazy Teacher's Handbook: How Your Students Learn More When You Teach Less* (Smith, 2017) reflect the mantra 'learning, not teaching'. Of course, learning should be emphasised because outcomes matter. And yet, conceptually, the point of teaching is simply to bring about learning. This can be achieved through inquiry-based approaches, led by pupils, but also through instruction. Alexander (1984) notes that those who reject the word 'teaching' fall into the trap of providing weapons for their critics and should instead recognise the more flexible, multifaceted meaning of 'teaching'. Good teachers certainly think flexibly about the methods and resources they use so that pupils can achieve learning objectives. While views about teachers talking less are new (Holt, 1964; 1972), they are problematic in diminishing the importance of *high quality* teaching through modelling, questioning, explaining and demonstrating. They can also lead to the adoption of arbitrary goals such as the '80:20' rule where teachers are advised to ensure that students talk for 80 per cent of the lesson and the teacher communicates 20 per cent of the time. It is sometimes overlooked that when well delivered, old-fashioned talks and lectures can prove cognitively challenging for all ages and provide the basis for fruitful discussion. Consider the phenomenal success of the Royal Institution Christmas Lectures or the Technology, Entertainment and Design (TED) Talks. What matters is not simply giving pupils more time to talk, but teachers regularly reflecting on the quality of communication in the classroom (between pupils and between pupils and adults) and how talk can be used more effectively to develop pupils' thinking. For example, this means planning to develop creative dialogues in the classroom, which are essential to learning and thinking (Fisher, 2009).

And in the future, these dialogues should increasingly focus on the global challenges that are likely to impact on pupils' lives. A good starting point to generate creative and critical thinking among young people is to show a video (of which there are various versions), which reduces the world to a community of one hundred people. This illustrates the inequalities in the world – 15 people would be malnourished and one starving, while 21 would be overweight. Overall, one person would control 50 per cent of all the money in the world (Osborne, 2016). If children and young people are to become genuine global citizens, they need to acquire the knowledge, skills, values and attitudes to enable them to behave in an ethical, responsible manner. As John Dewey (1916: 239) famously said, 'Education is not a preparation for life, it is life itself'.

Schools should prepare pupils *now* for living and working in a global society. This means engaging with issues such as climate change, poverty and social injustice. To do so well, pupils need to learn how to better express viewpoints, cooperate with others, share responsibility and actively engage in projects designed to improve the environment. As global citizens, pupils will need to respect diversity and be willing to take responsibility to make the world a more equitable and sustainable place to live. Many of the approaches we have mentioned can support teachers in achieving these goals. Thinkers Keys, for instance, were developed very much with environmental education in mind. Weil (2014) talks about giving students the tools so that they begin to learn how to address global challenges from an early age. For instance, figuring out the 'true price' of an everyday item and encouraging them to work in 'solutionary' teams to come up with an innovative, cost-effective solution to a real-life problem.

Technologies are a major force for globalisation, notably through social networking. Policy-makers and educationalists around the world are mindful of the double-edged sword that technologies present. On the one hand, educational systems need to ensure that young people are equipped with the digital literacy skills they need to flourish and which the economy cries for. And yet the fast-changing world of virtual reality, artificial intelligence and smart technologies put considerable pressures on educators to keep up to speed (e.g. in terms of training) and ensure that any provision is safe and secure. Ann Longfield (2018), the Children's Commissioner in England, calls on schools and parents to prepare older primary children for the 'cliff edge' they face in using social media as they enter secondary school. The playful, creative use of social media (e.g. through games) changes to one where social validation matters more than anything else (i.e. 'likes' and 'comments'). Longfield wants schools to provide online courses on building children's resilience and the survey provides further evidence of the importance of promoting dispositional thinking.

Levels of digital literacy are likely to be increasingly demanding. At a fundamental level, as touched upon in Chapter 3, pupils need the critical skills to locate and evaluate online information. It has become something of a cliché to say that pupils need to move from being consumers to producers of knowledge using technologies as an aid. Developments such as including computer programming within the curriculum, 'flipped classrooms', gamification of lessons[1] and collaborative web-based projects such as 'The School in the Cloud',[2] are pointers to what may become common educational practices. Businesses will require a workforce adept at identifying the kind of thinking that different tasks require, and then adjusting their work environments to enhance their ability to accomplish these tasks. The Institute for the Futures calls this 'design mindset' (2011: 11). However, one leading expert in technology and education reckons:

> We are at the ground floor of a new world full of imagination, creativity, innovation and digital wisdom. We are going to have to create the education of the future because it doesn't exist anywhere today. (Wakefield, 2015)

A review of research evidence over forty or so years suggests that the impact of technologies on learning has consistently brought benefits (Higgins et al., 2012). However, despite all the hype and occasional hysteria, we simply do not know if the use of technologies is making the difference. While many experts conclude that the digitalisation of education will continue to be a welcome and inevitable area of growth, Selwyn (2016) questions the underlying values, agenda and interests of those who stand to gain most from an increasingly digital-based education. The key point relevant to our discussion is that pupils need the skills of thinking creatively to make the most *appropriate* use of technologies in their lives. This includes developing self-regulating habits to cope with decreasing attention spans, fear-of-missing-out syndromes and digital withdrawal disorders.

Globalisation and the rise of technologies illustrate most powerfully the need to teach children and young people the skills of creative and critical thinking so that they are well placed to navigate the future with confidence and capability. A new science of learning is beginning to emerge, based on controlled psychology experiments, brain scanning,

---

[1] e.g. Classcraft at www.classcraft.com (accessed 20 June 2018).

[2] https://theschoolinthecloud.org (accessed 20 June 2018).

classroom observations and computational models of machine learning. By combining these sources, researchers are gaining much greater insight into how people learn, both as individuals and together, at different ages, with and without the teacher and across different cultures (Sharples et al., 2016). For example, we know that all new learning is built on a foundation of prior knowledge. We also know how memory works, how learning is affected by factors such as regular sleep and exercise, the importance of developing sensory experiences in the early years, why mindset matters and how thinking is shaped by emotions. There are also principles of learning that have endured over the centuries. Structure, motivation and high quality instruction remain essential. Successful learners do more than retrieve knowledge and apply skills in a technical manner. They *think* intelligently about their actions, beliefs and values. The good news is that children and young people can be taught to be more intelligent and better thinkers. But if we want students of all ages to improve their thinking, we can't think for them. They need the guidance, time and space to figure things out for themselves. It is hoped that the approaches reviewed in this book will provide such support.

APPENDIX – PLANNING

1 MEDIUM TERM PLANNING FOR THINKING MAPS IN ENGLISH (SEE CHAPTER 6)

Structure/ Parts	Tips	Examples	Sentence and word level teaching points
Headline	No more than 7 words	Pop Star's Shoplifting Shame! Father Christmas Sees Red!	• Alliteration • Rhyme • Puns/play on words • Exclamation marks
By-line	Writer's name, title and location (if an international story)	Ivor Pen, weather correspondent, London	• Commas to separate items in a list
Lead	5 bare bums on a rugby post – no more than 3 sentences	Britain came to a standstill this morning as temperatures crashed to minus ten and snow covered the whole country	• Causal connectives • 3rd person narrative • Tenses may change
Body	• Details about each of the Ws, some will be more important • Balanced (explain both sides) • Factual information • Short paragraphs • Emotive language (where appropriate) • Event-specific language		• Formal style
Sources	• Names, ages and/or titles of people who provided information • Use of direct and reported speech		• Direct speech – using inverted commas correctly • Reported speech Y4, 5, 6

(Continued)

(Continued)

Structure/ Parts	Tips	Examples	Sentence and word level teaching points
Illustration and caption	• No need to draw picture until publishing stage • Decide what the picture will be and write a caption underneath – short and snappy		

Thinking Maps which may be helpful in structuring writing or deconstructing exemplar texts:

What happened? What is the sequence of events? What are the sub-stages?

Flow Map

What are the causes and effects of this event?

Multi-Flow Map

Source: Danescourt Primary School

2 PLANNING FOR THINKING MAPS (SEE CHAPTER 6)

Pupils consider what options are available to them at 16 and 18.

Draw a flow chart of each age on the board with each of the options on there.

Pupils giving examples

Pupils reflect on their performance, the roles they fell into and the success of the task and team.

Split into small groups. Group task is to produce a bubble map for each age looking at the options, a brief description of what they are, the advantages of each and examples. They need to think about how to lay it out.

Teacher observations

Completion of bubble map

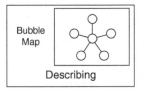

Bubble Map

Describing

Each group member must contribute.

Resources: Task 3 Notes, Careers Pilot website, laptops. Bubble maps.

ALP: place in appropriate group Task 4: Two different work or study opportunities

60 mins

Teacher observations
Completion Tree Maps
Teacher and pupil feedback

Pupils start to look at specific pathways and how they can help with career progression.

Use PPT to guide pupils through this task

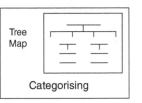

Tree Map

Categorising

Select a few pupils to show what they have produced.

Resources: Tree Maps and/or laptops

ALN: Help given with choices and producing the tree map

Task 5: Progression of a job role

Peer assessment on presentations at the end

(Continued)

(Continued)

Pupils take one specific job role or opportunity and look at how they can progress	Use PPT to guide pupils through this task.	45 mins	Teacher observations
			Quality of pupils flow map
			Verbal feedback after the activity

Flow Map

Sequencing

Select a few pupils to show what they have produced.

Resources: Flow Maps and/or laptops

ALN: Help given with choice and producing the flow map.

Source: Castle School

3 LESSON PLAN FOR 'BEANBAG PICKUP' (SEE CHAPTER 9)

Detailed Lesson Plan – KS2			
Date: 22.4.15	**Year Group:** Year 5 (9 chn.) Year 6 (19 chn.)	**Subject:** Maths – Problem Solving	**Observer:**

WALT: be systematic when problem solving and to find a rule. SOME – to express a rule using algebra.	**WILF:** WANT: identify and explain verbally patterns in the Beanbag Competition. EXPECT: As above but will also be able to use a given algebraic formula to predict future levels of the game. WOW: Can identify and explain patterns in the beanbag competition and can create an algebraic rule for this.
Assessment Opportunities/methods: Pupils will be assessed against the objective through the methods of observation, while pupils work. Through questioning of pupils and through discussion with pupils about their work and findings. *Self Assessment: thumbs, fist to five throughout, use of plenary cards at the end of the session.*	**TIB:** Pupils need to be able to spot patterns in numbers and explain these using mathematical language. Year 6 pupils need to be aware of algebra ready for going to high school and some pupils need to be challenged to do this as it is the next step in their learning.

Skills Framework:

Thinking Skills	ICT
Planning: Gathering information **Develop:** Generating and developing ideas Thinking logically and seeking patterns **Reflect:** Linking and lateral thinking Evaluating own thinking and learning	Use of ICT to enhance teaching and learning ⊗ ⑦

Subject Specific Skills:

KS2 – SKILLS	KS2 - RANGE
1. Solve mathematical problems Develop their own mathematical strategies and ideas and consider those of others	**Calculate in a variety of ways**

(Continued)

(Continued)

Try different approaches	Use of a variety of mental method of computation
2. Communicate mathematically	**Number – Investigate pattern and relationship**
Recognise and generalise in words, patterns that arise in numerical situations.	
Explain strategies, methods, choices and conclusions to others in a variety of ways	Explore features of numbers – square numbers
3. Reason mathematically	
Develop early ideas of algebra and mathematical structure by exploring number sequences and relationships; explain and predict subsequent terms	
LNF – NUMERACY	LNF – LITERACY
Developing numerical reasoning	**Oracy**
N2 – Identify the appropriate steps and information needed to complete a task or reach a solution	Year 6 O7 – contribute purposefully to a group discussion to achieve agreed aims
N3 – Select appropriate mathematics and techniques to use	
N7 – Explain results and procedures using mathematical language	
N9 – Use appropriate notation, symbols and units of measurement	

Previous Learning:	Resources:
Pupils have had some experience of identifying rules within problem solving sessions but further consolidation and work is needed on this in order to ensure that MAT pupils in particular demonstrate this level 5 skill.	Mini whiteboards
	Interactive board
	Squared paper
	Beanbags and chalk
	Count Fourways PPT – Step 5 in 2s
	Jigsaw Numbers PPT – Step 5
	Plenary Cards

Key Vocabulary:

CLIC – proper, improper and mixed number fractions, jigsaw numbers

Algebra

Pattern

Rule
Horizontally
Vertically
Square numbers

Key Questions:

What is the shortest route I can take?

What patterns do you notice in your results?

How would you explain this pattern?

Can you predict what will happen at level ... of this competition?

Why do you think that the shortest walk is one less than the number of beanbags?

Introduction:

BLP: collaboration, revising, noticing

Remind the children of what CLIC means

CLIC – First 20 minutes

Counting – Count Fourways Step 6 – for 2s – I can count in decimals. Use the PowerPoint to practise counting forward and backwards in decimals. Ask pupils about fraction equivalents.

Learn its – Chant 8 times table. Randomised names to answer a jumbled times table question.

It's nothing new – Jigsaw Numbers Step 5 – I can find the missing decimal piece. Recap 'remember to's for this step (completed yesterday). Using PPT go over some of these together as a class, with pupils showing their answers on the mini whiteboards.

Calculation Multiplication Step 17 – I can solve a 1d x a 1d.p. On mini whiteboards pupils practise multiplication strategies. Remind pupils to make links to Squiggleworth and the 'remember to's for this step. Differentiation for this is as follows:

JP, SR, KL, MR, ZT – practise full written method for step 17 – with SH.

Class and MAT – start to move pupils onto abridged part of step 17 – Teacher models how we can complete 4 x 2.3 using an abridged method. Pupils practise this on mini whiteboards and show me!

- **Introduce the objective to the children.** Share the success criteria to the lesson with them and discuss the skills and learning muscles that we will be using. Go over the structure of the lesson with the pupils.
- **Explain to pupils that there is a new Olympic sport.** What do you think it is?
- **Show pupils grid on IWB.** Explain that this is level three of the competition. Explain that in order to win they need to pick up all the beanbags in the shortest time by only walking horizontally or vertically. Demonstrate a route on the board – what is wrong with this route?

(Continued)

(Continued)

- **Take children outside with a grid already set up.** In pairs – can you work out a route? Snowball and share ideas with another pair. Get a child from each pair to show route. Which is the shortest? How did you know? How can we describe how far we have walked? Ensure pupils have found the shortest route.

Main Activity:

BLP: collaboration, noticing, reasoning, perseverance

- **Group Task** – draw grids for the next two levels of the competition – 4x4, 5x5 and 6x6 (time permitting). Work out the shortest possible route. Rough paper to record results – how can we record them systematically?

Differentiation:

LA pupils – Support by SH for this part of the activity.

MAT – through questioning get pupils to start to think of the algebraic formula and make predictions – Can you tell me any patterns you see in your results? How could we record this pattern using algebra, e.g. if n is the number of sides? How would you explain it to someone else? Can you predict how many steps are needed for level 10?

- **Record pupils' results on the board.** Show pupils the results table so far. Can you predict what the number of steps will be for level 6 or 7? How did you work that out?

- **Paired TALK – what patterns or rules can you see?** Why do you think that the shortest walk is one less than the number of beanbags? Snowball discussion. Record pattern in words on the board. Explain that mathematicians hate writing and so like to shorten things down.

- **If MAT were able to do this during the group activity ask some of them to explain the rule to the children using some algebra.** This can be reinforced with the use IWB, to explore how we could represent this as an algebraic rule. Check pupils can remember their square numbers.

- **Using mini whiteboards get pupils to confirm this rule by using the example of 7 sides.** LA pupils are supported throughout this part of the lesson by SH. MAT pupils could use the formula to calculate the number of steps for the 20th, 43rd and 113th levels.

- Throughout the session reinforce the learning objective and the success criteria – use of thumbs and fist to five to do so.

Plenary:

BLP: meta learning

- **Go over the learning objective** with the children and get an initial thumbs for the LO.

- **Pupils chose the plenary for the session using the plenary cards** – random plenary selected and completed by the children! Ensure that plenary enables pupils to reflect on the LO and the success criteria as well as skills used in the session and the BLP muscles used.

- **Go away and have a think** – housepoint for those that come back with an answer! - Would our results be the same if we did a rectangle format instead of a square? Why? Can you think of any real-life examples of this?

Teacher/SLSO Evaluation:

Source: St Roberts RC Primary School

REFERENCES

Academies Commission (2013) *Unleashing Greatness: Getting the Best from an Academised System. The Report of the Academies Commission.* London: Pearson/RSA.

Adey, P. (2002) *Learning Intelligence: Cognitive Acceleration Across the Curriculum from 5 to 15 Years.* Maidenhead: Open University Press.

Adey, P. (2005) 'Issues arising from the long-term evaluation of cognitive acceleration programs', *Research in Science Education*, 35(1): 3–22.

Adey, P., Robertson, A. and Venville, G. (2001) *Let's Think!* Windsor: NFER-Nelson.

Adey, P., Robertson, A. and Venville, G. (2002) 'Effects of a cognitive acceleration programme on Year 1 pupils', *British Journal of Educational Psychology*, 72: 1–75.

Adey, P. and Shayer, M. (1994) *Really Raising Standards: Cognitive Intervention and Academic Achievement.* London: Routledge.

Adey, P. and Shayer, M. (2011) 'The effects of Cognitive Acceleration – and speculation about causes of these effects', presentation at AERA, Learning, Research and Development Centre, University of Pittsburgh, available at: www.letsthinkinenglish. org/wpcontent/uploads/2012/06/TheEffectsofCognitiveAcceleration.pdf (accessed 14 February 2017).

Adey, P., Shayer, M. and Yates, C. (1989) *Thinking Science: The Curriculum Materials of the CASE Project.* London: Thomas Nelson and Sons.

Adhami, M., Johnson, D. and Shayer, M. (1995) *Thinking Maths: The Curriculum Materials of the Cognitive Acceleration through Mathematics Education (CAME) Project – Teacher's Guide.* London: CAME Project/King's College.

Adhami, M., Robertson, A. and Shayer, M. (2004) *Let's Think Through Maths! Developing Thinking in Mathematics with Five and Six-year-olds.* Windsor: NFER-Nelson.

Affley, P. (2012) 'Putting thinking at the heart of learning', *Primary Teacher Update*, December: 19–20.

Aiston, S., Rudd, P. and O'Donnell, L. (2002) *School Partnerships in Action: A Case Study of West Sussex Specialist Schools.* Slough: NFER.

Albrecht, K. (2006) *Social Intelligence: The New Science of Success.* San Francisco: Wiley.

Alexander, R.J. (1984) *Primary Teaching.* London: Cassell.

Alexander, R.J. (2008) *Towards Dialogic Teaching, Rethinking Classroom Talk.* York: Dialogos.

Alexander, R.J. (ed.) (2010) *Children, Their World, Their Education: Final Report and Recommendations of the Cambridge Primary Review*. Abingdon: Routledge.

Ali, A. (2015) 'Schools are "too focused on exam results and don't prepare pupils for the workplace", survey finds', *The Independent*, 24 August.

Alleyne, R. (2011) 'Welcome to the information age', *The Telegraph*, 11 February.

All-Party Parliamentary Group (2015) *A Report by the All-Party Parliamentary Group on a Fit and Healthy Childhood*. London: APPG.

Almila, A. (2016) 'How to spot a good conductor', *The Economist*, 6 July.

Anderson, C. (2018) *TED Talks: The Official TED Guide to Public Speaking*. New York: Headline.

Andrews, P. (2004) 'Creativity in Maths is the solution', *TES*, 22 October.

Antidote (2003) *The Emotional Literacy Handbook*. London: David Fulton.

Apple, M. and Beane, J. (1995) *Democratic Schools*. Buckingham: Open University Press.

Ariely, D. (2010) *The Upside of Irrationality*. London: HarperCollins.

Armstrong, P. (2015) *Effective School Partnerships and Collaboration for School Improvement. A Review of the Evidence*. London: Department of Education.

Armstrong, T. (2017) *Multiple Intelligences in the Classroom* (4th edn), Alexandria, VA: Association for Supervision & Curriculum Development.

Arts Education Partnership (1999) *Champions of Change: The Impact of the Arts on Learning. Arts Education Partnership*, available at: http://artsedge.kennedy-center.org/champions/pdfs/champsreport.pdf (accessed 27 November 2017).

Arum, R. and Roksa, J. (2010) *Academically Adrift: Limited Learning on College Campuses*. Chicago: University of Chicago Press.

Atavar, M. (2011) *12 Rules of Creativity*. London: Kiosk Publishing.

Attard, C. (2012) 'Applying a framework for engagement with mathematics in the primary classroom', *Australian Primary Mathematics Curriculum*, *17*(4): 22–27.

Attfield, R. (2012) *Improving the Quality of Teaching*. Nottingham: National College for School Leadership.

Babauta, L. (2009) *The Power of Less: The Fine Art of Limiting Yourself to the Essential … in Business and in Life*. New York: Hachette Books.

Backwell, J. and Hamaker, T. (2004) 'Cognitive acceleration through technology education (CATE): Implications for teacher education', paper presented at epiSTEME -1 International Conference to review research on Science, Technology and Mathematics Education, Goa, India.

Bae, B. (2009) 'Children's right to participate – challenges in everyday interactions', *European Early Childhood Education Research Journal*, *17*(3): 391–406.

Baines, E., Blatchford, P. and Kutnick, P. (2016) *Promoting Effective Group Work in the Primary Classroom: A Handbook for Teachers and Practitioners*. Abingdon: Routledge

Bakhshi, H., Downing, J., Osborne, M. and Schneider, P. (2017) *The Future of Skills: Employment in 2030*. London: Pearson and Nesta.

Banas, J.A., Dunbar, N., Rodriguez, D. and Liu, S. (2011) 'A review of humor in education settings: Four decades of research', *Communication Education*, 60(1): 115–144.

Bantock, G.H. (1969) 'Discovery methods', in C.B. Cox and A.E. Dyson (eds), *Black Paper Two*. London: Critical Quarterly Society, 110–118.

Barnhart, R.K. (ed.) (1988) *Chambers Dictionary of Etymology*. London: Chambers.

Baron-Cohen, S. (2011) *Zero Degrees of Empathy*. London: Penguin.

Barrett, P.S., Zhang, Y., Moffat, J. and Kobbacy, K. (2013) 'An holistic, multi-level analysis identifying the impact of classroom design on pupils' learning', *Building and Environment*, 59: 678–689.

Bassey, M. (2012) *Teachers and Government*. London: ATL.

Bee, F. and Bee, R. (1998) *Facilitation Skills*. London: Institute of Personnel and Development.

Belfer, K. (2001) 'De Bono's Six Thinking Hats Technique: A metaphorical model of communication in computer mediated classrooms', in C. Montgomerie and J. Viteli (eds), *Proceedings of ED-MEDIA 2001 – World Conference on Educational Multimedia, Hypermedia & Telecommunications*. Norfolk, VA: 113–116.

Bennett, N. (1976) *Teaching Styles and Pupil Progress*. London: Open Books Publishing.

Bennett, T. (2012) 'School councils: Shut up, we're listening', *The Guardian*, 12 March.

BERA (British Educational Research Association) (2014) *Research and the Teaching Profession Building the Capacity for a Self-improving Education System*. London: BERA.

Beveridge, W.I.B. (1950) *The Art of Scientific Investigation*. New York: Norton.

Birkett, D. (2011) 'The school I'd like: Who made the grade?', *The Guardian*, 20 October.

Blackwell, L., Trzesniewski, K. and Dweck, C.S. (2007) 'Implicit theories of intelligence predict achievement across an adolescent transition: A longitudinal study and an intervention', *Child Development*, 78(1): 246–263.

Blake, M. (2008) *Comfortably Numb: The Inside Story of Pink Floyd*, Cambridge: De Capro Press.

Blatchford, P., Galton, M., Kutnick, P. and Baines, E. (2005) *Improving the Effectiveness of Pupils Groups in Classrooms. ESRC/TLRP Final Report*.

Blishen, E. (1973) *The School I'd Like*. London: Penguin.

Bloom, B.S. (1956) *Taxonomy of Educational Objectives*. New York: Longmans Green.

Bloom, S.A. (2017) 'Government pledges £215m to bring mental health treatment into schools', *TES*, 3 December.

Blyth, A. (1965) *English Primary Education: A Sociological Description*. London: Routledge and Kegan Paul.

Boaler, J. (1997) *Experiencing School Mathematics*. Maidenhead: Open University Press.

Boaler, J. (2016) *Mathematical Mindsets: Unleashing Students' Potential through Creative Math, Inspiring Messages and Innovative Teaching*. San Francisco: Jossey-Bass.

Board of Education (1931) *Report of the Consultative Committee on the Primary School*. London: HMSO.

Bond, M. (2015) *The Power of Others: Peer Pressure, GroupThink, and How the People Around Us Shape Everything We Do*. London: Oneworld Publications.

Bowkett, S. (2004) *Philosophy Bear and the Big Sky (But Why? – Developing Philosophical Thinking in the Classroom)*. Stafford: Network Education Press Ltd.

Bragg, S. and Manchester, H. (2011) *Creativity, School Ethos and the Creative Partnerships Programme*. London: Creative Partnerships.

Brown, J.S., Collins, A. and Duguid, P. (1989) 'Situated cognition and the culture of learning', *Educational Researcher*, 18(1): 32–42.

Brown, S. (2014) *The Doodle Revolution*. New York: Penguin.

Bruner, J.S. (1983) *Child's Talk: Learning to Use Language*. Oxford: Oxford University Press.

Bruno, D. (2017) *Cave Art*. London: Thames and Hudson Ltd.

Bryant, B. (2011) 'Judges are more lenient after taking a break, study finds', *The Guardian*, 11 April.

Bullard, P. (2016) 'Eighteenth-century minds: From Associationism to Cognitive Psychology', in *Literature, Literary Studies – 1701 to 1800, Literary Theory and Cultural Studies*. Oxford Handbooks Online, 1–27.

Burden, B. (2006) 'Is there any such thing as a "Thinking School"?', available at: www.thinkingschoolsinternational.com (accessed 4 January 2018).

Burmark, L. (2002) *Visual Literacy: Learn To See, See To Learn*. Alexandria: VA: Association for Supervision and Curriculum Development.

Burton, N. (2015) *Heaven and Hell: The Psychology of the Emotions*, Exeter: Acheron Press.

Burton-Hill, C. (2014) 'What does a conductor actually do?', *BBC Culture*, available at: www.bbc.com/culture/story/20141029-what-do-conductors-actually-do (accessed 7 January 2018).

Cabinet Office (2012) *Applying Behavioural Insights to Reduce Fraud, Error and Debt*. London: Cabinet Office.

Cale, E. (2011) 'A culture of thinking', available at http://acultureofthinking.weebly.com (accessed 15 January 2018).

Canny, B. (2016) *The New Basics: Big Data Reveals the Skills Young People Need for the New Work Order. Foundation for Young Australians*, available at: www.fya.org.au/wp-content/uploads/2016/04/The-New-Basics_Update_Web.pdf (accessed 5 November 2017).

Caproni, P. (2017) *The Science of Success: What Researchers Know*. Michigan: Van Rye Publishing, LLC.

Catalanotto, P. (2006) *Emily's Art*. New York: Aladdin Paperbacks.

CBI/Pearson (2016) *The Right Combination*. London: CBI/Pearson.

Chambliss, D.F. (1989) 'The mundanity of excellence: An ethnographic report on stratification and Olympic swimmers', *Sociological Theory*, 7(1): 70–86.

Channel4.com (2017) 'C4 study reveals only 4 per cent surveyed can identify true or fake news', *Channel 4 News*, available at: www.channel4.com/info/press/news/c4-study-reveals-only-4-surveyed-can-identify-true-or-fake-news (accessed 25 November 2017).

Cholle, F. (2011) *The Intuitive Compass: Why the Best Decisions Balance Reason and Instinct*, San Francisco: John Wiley & Sons.

Chouinard, M. (2007) *Children's Questions: A Mechanism for Cognitive Development*. Oxford: John Wiley & Sons.

CLA (Cultural Learning Alliance) (2017) *ImagineNation: The Value of Cultural Learning*, available at: https://culturallearningalliance.org.uk/wp-content/uploads/2017/08/ImagineNation_The_Case_for_Cultural_Learning.pdf (accessed 26 June 2018).

Clapp, E. (2017) *Participatory Creativity*. New York: Routledge.

Clark, J. and Paivio, A. (1991) 'Dual Coding Theory and education', *Educational Psychology Review 3*(3): 149–210.

Claxton, G. (2002) *Building Learning Power: Helping Young People Become Better Learners*. Bristol: TLO Limited.

Claxton, G. (2008a) 'Cultivating positive learning dispositions', in H. Daniels, H. Lauder and J. Porter (eds), *The Routledge Companion to Education*, London: Routledge, 177–187.

Claxton, G. (2008b) *What's the Point of School?* Oxford: One World.

Claxton, G. (2015) *Intelligence in the Flesh: Why Your Mind Needs Your Body Much More Than it Thinks*. Yale: Yale University Press.

Claxton, G., Chambers, M., Powell, G. and Lucas, B. (2011) *The Learning Powered School: Pioneering 21st-century Education*. Bristol: TLO Limited.

Cleese, J. (1991) 'John Cleese on creativity', available at www.youtube.com/watch?v=Gg-6LtfB5JA (accessed 7 January 2018).

Coe, R., Aloisi, C., Higgins, S. and Major, L.E. (2014) *What Makes Great Teaching?* London: The Sutton Trust.

Coffield, F., Moseley, D., Hall, E. and Ecclestone, K. (2004) *Learning Styles in Pedagogy Post-16 Learning: A Systematic and Critical Review*. London: Learning and Skills Research Centre.

Coltman, P., Warwick, J., Willmott, J. and Whitebread, D. (2013) 'Teachers co-constructing pedagogical practices to support children's exploratory talk and self-regulation: The Children Articulating Thinking (ChAT) project', in D. Whitebread, N. Mercer, C. Howe and A. Tolmie (eds), *British Journal of Educational Psychology Monograph Series II: Psychological Aspects of Education- Current Trends*, 10: 174–146.

Colvin, G. (2008) *Talent Is Overrated: What Really Separates World-Class Performers from Everybody Else*. London: Penguin.

Conkbayir, M. and Pascal, C. (2015) *Early Childhood Theories and Contemporary Issues: An Introduction*. London: Bloomsbury Publishing.

Conn, D. (2017) 'Football's biggest issue: The struggle facing boys rejected by academies', *The Guardian*, 6 October.

Coolidge, F. L. and Wynn, T. (2009) *The Rise of Homo Sapiens: The Evolution of Modern Thinking*. Oxford: John Wiley & Sons.

Cooper, B.B. (2013) '10 of the most counterintuitive pieces of advice from famous entrepreneurs', in *The Creativity Post*, 19 August, available at: www.creativitypost.com/business/10_of_the_most_counterintuitive_pieces_of_advice_from_famous_entrepreneurs (accessed 28 November 2017).

Coplan, R.J. and Rudasill, K.M. (2016) *Quiet at School: An Educator's Guide to Shy Children*. New York: Teachers College Press.

Costa, A. (1981) 'Teaching for intelligent behavior', *Educational Leadership*, 39(1): 29–32.

Costa, A. and Kallick, B. (2000a) *Discovering and Exploring Habits of Mind*. Alexandria, VA: Association for Supervision & Curriculum Development.

Costa, A. and Kallick, B. (2000b) *Assessing & Reporting (Habits of Mind)*. Alexandria, VA: Association for Supervision & Curriculum Development.

Costa, A. and Kallick, B. (2008) *Learning and Leading with Habits of Mind*. Alexandria, VA: Association for Supervision & Curriculum Development.

Costa, A. and Kallick, B. (2009) *Habits of Mind Across the Curriculum: Practical and Creative Strategies for Teachers*. Alexandria, VA: Association for Supervision & Curriculum Development.

Coughlan, S. (2011) 'Spelling mistakes "cost millions" in lost online sales', 14 July, available at www.bbc.co.uk/news/education-14130854 (accessed 7 January 2018).

Coyle, D. (2010) *The Talent Code: Greatness Isn't Born. It's Grown*. London: Arrow.

Crehan, L. (2016) *Cleverlands*. London: Unbound.

Cremin, T. (2015) *Teaching English Creatively*. Abingdon: Routledge.

Crystal, D. (2010) *A Little Book of Language*. London: Yale University Press.

Csikszentmihalyi, M. (1996) *Creativity: Flow and the Psychology of Discovery and Invention*. New York: HarperCollins.

Currey, M. (2014) *Daily Rituals*. London: Picador.

Currie, C., Zanotti, C., Morgan, A., Currie, D., de Looze, M., Roberts, C., Samdal, O., Smith, O.R. and Barnekow, V. (2010) *Social Determinants of Health and Well-being Among Young People*. Copenhagen: World Health Organization.

Curtis, S.J. and Boultwood, M.E.A. (1965) *A Short History of Educational Ideas*. London: University Tutorial Press.

Cutting, R. and Kelly, O. (2015) *Creative Teaching and Science*. London: Sage.

Dalton, J. (1986) *Adventures in Thinking*. Melbourne: Thomas Nelson.

Davidson, C.N. (2011) *Now You See It*. New York: Penguin.

Davidson, L. (2017) 'Blue sky thinking? The 10 business phrases most likely to make you scream', *The Independent*, 17 June.

Davidson, N. and Worsham, T. (1992) *Enhancing Thinking Through Cooperative Learning*. New York: Teachers College Press.

Davies, D., Jindal-Snape, D., Collier, C., Digbya, R., Hay, P. and Howe, A. (2013) 'Creative learning environments in education: A systematic literature review', *Thinking Skills and Creativity*, 8: 80–91.

Dawes, R. (1848) *Hints on an Improved and Self-Paying System of National Education: Suggested From the Working of a Village School in Hampshire, With Observation, From … the Irish National Schools*. London: Groombridge and Sons.

Dawes, L. and Warwick, P. (2012) *Talking Points: Discussion Activities in the Primary Classroom*. Abingdon: Routledge.

Deakin Crick, R. and Goldspink, C. (2014) 'Learner dispositions, self-theories and student engagement', *British Journal of Educational Studies*: 62(1): 19–35.

De Bono, E. (1970) *Lateral Thinking*. New York: Harper Row.

De Bono, E. (1976) *Teaching Thinking*. London: Pelican.

De Bono, E. (1985) *Six Thinking Hats*. London: Penguin.

De Bono, E. (1991) *Six Action Shoes*. New York: HarperBusiness.

De Bono, E. (1992) *Teach Your Child How to Think*. London: Penguin.

De Bono, E. (1993) *Tactics: The Art and Science of Success*. London: HarperCollins.

De Bono, E. (1994) *Parallel Thinking*. London: Penguin.

De Bono, E. (1999) *Six Thinking Hats* (revised edn). London: Penguin.

DeHaan, R. (2009) 'Teaching creativity and inventive problem solving in science', *Life Science Education*, 8(3): 172–181.

DES (1967) *Children and their Primary Schools* [The Plowden Report]. London: HMSO.

DES (1977) *Education in Schools: A Consultative Document*. London: HMSO.

Dewey, J. (1910) *How We Think*. Boston: D C Heath & Co.

Dewey, J. (1916) *Democracy and Education*. New York: MacMillan.

DfE (2014) *National curriculum in England: English Programmes of Study*. London: DfE.

DfE (2017) *Statutory Framework for the Early Years Foundation Stage*. London: DfE.

DfEE/QCA (1999) *The National Curriculum: Handbook for Primary Teachers in England*. London: DfEE/QCA.

DfES (2004) *Excellence and Enjoyment*. London: DFES.

DfES (2005) *14–19 Education and Skills*. London: DFES.

Dhanapal, S. and Wern Ling, K.T. (1999) 'A study to investigate how Six Thinking Hats enhance the learning of Environmental Studies', *Journal of Research & Method in Education*, 1(6): 20–29.

Didau, D. (2016) *What If Everything You Knew About Education Was Wrong?* Carmarthen: Crown House.

Dillner, L. (2017) 'Can optimism make you live longer?', *The Guardian*, 6 March.

Dodgson, L. (2017) 'Scientists have created brain implants that could boost our memory by up to 30%', *Business Insider*, 14 November.

Donaldson, G. (2015) *Successful Futures*. Cardiff: Welsh Government.

Doward, J. (2017) 'Revealed: The more time that children chat on social media, the less happy they feel', *The Guardian*, 9 April.

Dowling, J.E. (2007) *The Great Brain Debate: Nature or Nurture?* Princeton, NJ: Princeton University Press.

Duckworth, A. (2017) *Grit: Why Passion and Resilience Are the Secrets to Success*. London: Vermilion.

Dweck, C.S. (1989) 'Motivation', in A. Lesgold and R. Glaser (eds), *Foundations for a Psychology of Education*. Hillsdale, NJ: Lawrence Erlbaum Associates, 87–136.

Dweck, C.S. (2006) *Mindset: The New Psychology of Success*. New York: Random House.

Dweck, C.S. (2017) *Mindset – Updated Edition: Changing The Way You Think to Fulfil Your Potential*. New York: Ballatine Books.

Eaglesham, E. (1967) *Foundation of Twentieth Century Education in England*. London: Routledge and Kegan Paul.

Eberle, B. (2008) *Scamper: Creative Games and Activities for Imagination Development*. Waco: Prufrock Press.

Education Scotland (2012) *A Curriculum for Excellence – Literacy and English Experiences and Outcomes*. Livingston: Education Scotland.

Education Scotland (2015) *How Good Is Our School?* Livingston: Education Scotland.

Edwards, J. (2014) *Habits of Mind: A Synthesis of the Research*. Westport, CT: Institute for Habits of Mind International.

Edwards, J. (2016) *Articles and Research on the Importance of the Habits of Mind*. Westport, CT: Institute for Habits of Mind International.

Egan, R. (2007) 'Reflections on cultural understanding', *English in Australia, 42*(2): 32–33.

Eichenbaum, A., Bavelier, D. and Green, C.S. (2014) 'Video games: Play that can do serious good', *American Journal of Play*, Fall, 50–72.

Eisenstein, E. (1982) *The Printing Press as an Agent of Change*. Cambridge: Cambridge University Press.

Ekman, R. (2004) *Emotions Revealed: Understanding Faces and Feelings*. London: Phoenix.

Elliot, J. (2015) 'Teacher expertise', in J.D. Wright (ed.), *International Encyclopaedia of the Social & Behavioral Sciences*, Vol *24*. Oxford: Elsevier, 56–59.

Ennis, R. (1985) 'Goals for a critical thinking curriculum', in A.L. Costa (ed.), *Developing Minds: A Resource Book for Teaching Thinking*. Alexandria, VA: Association for Supervision and Curriculum Development, 44–46.

Ericsson, K.A. (1993) 'The role of deliberate practice in the acquisition of expert performance', *Psychological Review, 100*(3): 363–406.

Estyn (2010) *Inspection Report. Danescourt Primary School*. Cardiff: Estyn.

Estyn (2016) *A Report on Danescourt Primary School*. Cardiff: Estyn.

Estyn (2017) *Guidance Handbook for the Inspection of Primary Schools*. Cardiff: Estyn.

ETI (2017) *Effective Practice and Self-Evaluation Questions for Primary*, available at: www.etini.gov.uk (accessed 23 November 2017).

European Commission (2016) *EntreComp: The Entrepreneurship Competence Framework*. Brussels: European Commission.

Feist, G. (1999) 'The influence of personality on artistic and scientific creativity', in Feldman, D.H., Csikszentmihalyi, M. and Gardner, H. (1999) *Changing the World: A Framework for the Study of Creativity*. Santa Barbara: Praeger.

Feuerstein, R.R. (1980) *Instrumental Enrichment: An Intervention Program for Cognitive Modifiability*, Baltimore: University Park Press.

Feuerstein, R.R. (2003) 'The theory of structural cognitive modifiability and mediated learning experience', in R.R. Feuerstein, *Theory and Applied Systems: A Reader*. Jerusalem: ICELP, 37–45.

Feuerstein, R.R., Falik, L.H. and Feuerstein, R.S. (2015) *Changing Minds & Brains – The Legacy of Reuven Feuerstein: Higher Thinking and Cognition Through Mediated Learning*. New York: Teachers College Press.

Fidan, T. and Balci, C. (2017) 'Managing schools as complex adaptive systems: A strategic perspective', *International Electronic Journal of Elementary Education*, *10*(1): 11–26.

Finn, P. (2015) *Critical Conditioning*. Ontario: Wilfred Laurier University Press.

Fisher, R. (1998) *Teaching Thinking*. London: Cassell.

Fisher, R. (2005) *Teaching Children to Learn*. Cheltenham: Nelson Thornes.

Fisher, R. (2008) *Teaching Thinking: Philosophical Enquiry in the Classroom*. London: Continuum.

Fisher, R. (2009) *Creative Dialogue: Talk for Thinking in the Classroom*. Abingdon: Routledge.

Fiskaa, M. (no date) *Our Journey Towards a Thinking School*, available at: www.thinkingschoolsinternational.com/site/wp-content/uploads/2015/07/Info-til-presentasjonsmappeLjan-Schoolmed-bilder.pdf (accessed 5 January 2018).

Flavell, J.H. (1976) 'Metacognitive aspects of problem solving', in L. Resnick (ed.), *The Nature of Intelligence*. Hillsdale, NJ: Lawrence Erlbaum Associates, 231–235.

Flood, A. (2013) 'Four million UK adults never read books for pleasure', *The Guardian*, 14 February.

Flood, A. (2015) 'National curriculum is damaging children's creative writing, say authors', *The Guardian*, 23 June.

Flood, A. (2016) 'Winnie-the-Pooh beats Harry Potter in best-loved book character poll', *The Guardian*, 15 July.

Folkman, J. (2015) 'Which superpower would you choose: To fly or to be invisible?', 17 August, available at: www.forbes.com/sites/joefolkman/2015/08/17/which-superpower-would-you-choose-to-fly-or-to-be-invisible/#5400661e1a7d (accessed 12 December 2017).

Forward, T. and Cohen, I. (2006) *The Wolf's Story: What Really Happened to Little Red Riding Hood*. London: Walker Books.

Freestone, S. (2016) 'Schools should be more than factories churning out Gradgrindian three Rs and imparting "facts" with little space for creativity', *The Telegraph*, 20 July.

Fried, R. (2001) *The Passionate Teacher: A Practical Guide*. Boston, MA: Beacon Press.

Gaarder, J. (1995) *Sophie's World*. London: Phoenix.

Galton, M. (1995) *Crisis in the Primary Classroom*. London: David Fulton.

Galton, M., Simon, B. and Croll, P. (1980) *Inside the Primary Classroom*. London: Routledge & Kegan Paul.

Gardner, H. (1993) *Frames of Mind*. New York: Basic Books.

Gardner, H. (2000) *Intelligence Reframed: Multiple Intelligences for the 21st Century*. New York: Basic Books.

Gardner, H. (2007) *Five Minds for the Future*. Cambridge, MA: Harvard Business School Press.

Gardner, H. (2011) *Creating Minds: An Anatomy of Creativity Seen Through the Lives of Freud, Einstein, Picasso, Stravinsky, Eliot, Graham, and Ghandi*. New York: Basic Books.

Garner, R. (2014) 'A more creative approach to education', *The Independent*, 4 November.

Garrison, D.R. (2015) *Thinking Collaboratively: Learning in a Community of Inquiry*. New York: Routledge.

Geake, J.G. (2009) *The Brain at School*. Maidenhead: Open University Press.

Gilbert, I. (2004) *Little Owl's Book of Thinking: An Introduction to Thinking Skills*. Carmarthen: Crown House.

Gill, N. (2014) 'Loneliness: a silent plague that is hurting young people most', *The Guardian*, 20 July.

Gladwell, M. (2009) *Outliers: The Story of Success*. London: Penguin.

GL Assessment (2017) *Hidden Talents: The Overlooked Children Whose Poor Verbal Skills Mask Potential*. London: GL Assessment.

Gleck, J. (2012) *The Information*. London: Fourth Estate.

Godfrey, E. (1907) *English Children in the Olden Time*. London: Methuen & Co.

Goldberg, E. (2009) *The New Executive Brain: Frontal Lobes in a Complex World*. New York: Oxford University Press.

Goleman, D. (1995) *Emotional Intelligence*. New York: Bantam Books.

Goleman, D. (2011) *Social Intelligence*. New York: Bantam Books.

Gorard, S., Siddiqui, N. and Huat See, B. (2015) *Philosophy for Children: Evaluation Report and Executive Summary*. Millbank: Education Endowment Foundation.

Gouge, K. and Yates, C. (2002) *Learning Intelligence: Cognitive Acceleration Across the Curriculum*. Buckingham: Open University Press.

Gove, M. (2013) 'Michael Gove speaks about the importance of teaching', available at: www.gov.uk/government/speeches/michael-gove-speaks-about-the-importance-of-teaching (accessed 20 November 2017).

Government Office for Science (2017) *Future of Skills & Lifelong Learning*, available at: www.gov.uk/government/collections/future-of-skills-and-lifelong-learning (accessed 17 February 2018).

Gray, C. and MacBlain, S. (2015) *Learning Theories in Childhood*. London: Sage.

Gregory, J. (2006) 'Facilitation and facilitator style', in P. Jarvis (ed.), *The Theory and Practice of Teaching*. London: Routledge, 98–113.

Grigg, R. and Hughes, S.V. (2018) *Teaching Primary Humanities* (2nd edn). Abingdon: Routledge.

Grigg, R. and Lewis, H. (2017) 'What makes someone a hero or a villain?', *Teach Primary*, 104–105.

Gruwell, E. (2009) *The Freedom Writers Diary*. New York: Broadway Books.

Guilford, J.P. (1967) *The Nature of Human Intelligence*. New York: McGraw-Hill.

Gunter, M.A., Estes, T.H. and Mintz, S.L. (2007) *Instruction. A Models Approach*. Boston: Pearson.

Hall, E., Higgins, S. and Baumfield, V. (2005) 'The impact of thinking skills: The results from three reviews'. Presented to the EPPI-Centre conference, Institute of Education, May.

Hallam, S. (2010) 'The power of music: Its impact on the intellectual, social and personal development of children and young people', *International Journal of Music Education*, 28(3): 269–289.

Halpern, D. (2002) *Thinking Critically about Critical Thinking*. Hillsdale, NJ: Lawrence Erlbaum Associates.

Hampson, M., Patton, A. and Shanks, L. (2010) *10 Ideas for 21st Century Education*, Innovation Unit, available at: www.innovationunit.org/wp-content/uploads/2017/04/10-Ideas-for-21st-Century-Education.pdf (accessed 3 January 2018).

Hancock, D. (2013) *Gundogs: Their Past, Their Performance and Their Prospects*. Marlborough: The Crowood Press.

Hargie, O. (2017) *Skilled Interpersonal Interaction: Research, Theory, and Practice*. London: Routledge.

Hargreaves, A. (1994) *Changing Teachers, Changing Times*. London: Cassell.

Hargreaves, D.H. (2012) *A Self-improving School System: Towards Maturity*. Nottingham: National College for School Leadership.

Harris, C. (2016) '"Our curriculum is so narrow that it bores both pupils and teachers – and crushes creativity"', *TES*, 21 October.

Hatano, G. and Inagaki, K. (1986) 'Two courses of expertise', in H. Stevenson, H. Azuma and K. Hakuta (eds), *Children Development and Education in Japan*. New York: Freeman, 262–272.

Hattie, J. (2009) *Visible Learning: A Synthesis of Over 800 Meta-analyses Relating to Achievement*. London: Routledge.

Hattie, J. (2012) *Visible Learning for Teachers, Maximising Impact on Learning*. London: Routledge.

Hattie, J. (2015) *What Doesn't Work in Education: The Politics of Distraction*. London: Pearson.

Hattie, J. and Zierer, K. (2018) *10 Mindframes for Visible Learning: Teaching for Success*. Abingdon: Routledge.

Hay McBer (2000) *Research into Teacher Effectiveness A Model of Teacher Effectiveness*. London: DfEE.

Haynes, J. (2002) *Children as Philosophers*. London: Routledge.

Henley, J. (2010) 'Why our children need to get outside and engage with nature', *The Guardian*, 16 August.

Hennessey, B.A. and Amabile, T.M. (1988) 'The conditions of creativity' in R.J. Sternberg (ed.), *The Nature of Creativity*. Cambridge: Cambridge University Press, 11–38.

Henry, J. (2017) *Knowledge Is Power*. Cambridge: Icon Books.

Heron, J. (1999) *The Complete Facilitator's Handbook*. London: Kogan Page.

Hevrdejs, J. (2012) 'Patterns of behavior, properly harnessed, help keep life on track', *Tribune Newspapers*, available at: http://articles.chicagotribune.com/2012-09-13/features/sc-fam-0911-routine-blessing-20120911_1_habits-cues-and-rewards-charles-duhigg (accessed 1 January 2018).

Higgins, S., Baumfield, V., Lin, M., Moseley, D., Butterworth, M., Downey, G., Gregson, G., Oberski, I., Rockett, M. and Thacker, D. (2004) *Thinking Skills Approaches to Effective Teaching and Learning: What Is the Evidence for Impact on Learners?* London: EPPI Centre, Institute of Education.

Higgins, S., Hall, E., Baumfield, V. and Moseley, D. (2005) *A Meta-analysis of the Impact of the Implementation of Thinking Skills Approaches on Pupils*. London: EPPI-Centre.

Higgins, S., Katsipataki, M., Kokotsaki, D., Coleman, R., Major, L.E. and Coe, R. (2014) *The Sutton Trust-Education Endowment Foundation Teaching and Learning Toolkit*. London: Education Endowment Foundation.

Higgins, S., Xiao, Z. and Katsipataki, M. (2012) *The Impact of Digital Technology on Learning: A Summary for the Education Endowment Foundation*. London: Education Endowment Foundation.

Hill, K., Davis, A., Hirsch, D. and Marshall, L. (2016) *Falling Short: The Experiences of Families Living Below the Minimum Income Standard*. York: Joseph Rowntree Foundation.

Hines, B. (1969) *A Kestrel for a Knave*. London: Penguin.

Hoff, B. (2015) *The Tao of Pooh & The Te of Piglet (Wisdom of Pooh)*. London: Egmont Books.

Hollingsworth, J.R. and Ybarra, S. (2018) *Explicit Direct Instruction (EDI): The Power of the Well-Crafted, Well-Taught Lesson*. Thousand Oaks, CA: Corwin.

Holt, J. (1964) *How Children Fail*. New York: Pitman.

Holt, J. (1972) *How Children Learn*. New York: Dell.

Horsfall, P. and Bennett, L. (2005) 'Thinking hats in the primary school: from thinking skills to thinking curriculum', *Education Today*, 55(1): 20–29.

Horton, H. (2015) 'More people have died by taking selfies this year than by shark attacks', *The Telegraph*, 22 September.

House of Commons (2014–15) *Adult Literacy and Numeracy: Fifth Report of Session*. London: House of Commons, Business, Innovation and Skills Committee.

House of Commons (2016) *Digital Skills Crisis. Second Report of Session 2016–17*. London: House of Commons.

Hu, W., Wu, B., Jia, X., Yi, X., Duan, C., Meyer, W. and Kaufman, J.C. (2013) 'Increasing students' scientific creativity: The "Learn to Think" intervention program', *The Journal of Creative Behavior, 47*(1): 3–21.

Hudson, H. (2012) 'Kelvin Doe, self-taught engineering whiz from Sierra Leone, wows MIT experts', *Huffington Post*, 19 November, available at: www.huffingtonpost.co.uk/entry/kelvin-doe-self-taught-en_n_2159735 (accessed 8 January 2018).

Husbands, C. and Pearce, J. (2012) *What Makes Great Pedagogy? Nine Claims from Research.* Nottingham: National College for School Leadership.

Hutchings, M. (2015) *The Impact of Accountability Measures on Children and Young People.* London: National Union of Teachers.

Hyerle, D. and Alper, L. (2011) *Student Successes with Thinking Maps.* Thousand Oaks, CA: Corwin Press.

Hyerle, D. and Yeager, C. (2007) *Thinking Maps: A Language for Learning.* Cary, NC: Thinking Maps, Inc.

Immordino-Yang, M.H. and Damasio, A. (2007) 'We feel, therefore we learn', *Mind, Brain and Education, 1*(1): 3–10.

Ings, R., Crane, N. and Cameron, M. (2012) *Be Creative. Be Well.* London: Arts Council.

Institute for the Futures (2011) *Future Work Skills 2020.* Phoenix: University of Phoenix Research Institute.

Janis, I.L. (1972) *Victims of Group Think.* Boston: Houghton Mifflin.

Jeffers, O. (2011) *The Heart and the Bottle.* New York: Philomel Books.

Jewell, H. (1998) *Education in Early Modern England.* New York: St Martin's Press.

Johnson, D.W. and Johnson, R.T. (1999) *Learning Together and Alone: Cooperative, Competitive, and Individualistic Learning.* Boston: Allyn and Bacon.

Johnson, D.W., Johnson, R.T. and Stanne, M.B. (2000) *Cooperative Learning Methods: A Meta-Analysis.* The Cooperative Learning Center, The University of Minnesota.

Johnson, S. (2010) 'Teaching Thinking Skills', in C. Winch (ed.), *Teaching Thinking Skills.* London: Continuum, 1–50.

Johnson, S. (2011) *Where Good Ideas Come From: The Seven Patterns of Innovation.* London: Penguin.

Kagan, S. (1994) *Cooperative Learning.* San Clemente, CA: Kagan Publishing.

Kahneman, D. (2012) *Thinking, Fast and Slow.* London: Penguin.

Katz, L.G. (1988) 'What should young children be doing?', *American Educator: The Professional Journal of the American Federation of Teachers, 12*(2): 29–45.

Katz, L. (1993) 'Dispositions: Definitions and implications for early childhood practices', *ERIC Clearinghouse on Elementary and Early Childhood Education.* Urbana, IL: ERIC Clearinghouse.

Kaufman, J.C. and Sternberg, R.J. (eds) (2010) *Cambridge Handbook of Creativity.* Cambridge: Cambridge University Press.

Kelly, T. (1970) *A History of Adult Education in Great Britain*. Liverpool: Liverpool University Press.

Kerry, T. (1982) *Effective Questioning*. London: MacMillan.

Kershaw, A. (2017) 'School children should be taught to recognise fake news', *The Independent*, 18 March.

Keys, D. (2008) 'Stonehenge builders had geometry skills to rival Pythagoras', *The Independent*, 25 May.

Khaleeli, H. and Dowling, T. (2017) 'The stiff upper lip: Why the royal health warning matters', *The Guardian*, 18 April.

Khomami, N. (2017) 'Primary school encourages pupils to wear slippers in class', *The Telegraph*, 31 January.

Kikas, E., Peets, K. and Hodges, E.V.E. (2014) 'Collective student characteristics alter the effects of teaching practices on academic outcomes', *Journal of Applied Developmental Psychology*, 35: 273–283.

King, M.L. (1947) 'The purpose of education', in *The Maroon Tiger*, available at: https://kinginstitute.stanford.edu/king-papers/documents/purpose-education (accessed 2 February 2018).

King's College London (2017) 'My Primary School Is at the Museum project', available at www.kcl.ac.uk/Cultural/-/Projects/My-Primary-School-is-at-the-Museum.aspx (accessed 21 January 2017).

Kipling, R. (1889) 'An interview with Mark Twain', *From Sea to Sea: Letters of Travel*. Doubleday & McClure Company.

Kirkup, C., Sizmur, J., Sturman, L. and Lewis, K. (2005) *Schools' Use of Data in Teaching and Learning*. London: DFES.

Knapton, S. (2017) 'Babies can recognise faces while still in the womb, scientists find', *The Telegraph*, 8 July.

Koch, C. (2009) 'When does consciousness arise in human babies?', *Scientific American Mind*, 1 September.

Kounios, J. and Beeman, M. (2015) *The Eureka Factor*. London: William Heinemann.

Kovas, Y., Malykh, S. and Petrill, S.A. (2013) 'Genetics for education', in D. Mareschal, B. Butterworth and A. Tolmie (eds), *Educational Neuroscience*. Oxford: John Wiley & Sons, 77–109.

Kuhn, D. and Dean, D. (2004) 'Metacognition: A bridge between cognitive psychology and educational practice', *Theory Into Practice*, 43(4): 268–273.

Langer, E. and Piper, A. (1987) 'The prevention of mindlessness', *Journal of Personality and Social Psychology*, 53(2): 280–287.

Larkin, S. (2010) *Metacognition in Young Children*. Abingdon: Routledge.

Lawson, J. and Silver, H. (1973) *A Social History of Education in England*. London: Methuen.

Lazarus, R.S. and Lazarus, B.N. (1994) *Passion and Reason*. Oxford: Oxford University Press.

Lazear, D. (1991) *Eight Ways of Knowing: Teaching for Multiple Intelligences*. Palatine, IL: SkyLight Publishing.

Leat, D. (2017) *Enquiry and Project Based Learning: Students, School and Society*. London: Routledge.

LeDoux, J. (1998) *The Emotional Brain*. London: Weidenfeld & Nicholson.

Lemov, D. (2015) *Teach Like a Champion 2.0*. San Francisco: Wiley.

Leontiev, A.N. (1978) *Activity, Consciousness, and Personality*. Englewood Cliffs: Prentice-Hall.

Levy, J. (2011) *A Bee in a Cathedral: And 99 Other Scientific Analogies*. New York: Firefly.

Lewis, A., Sarwar, S., Tyrie, J., Waters, J. and Williams, J. (2017) 'Exploring the extent of enactment of young children's rights in the education system in Wales', *Wales Journal of Education, 19*(2): 27–50.

Lewis, H. (2017a) 'Tales with tails: How can reading with dogs improve pupil outcomes and motivation?', *English 4–11, 60*: 11–13.

Lewis, H. (2017b) 'Canines in the classroom', *SENCO, 3*(2): 40–41.

Lewis, H. (2017c) 'An investigation into thinking skills and young children's metacognition in the Foundation Phase in Wales', unpublished PhD thesis, University of Wales Trinity Saint David.

Lewis, H. and Grigg, R. (2017) 'The mystery of the dog in the classroom', *School Leadership Today, 8*(3): 68–72.

Li, N. (2012) *Approaches to Learning: Literature Review. International Baccalaureate Organization*, available at: www.ibo.org/globalassets/publications/ib-research/approachestolearnin geng.pdf (accessed 17 January 2018).

Li, Y. and Bates, T.C. (2017) 'Does growth mindset improve children's IQ, educational attainment or response to setbacks? Active-control interventions and data on children's own mindsets', *SocArXiv Papers*, available at: https://osf.io/preprints/socarxiv/tsdwy (accessed 17 January 2018).

Lindsay, G., Muijs, D., Harris, A., Chapman, C., Arweck, E. and Goodall, J. (2007) *School Federations Pilot Study: 2003–2007*. Nottingham: Department for Children, Schools and Families (DCSF).

Lipman, M. (2003) *Thinking in Education* (2nd edn). Cambridge: Cambridge University Press.

Lipman, M. (2008) *A Life Teaching Thinking*. Montclair, NJ: IAPC.

Lipman, M., Sharp, A.M., and Oscanyan, F.S. (1980) *Philosophy in the Classroom*. Philadelphia: Temple University Press.

Lipton, L. and Wellman, B. (1998) *Patterns and Practices in the Learning-focused Classroom*. Guilford, VT: Pathways Publishing.

Littleton, K. and Mercer, N. (2013) *Interthinking: Putting Talk to Work*. Abingdon: Routledge.

Livingstone, T. (2005) *Child of Our Time*. London: BBC Books.

Locke, J. (1693) *Some Thoughts Concerning Education*. London: A. and J. Churchill. Available at: https://archive.org/stream/somethoughtsconc00lockuoft/somethoughts conc00lockuoft_djvu.txt (accessed 17 July 2018).

Locke, J. (1690) *An Essay Concerning Human Understanding*, Chapter XXXIII, point 8, available at: http://enlightenment.supersaturated.com/johnlocke/BOOKIIChapterXXXIII. html (accessed 17 November 2017).

Longfield, A. (2018) *Life in 'Likes'. Children's Commissioner Report into Social Media Use Among 8–12 Year Olds*. London: Children's Commission.

Lowndes, G.A.N. (1937) *The Silent Social Revolution*. Oxford: Oxford University Press.

Lucado, M. (1997) *You Are Special*. Wheaton, IL: Crossway.

Lucas, B., Claxton, G. and Spencer, E. (2012) 'Progression in creativity: Developing new forms of assessment', *OECD Paper*, April, available at: www.oecd.org/edu/ceri/50153675. pdf (accessed 2 January 2017).

Lucas, B. and Spencer, E. (2017) *Teaching Creative Thinking*. Carmarthen: Crown House.

Lynch, J. (ed.) (2004) *Samuel Johnson's Dictionary*. Florida: Levenger Press.

Mareschal, D., Butterworth, B. and Tolmie, A. (eds) (2013) *Educational Neuroscience*. Oxford: Wiley Blackwell.

Marrou, H.I. (1956) *A History of Education in Antiquity*. London: Sheed and Ward.

Martin, C. (1979) *A Short History of English Schools*. Hove: Wayland.

Marzano, R.J. (2001) *Classroom Instruction that Works: Research-based Strategies for Increasing Student Achievement*. Alexandria, VA: Association for Supervision and Curriculum Development.

Marzano, R.J. (2003) *What Works in Schools: Translating Research into Action*. Alexandria, VA: Association for Supervision and Curriculum Development.

Matthews, D. (2016) 'Chinese students lack critical thinking 'due to propaganda', *Times Higher Education*, 10 February.

Matthews, G. (1980) *Philosophy and the Young Child*. Cambridge, MA: Harvard University Press.

Matthews, G. (1994) *The Philosophy of Childhood*. Cambridge, MA: Harvard University Press.

Mayer, R. (2004) 'Should there be a three-strikes rule against pure discovery learning? The case for guided methods of instruction', *American Psychologist*, 9(1): 14–19.

McCall, C. (2009) *Transforming Thinking: Philosophical Inquiry in the Primary and Secondary Classroom*. Abingdon: Routledge.

McDonalds UK (2015) *The Value of Soft Skills to the UK Economy*, available at www.backing softskills.co.uk/ (accessed 3 July 2018).

McGuinness, C. (1999) *From Thinking Skills to Thinking Classrooms: A Review and Evaluation of Approaches for Developing Pupils' Thinking*. London: DfEE (Research Report RR115).

McGuinness, F. (2016) *Poverty in the UK: Statistics*. London: House of Commons.

McLeish, K. (1993) *Bloomsbury Guide to Human Thought*. London: Bloomsbury.

Mercer, N. and Dawes, L. (2008) 'The value of exploratory talk', in N. Mercer and S. Hodgkinson (eds), *Exploring Talk in School: Inspired by the Work of Douglas Barnes*. Thousand Oaks, CA: Sage, 55–72.

Mercer, N. and Littleton, K. (2007) *Dialogue and Development of Children's Thinking*. Abingdon: Routledge.

Middleton, C. (2011) 'Dissertation: A first-class essay? Yours for just £660', *The Telegraph*, 7 December.

Miller, H. (no date) 'The impact of thinking skills at Rochester Grammar School', available at: www.thinkingschoolsinternational.com/site/wp-content/uploads/2013/11/Rochester-pictures-and-evidence2.pdf (accessed 5 January 2018).

Mithen, S. (1996) *The Prehistory of the Mind*. London: Thames & Hudson.

Mitra, S. and Negroponte, N. (2012) *Beyond the Hole in the Wall: Discover the Power of Self-Organized Learning*. New York: TED Books.

Moffitt, T.E., Arseneault, L., Belsky, D., Dickson, N., Hancox, R.J., Harrington, H. and Sears, M.R. (2011) 'A gradient of childhood self-control predicts health, wealth, and public safety', *Proceedings of the National Academy of Sciences*, 108(7): 2693–2698.

Mooney, C.G. (2013) *Theories of Childhood* (2nd edn). St Paul: Redleaf Press.

Morris, E. (2013) 'Schools work best when they work together', *The Guardian*, 21 January.

Moseley, D., Baumfield, V., Elliot, J., Gregson, M., Higgins, S., Miller, J. and Newton, D.P. (2005) *Frameworks for Thinking*. Cambridge: Cambridge University Press.

Muller, U., Carpendale, J.I.M. and Smith, L. (2009) *The Cambridge Companion to Piaget*. New York: Cambridge University Press.

Mulvey, K. (2017) '80% of New Year's resolutions fail by February — here's how to keep yours', *Business Insider UK*, 4 January, available at: http://uk.businessinsider.com/new-years-resolutions-courses-2016-12 (accessed 5 January 2018).

NASUWT (2017) *Creativity and the Arts in the Curriculum*. London: NASUWT.

National Advisory Committee on Creative and Cultural Education (1999) *All Our Futures: Creativity, Culture and Education*. London: DFEE.

National College for Leadership of Schools and Children's Services (2010) *10 Strong Claims About Successful School Leadership*, available at: http://dera.ioe.ac.uk/2082/1/10-strong-claims-about-successful-school-leadership.pdf (accessed 2 January 2018).

National Education Union (2015) 'Why are so many children so unhappy at school?', Blog, available at: www.atl.org.uk/latest/blog/why-are-so-many-children-so-unhappy-school (accessed 17 January 2018).

Naylor, L. (2013) 'A guide to philosophical enquiry in the primary classroom', *The Guardian*, Blog, 7 May.

NCSL (National College for School Leadership) (2012) *School Leadership for a Self-improving System*. Nottingham: National College for School Leadership.

Neill, A.S. (1972) *Neill Neill! Orange Peel!* New York: Hart Publishing Company.

Nelson, J. and Sharples, J. (2017) 'How research-engaged are you? *Impact*, 16–20.

Newton, D. (2014) *Thinking with Feeling*. London: Routledge.

Nottingham, J. (2013) *The Learning Challenge: How to Guide Your Students Through the Learning Pit to Achieve Deeper Understanding*. Abingdon: Routledge.

Nussbaum, M. (2010) *Not for Profit: Why Democracy Needs the Humanities*. Princeton, NJ: Princeton.

Obenchain, T.G. (2016) *Genius Belabored: Childbed Fever and the Tragic Life of Ignaz Semmelweis*. Alabama: The University of Alabama Press.

OECD (2016) *Global Competence for an Inclusive World*. Paris: OECD.

Ofsted (2006) *Creative Partnerships: Initiative and Impact*. Manchester: Ofsted.

Ofsted (2011) *Good Practice in Primary Mathematics: Evidence from 20 Successful Schools*. London: Ofsted.

Ofsted (2013) *School Inspection Report: Whitchurch Junior School 10–11ᵗʰ January 2013*, available at: https://reports.ofsted.gov.uk/provider/files/2170043/urn/131316.pdf (accessed 4 January 2018).

Ofsted (2014) *Teaching, Learning and Assessment in Further Education and Skills: What Works and Why?* London: Ofsted.

Ofsted (2015) *Inspection Report: Barbara Priestman Academy*, 28–29 January. London: Ofsted.

Ofsted (2017) *School Inspection Handbook*. London: Ofsted.

Ohreen, D. (2004) *The Scope and Limits of Folk Psychology: A Socio-linguistic Approach*. Bern: Verlag Peter Lang.

Oliver, M. and Venville, G. (2017) 'Bringing CASE in from the cold: The teaching and learning of thinking', *Research in Science Education*, *47*(1): 49–66.

Ontario Ministry of Education (2018) *Essential Skills in the OPS: Thinking Skills*, available at: www.skills.edu.gov.on.ca/OSP2Web/EDU/DisplayEssentialSkills.xhtml (accessed 15 June 2018).

O'Reilly, F., Chande, R., Sanders, M. and Groot, B. (2017) *Behavioural Insights for Education: A Practical Guide for Parents, Teachers and School Leaders*. London: Behavioural Insight Team/Pearson.

Orme, N. (2006) *Medieval Schools*. New Haven: Yale University Press.

Osborne, S. (2016) 'If the world were 100 people: One video that explains how unequal the world is', *The Independent*, 15 March.

Paton, G. (2009) 'School is boring and irrelevant, say teenagers', *The Telegraph*, 21 January.

Paton, G. (2012) 'New-style "nappy curriculum" will damage childhood', *The Telegraph*, 6 February.

Peal, R. (2014) *Progressively Worse*. London: Civitas.

Peirce, C.S. (1877) 'The fixation of belief', in P. Wiener (ed.) (1958), *Charles Sanders Peirce: Selected Writings*. New York: Dover Publications, 91–112.

Pells, R. (2016) 'Children with no shoes on "do better in classroom", major study finds', *The Independent*, 24 May.

Perkins, D. (1985) 'What creative thinking is', in A.L. Costa (ed.), *Developing Minds: A Resource Book for Teaching Thinking*. Alexandria, VA: Association for Supervision and Curriculum Development, 85–88.

Perkins, D. (2003) *King Arthur's Round Table: How Collaborative Conversations Create Smart Organizations*. Hoboken, NJ: John Wiley & Sons.

Perkins, D., Tishman, S., Ritchhart, R., Donis, K. and Andrade, A. (2000) 'Intelligence in the wild: A dispositional view of intellectual traits', *Educational Psychology Review*, *12*(3): 269–293.

Peters, M. (2017) 'Education in a post-truth world', *Educational Philosophy and Theory*, *49*(6): 563–566.

Peterson, C. and Seligman, M.E.P. (2004) *Character Strengths and Virtues: A Handbook and Classification*. Washington, DC: American Psychological Association.

Petty, G. (2006) *Evidence-Based Teaching: A Practical Approach*. Cheltenham: Nelson Thornes.

Pfenninger, K.H. and Shubik, V.R. (2001) *The Origins of Creativity*. Oxford: Oxford University Press.

Phelps, E.A. (2006) 'Emotion and cognition: Insights from studies of the human amygdala', *Annual Review of Psychology*, *57*: 27–53

Phillips, M. (1996) *All Must Have Prizes*. London: Little, Brown and Company.

Piaget, J. (1950) *The Psychology of Intelligence*. London: Routledge.

Picton, I. and Teravainen, A. (2017) *Fake News and Critical Literacy: An Evidence Review*. London: National Literacy Trust.

Pink, D. (2011) *Drive*. London: Canongate Books.

Pinker, S. (2018) *Enlightenment Now*. London: Allen Lane.

Plutchik, R. (1980) *A General Psychoevolutionary Theory of Emotion*. New York: Academic Press.

Polderman, T.C.J., Benyamin, B., De Leeuw, C.A., Sullivan, P.F., Van Bochoven, A., Visscher, P.M. and Posthuma, D. (2015) 'Meta-analysis of the heritability of human traits based on fifty years of twin studies', *Nature Genetics*, *47*(7): 702–709.

Pope, R. (2005) *Creativity: Theory, History, Practice*. Abingdon: Routledge.

Preskill, H. and Torres, R. (1999) 'The role of evaluative enquiry in creating learning', in M. Easterby-Smith, L. Araujo and J. Burgoyne (eds), *Organizational Learning and the Learning Organization: Developments in Theory and Practice*. London: Sage, 92–114.

Prinz, J.J. (2012) *Beyond Human Nature: How Culture and Experience Shape Our Lives*. New York: Allen Lane.

Pritchard, A. and Woollard, J. (2010) *Psychology for the Classroom: Constructivism and Social Learning*. Abingdon: Routledge.

Provine, R. (2001) *Laughter: A Scientific Investigation*. London: Penguin.

Quick, R.H. (1907) *Essays on Educational Reformers*. London: Longmans, Green and Co.

Ramachandran, V.S. (2011) *The Tell-Tale Brain*. New York: W.W. Norton & Co.

Relate (2015) *The Way We Are Now: The State of the UK's Relationships 2015*, available at: relate.org.uk/waywearenow (accessed 17 December 2017).

Renfrew, C. (2007) *Prehistory*. London: Phoenix.

Resnick, L. (1987) *Education and Learning to Think*. Washington: National Academy Press.

Resnick, L. (1999) 'Making America smarter', *Education Week*, 38–40.

Reynolds, G. (2017) 'Walk, stretch or dance? Dancing may be best for the brain', *New York Times*, 29 March.

Richardson, K. (1999) *The Making of Intelligence*. Maidenhead: Open University Press.

Ridley, M. (2003) *Nature Via Nurture*. London: Fourth Estate.

Ritchhart, R. (2002) *Intellectual Character: What It Is, Why It Matters, and How to Get It*. Hoboken, NJ: John Wiley & Sons.

Ritchhart, R. (2015) *Creating Cultures of Thinking: The 8 Forces We Must Master to Truly Transform Our Schools*. San Francisco: Jossey-Bass.

Ritchhart, R., Church, M. and Morrison, K. (2011) *Making Thinking Visible: How to Promote Engagement, Understanding, and Independence for All Learners*. Hoboken, NJ: John Wiley & Sons.

Ritchhart, R. and Perkins, D. (2008) 'Making thinking visible', *Educational Leadership*, 65(5): 57–61.

Rittle-Johnson, B., Saylor, M. and Swygert, K.E. (2008) 'Learning from explaining: Does it matter if Mom is listening?', *Journal of Experimental Child Psychology*, 100(3): 215–224.

Roberts, N. and Perry, J. (1999) *Hold Ye Front Page! 2000 Years of History on the Front Page of The Sun*. London: HarperCollins.

Robertson, A. (2006) *Let's Think Early Years!* Windsor: NFER-Nelson.

Robinson, C. (2014) *Children, Their Voices and Their Experiences of School: What Does the Evidence Tell Us?* York: Cambridge Primary Review Trust.

Robinson, M. (2013) *Trivium21c*. Carmarthen: Independent Thinking Press.

Robson, S. and Hargreaves, D.J. (2005) 'What do early childhood practitioners think about young children's thinking?', *European Early Childhood Education Research Journal*, 13(1): 81–96.

Rowe, M.B. (1986) 'Wait time: Slowing down may be a way of speeding up!', *Journal of Teacher Education*, 37: 43–50.

Rugg, H. (1963) *Imagination*. New York: Harper & Row.

Runco, M.A. and Pagnani, A.R. (2011) 'Psychological research on creativity', in J. Sefton-Green, P. Thomson, K. Jones and L. Bresler (eds), *The Routledge International Handbook of Creative Learning*. Abingdon: Routledge, 63–71.

Russell, B. (2016) 'Bernadette Russell's top 10 philosophical questions children should ask', *The Guardian*, 14 February.

Russell, B. (2017) *The Little Book of Kindness: Everyday Actions to Change Your Life and the World Around You*. London: Orion Spring.

Ryan, T. (1990) *Thinkers Keys for Kids*, available at: www.tonyryan.com.au/blog/wp-content/uploads/Thinkers_Keys_Version1.pdf (accessed 12 November 2017).

Ryan, T. (2014) *Thinkers Keys: A Powerful Program for Teaching Children to Become Extraordinary Thinkers*. Queensland: Greenslade Creations.

Ryan, T. (2017) *The Next Generation: Preparing Today's Kids for an Extraordinary Future.* Melbourne: Wiley.

Ryan, T. (no date) *Thinkers Keys Cards*, available at: www.tonyryan.com.au/home/projects/ (accessed 5 December 2017).

Sabol, T. and Pianta, R.C. (2012) 'Recent trends in research on teacher-child relationships', *Attachment & Human Development, 14*(3): 213–231.

Sahlberg, P. (2012) 'Global educational reform movement is here!', available at: https://pasisahlberg.com/global-educational-reform-movement-is-here/ (accessed 27 June 2017).

Saini, A. (2013) 'Newborn babies may be more developed than we think', *The Observer*, 8 December.

Salmon, A. (2008) 'Promoting a culture of thinking in the young child', *Early Childhood Journal, 35*(5): 457–461

Sammons, P., Sylva, K., Melhuish, E., Siraj-Blatchford, I., Taggart, B., Smees, R., Draghici, D. and Toth, K. (2012) *Influences on Students' Dispositions in Key Stage 3: Exploring Enjoyment of School, Popularity, Anxiety, Citizenship Values and Academic Self-Concepts in Year 9.* London: Institute of Education.

Sawyer, K. (2013) *Zig Zag: The Surprising Path to Greater Creativity.* San Francisco: Jossey-Bass.

Schleicher, A. (no date) 'The case for 21st-century learning', available at: www.oecd.org/general/thecasefor21st-centurylearning.htm (accessed 26 June 2018).

Schoemaker, P. (2011) *Brilliant Mistakes. Finding Success on the Far Side of Failure.* Philadelphia: Wharton Digital Press.

Schön, D. (1991) *The Reflective Practitioner: How Professionals Think in Action.* New York: Routledge.

Scieszka, J. (1989) *True Story of the Three Little Pigs.* London: Harper Collins.

Seligman, M. (2002) *Authentic Happiness: Using the New Positive Psychology to Realize Your Potential for Lasting Fulfillment.* New York: Simon & Schuster.

Selwyn, N. (2016) *Is Technology a Good Thing?* Cambridge: Polity Press.

Service, T. (2012) *Music as Alchemy: Journeys with Great Conductors and Their Orchestras.* London: Faber & Faber.

Shallcross, D.J. (1981) *Teaching Creative Behaviour: How to Teach Creativity to Children of All Ages.* Eaglewood Cliffs, NJ: Prentice-Hall.

Shamas, V. (2018) *Deep Creativity: Inside the Creative Mystery.* New York: Morgan James Publishing.

Sharot, T. (2017) *The Influential Mind: What the Brain Reveals About Our Power to Change Others.* Boston: Little, Brown.

Sharp, A.M. and Reed, R.E. (1991) *Studies in Philosophy for Children: Harry Stottlemeier's Discovery.* Philadelphia: Temple University Press.

Sharples, M., de Roock, R., Ferguson, R., Gaved, M., Herodotou, C., Koh, E., Kukulska-Hulme, A., Looi, C.-K., McAndrew, P., Rienties, B., Weller, M. and Wong, L.H. (2016)

Innovating Pedagogy 2016: Open University Innovation Report 5. Milton Keynes: The Open University.

Shaskan, T. (2012) *Honestly, Red Riding Hood Was Rotten! The Story of Little Red Riding Hood as Told by the Wolf*. London: Raintree.

Shayer, M. (1988) *Cognitive Acceleration Through Science Education*. London: King's College.

Shayer, M. and Adey, P. (2002) *Learning Intelligence: Cognitive Acceleration Across the Curriculum from 5 to 15 Years*. Buckingham: Open University Press.

Shayer, M. and Adhami, M. (2007) 'Fostering cognitive development through the context of Mathematics: Results of the CAME Project Educational Studies in Mathematics', *64*(3): 256–291.

Sherwin, A. (2016) 'Winnie-the-Pooh "a philosopher to rival Plato and Confucius"', *iNews*, 14 October, available at: https://inews.co.uk/essentials/culture/books/winnie-pooh-philosopher-rival-plato-confucius/ (accessed 7 December 2017).

Siegel, D.J. and Bryson, T.P. (2012) *The Whole-Brain Child*. New York: Random House.

Siegel, H. (2010) 'On thinking skills', in C. Winch (ed.), *Teaching Thinking Skills*. London: Continuum, 51–84.

Siegler, R.S. and Alibali, M.A. (2005) *Children's Thinking*. Upper Saddle River, NJ: Pearson Education International.

Simonton, D. (2009) *Scientific Genius: A Psychology of Science*. Cambridge: Cambridge University Press.

Siraj, I. and Asani, R. (2015) 'The role of sustained shared thinking, play and metacognition in young children's learning', in S. Robson and S. Flannery Quinn (eds), *The Routledge International Handbook of Young Children's Thinking and Understanding*. Oxon: Routledge, 403–415.

Siraj-Blatchford, I. (2009) 'Conceptualising progression in the pedagogy of play and sustained shared thinking in early childhood education: A Vygotskian perspective', *Education and Child Psychology*, *26*(2): 77–89.

Siraj-Blatchford, I., Sammons, P., Taggart, B., Sylva, K. and Melhuish, E. (2006) 'Educational research and evidence-based policy: The mixed-method approach of the EPPE project', *Evaluation & Research in Education*, *19*(2): 63–82.

Siraj-Blatchford, I., Sylva, K., Muttock, S., Gilden, R. and Bell, D. (2002) *Researching Effective Pedagogy in the Early Years*. London: DfES.

Sizer, T.R. (1992) *Horace's School: Redesigning the American High School*. New York: Houghton Mifflin.

Slavin, R.E. (1991) 'Synthesis of research on cooperative learning', *Educational Leadership*, 48: 71–82.

Sloane, P. (2007) *The Innovative Leader: How to Inspire Your Team and Drive Creativity*. London: Kogan Page.

Smith, D. (2013) *Wallace & Gromit: Cracking Contraptions Manual: Volumes 1 & 2 (Haynes Manual)*. Yeovil: J.H. Haynes & Co Ltd.

Smith, F. (1992) *To Think in Language, Learning and Education*. Abingdon: Routledge.

Smith, J. (2017) *The Really Lazy Teacher's Handbook: How Your Students Learn More When You Teach Less* (2nd edn). Carmarthen: Crown House.

Solomon, T. (2015) 'The mystery of the incredible human brain: We've learned a lot, but think how much more there is to discover', *The Independent*, 19 March.

Stahl, R.J. (1990) *Using 'Think Time' Behaviours to Promote Students' Information Processing, Learning, and On-task Participation. An Instruction Module*. Temple, AZ: Arizona State University.

Standing, E.M. (1998) *Maria Montessori. Her Life and Work*. London: Penguin.

Stanley, S. and Bowkett, S. (2004) *But Why?* Stafford: Network Educational Press.

Stark, K. (2016) *When Strangers Meet: How People You Don't Know Can Transform You*. New York: Simon & Schuster.

Starko, A.J. (ed.) (1995) *Creativity in the Classroom: Schools of Curious Delight*. New York: Longman.

Sternberg, R.J. (ed.) (1988) *The Nature of Creativity*. Cambridge: Cambridge University Press.

Sternberg, R.J. (1996) *Successful Intelligence: How Practical and Creative Intelligence Determine Success in Life*. New York: Simon and Schuster.

Sternberg, R.J. (2003) *Wisdom, Intelligence and Creativity Synthesized*. Cambridge: Cambridge University Press.

Stewart, W. (2014) 'School leavers lack the critical thinking skills needed for university, exam board warns', *TES*, 25 January.

Stewart, W.A.C. and McCann, W.P. (1967) *The Educational Innovators 1750–1880*. London: MacMillan.

St John, R. (2010) *The 8 Traits Successful People Have in Common: 8 to Be Great*. Toronto: Train of Thought Arts.

Striraman, B. (2004) 'The characteristics of mathematical creativity', *The Mathematical Educator*, 14(1): 19–34.

Striraman, B. and Lee, K.H. (2010) *The Elements of Creativity and Giftedness in Mathematics*. Boston: Sense Publishers.

Swartz, R., Costa, A.L., Beyer, B.K., Reagan, R. and Kallick, B. (2008) *Thinking-Based Learning*. New York: Teacher College Press.

Swartz, R. and McGuinness, C. (2014) *Developing and Assessing Thinking Skills. The International Baccalaureate Project 2014*, available at: www.ibo.org/globalassets/publications/ib-research/continuum/student-thinking-skills-report-part-1.pdf (accessed 20 January 2018).

Sweller, J. (1988) 'Cognitive load during problem solving: Effects on learning', *Cognitive Science*, 12: 257–285.

Syed, M. (2011) *Bounce: The Myth of Talent and the Power of Practice*. London: Fourth Estate.

Sylva, K., Melhuish, E., Sammons, P., Siraj-Blatchford, I. and Taggart, B. (2004) *The Effective Provision of Pre-school Education (EPPE) Project: Final Report*. Nottingham: DfES.

Sylva, K., Melhish, E., Sammons, P., Siraj-Blatchford, I. and Taggart, B. (2010) *Early Childhood Matters: Evidence from the Effective Pre-school and Primary Education Project*. Abingdon: Routledge.

Taggart, G., Ridley, K., Rudd, P. and Benefield, P. (2005) *Thinking Skills in the Early Years: A Literature Review*. Slough: NFER.

Taie, E.S. and El Kamel, A.A. (2013) 'Six thinking hats as a creative approach in managing meetings in hospitals', *Journal of Nursing Education and Practice*, 3(9): 187–200.

Tannenbaum, S.I. and Cerasoli, C.P. (2013) 'Do team and individual debriefs enhance performance? A meta-analysis', *Human Factors*, 55(1): 231–245.

Taylor, C., Rhys, M., Waldron, S., Davies, R., Power, S., Maynard, T., Moore, L., Blackaby, D. and Plewis, I. (2015) *Evaluating the Foundation Phase: Final Report*. Cardiff: Welsh Government.

Thaler, R. and Sunstein, C.R. (2009) *Nudge: Improving Decisions About Health, Wealth and Happiness*. London: Yale University Press.

The Children's Society (2016) *The Good Childhood Report for 2015*. London: The Children's Society.

The Children's Society (2018) *The Children's Society Good Childhood Report 2017*. London: The Children's Society.

Thinking Maps, Inc. (2011) *Thinking Maps*, available at: www.thinkingmaps.com (accessed 15 November 2017).

Thomas, G. (2013) *Education: A Very Short Introduction*. Oxford: Oxford University Press.

Thompson, C. (2013) *Smarter Than You Think*. London: William Collins.

Thornburg, P. and Thornburg, D. (1989) *The Thinker's Toolbox*. Labanon, IN: Dale Seymour Publications.

Thorrington, D. (2017) *Written Evidence Submitted by Dominic Thorrington (FNW0010)*, available at: http://data.parliament.uk/writtenevidence/committeeevidence.svc/evidence document/culture-media-and-sport-committee/fake-news/written/46489.html (accessed 25 November 2017).

Tickell, C. (2011) *The Early Years: Foundations for Life, Health and Learning*. London: DfES.

Tishman, S. (2018) *Slow Looking: The Art and Practice of Learning Through Observation*. New York: Routledge.

Tochon, F. and Munby, H. (1993) 'Novice and expert teachers' time epistemology: A wave function from didactics to pedagogy', *Teaching and Teacher Education*, 9(2): 205–218.

Tolstoy, L. (1904) *What Is Art?* (transl.). New York: Funk & Wagnalls Company.

Tooley, S.H. (2009) *The Art in Teaching Writing*. Kentucky: Western Kentucky University.

Torrance, E.P. (1962) *Guiding Creative Talent*. Englewood Cliffs, NJ: Prentice-Hall.

Torrance, E.P. (1988) 'The nature of creativity as manifest in the testing', in R.J. Sternberg (ed.), *The Nature of Creativity*. Cambridge: Cambridge University Press, 43–75.

Tough, P. (2012) *How Children Succeed: Grit, Curiosity and Hidden Power of Character*. London: Arrow.

Tovey, H. (2014) 'All about … risk', *Nursery World*, 13–26 January, 21–24.

Tranter, G. (2011) *Using Humour in the English Classroom: Teaching Ideas and Activities*. Stuttgart: Ernst Klett.

Treffinger, D.J., Young, G.C., Selby, E.C. and Shepardson, C.A. (2002) *Assessing Creativity*. Storrs, CT: The National Research Center on the Gifted and Talented.

Trickey, S. and Topping, K.J. (2004) '"Philosophy for children": A systematic review', *Research Papers in Education, 19*(3): 365–380.

Trivizas, E. (1993) *The Three Little Wolves and the Big Bad Pig*. Portsmouth, NH: Heinemann Young Books.

Turner, R. (1979) 'The value of variety in teaching styles', *Education Leadership*, January, 257–258, available at: www.ascd.org/ASCD/pdf/journals/ed_lead/el_197901_turner.pdf (accessed 17 January 2018).

Twiselton, S. (2006) 'The problem with English: The exploration and development of student teachers' English subject knowledge in primary classrooms', *Literacy, 40*(2): 88–96.

UK Children's Commissioners (2015) *UN Committee on the Rights of the Child: Examination of the Fifth Periodic Report of the United Kingdom of Great Britain and Northern Ireland*. Belfast, Cardiff, Edinburgh and London: UK Children's Commissioners.

UNICEF (2017) 'Rights Respecting Schools Award', available at: www.unicef.org.uk/rights-respecting-schools/wp-content/uploads/sites/4/2017/01/Change-for-Children-through-RRSA.pdf (accessed 25 November 2017).

Vaughan, R. (2016) 'Schools turn to live in-ear coaching for teachers in the classroom', *TES*, 27 February.

Venninen, T., Leinonen, J., Lipponen, L. and Ojala, M. (2014) 'Supporting children's participation in Finnish child care centers', *Early Childhood Education Journal, 42*(3): 211–218.

Vlastos, G. (1991) *Socrates, Ironist and Moral Philosopher*. New York: Cambridge University Press.

Vohs, K.D, Redden, J.P. and Rahinel, R. (2013) 'Physical order produces healthy choices, generosity, and conventionality, whereas disorder produces creativity', *Psychological Science, 24*(9): 1860–1867.

Vorhaus, J., Litster, J., Frearson, M. and Johnson, S. (2011) *Review of Research and Evaluation on Improving Adult Literacy and Numeracy Skills: Research Paper Number 61*. London: Department for Business, Energy and Industrial Strategy.

Vygotsky, L.S. (1962) *Thought and Language*. Cambridge, MA: MIT Press.

Vygotsky, L. (1978) *Mind in Society: The Development of Higher Psychological Processes.* Cambridge, MA: Harvard University Press.

Wakefield, J. (2015) 'Technology in schools: Future changes in classrooms', *BBC News,* 2 February.

Wallace, B. (2001) *Teaching Thinking Skills Across the Primary Curriculum: A Practical Approach for All Abilities.* Abingdon: David Fulton.

Wallace, B. (2004) *Thinking Skills and Problem-Solving – An Inclusive Approach: A Practical Guide for Teachers in Primary Schools.* Abingdon: David Fulton.

Wallace, B. (2009) *Teaching Problem-Solving and Thinking Skills through Science: Exciting Cross-Curricular Challenges for Foundation Phase, Key Stage One and Key Stage Two.* Abingdon: Routledge.

Wallace, B. and Kirkman, L. (2014) *Talk-Less Teaching: Practice, Participation and Progress.* Carmarthen: Crown House.

Wallas, G. (1926) *The Art of Thought.* London: Johnathan Cape.

Wang, J., Lo, C.K., Chen, K., Shieh, J. and Ku, Y. (2002) 'The efficacy of teaching by professional nursing concept utilizing problem solving strategies for students enrolled in a 2-year baccalaureate nursing program', *The Journal of Nursing Research,* 10(2): 113–119.

Wartenberg, T. (2014) *Big Ideas for Little Kids: Teaching Philosophy through Children's Literature.* Lanham, MD: Rowman & Littlefield Publishers.

Warwick Commission (2015) *Enriching Britain: Culture, Creativity and Growth.* Coventry: University of Warwick.

Watson, R. (2012) *Future Files.* London: Nicholas Brearley.

Wegerif, R. (2010) *Mind Expanding. Teaching for Thinking and Creativity in Primary Education.* Maidenhead: Open University Press.

Weil, Z. (2014) 'How do we educate global problem solvers?', *Edutopia,* 10 June, available at: www.edutopia.org/blog/educating-global-problem-solvers-zoe-weil (accessed 21 January 2018).

Weir, K. (2018) 'Turning classrooms into learning laboratories', *Monitor on Psychology,* 49(1): 64, available at: www.apa.org/monitor/2018/01/classrooms-laboratories.aspx (accessed 17 January 2018).

Wells, G. (1999) *Dialogic Enquiry: Towards a Sociocultural Practice and Theory of Education.* Cambridge: Cambridge University Press.

Wells, K. (2009) 'Thinking hats on …', *Professional Focus,* 6–7.

Welser, W. (2018) 'Fake news 2.0: AI will soon be able to mimic any human voice', *WIRED,* 8 January.

Welsh Assembly Government (2009) *Optional Skills Assessment Materials. Developing Thinking.* Cardiff: Welsh Assembly Government.

Whitty, G. and Wisby, E. (2011) *Real Decision Making? School Councils in Action.* London: DCSF.

Wilce, H. (2006) 'University students: They can't write, spell or present an argument', *The Independent*, 24 May.

Williams, J.T. (2003) *Pooh and the Philosophers (Wisdom of Pooh)*. London: Egmont Books.

Williams, R. (1958) *Culture and Society: Coleridge to Orwell*. London: Hogarth Press.

Williams, S. (2009) 'Football academies: Kicking and screaming', *The Telegraph*, 4 March.

Willingham, D.T. (2008) 'Critical thinking: Why is it so hard to teach?', *Arts Education Policy Review*, *109*(4): 21–32.

Winch, C. (ed.) (2010) *Teaching Thinking Skills*. London: Continuum.

Winterman, D. (2007) 'Just another brick in the wall?', *BBC News*, 2 October 2007, available at: http://news.bbc.co.uk/1/hi/magazine/7021797.stm (accessed 8 January 2018).

Winthrop, R. and MGivney, E. (2016) *Skills for a Changing World: Advancing Quality Learning for Vibrant Societies*. Washington: Center for Universal Education.

Wolberg, R.I. and Goff, A. (2012) 'Thinking routines: Replicating classroom practices within museum settings', *Journal of Museum Education*, *37*(1): 59–68.

Wooldridge, A. (1994) *Measuring the Mind: Education and Psychology in England, c. 1860–1990*. Cambridge: Cambridge University Press.

World Economic Forum (2015) *New Vision for Education Unlocking the Potential of Technology*. Geneva: World Economic Forum.

Worthington, I. (ed.) (2007) *A Companion to Greek Rhetoric*. Oxford: Blackwell.

Wright, N. (1977) *Progress in Education*. London: Croom Helm.

Yorke, H. (2017) 'More than 20,000 university students buying essays and dissertations as Lords call for ban on "contract cheating"', *The Telegraph*, 13 January.

Young, S. (2017) 'Messy desks could be a sign of genius, say researchers', *The Independent*, 11 July.

Youth Enterprise (2016) *Young Enterprise Fiver Challenge Evaluation Report*, available at: www.fiverchallenge.org.uk/images/fiverUploads/Fiver_Challenge_Impact_Report_2016.pdf (accessed 2 February 2018).

Zeldin, T. (1994) *An Intimate History of Humanity*. London: Sinclair-Stevenson.

Zielinski, K., McLaughlin, T.F. and Derby, K.M. (2012) 'The effect of "cover, copy, and compare" on spelling accuracy of high school students with learning disabilities', *American Secondary Education*, *41*(1): 78–95.

INDEX

t = table; f = figure